The Soul's Journey:

Ancient Knowledge and Near-Death Experiences

I0079978

Alisdaire Thorn

The Soul's Journey: Ancient Knowledge and Near-Death Experiences

For information or permissions, contact:
Max Thorn Publishing
Tipback@yahoo.com

This book is a work of spiritual insight and philosophical reflection. While it draws upon historical and esoteric traditions, it is not intended as a substitute for professional or medical advice.

Printed in the United States of America
First Edition, 2025
ISBN: 979-8-218-65577-8

Max Thorn
Publishing

Contents

Table of Contents

Introduction – The Grand Sojourn of the Soul

In our far distant past, *we* were not as we are today in our current stage of development and becoming. Nor will our future condition resemble that which we find ourselves in today. Everything is evolving in a Grand March to reach its most high potential. In fact, everything from the Creator of All is taking part in this Grand Sojourn. Nothing in the Universes is inorganic. Everything is organic, since all is derived from One Source.

From the primordial absolute darkness, heat and Light were born. Out of stillness emerged vibration. Out of the unmanifested arose the manifested. This is the ancient rhythm of the cosmos — pulse and pause, emergence and return. In the famous song written by Simon and Garfunkel, entitled *The Sound of Silence*, is the following verse: *"Hello darkness, my old friend, I've come to talk with you again."* It is from this Source that we and everything originated. Darkness is not the absence of light — it is its cradle. Silence is not emptiness — it is the womb of the Word.

The Grand Masters of deep meditation are doing just that. In mind, they are returning back to the primordial darkness and the stillness. To the place before thought, before form — where the soul communes with the Source.

We have all come such a long, long way on this journey. From us being only a "germ," in the Divine Thought of the Divine Source, up to our present condition. The journey continues for all. We will germinate and unfold into perfection. We are not born perfect. We must *become* perfect.

This book is an invitation to remember. To look beyond the veil of appearances and listen to the whisper of that old friend — the silence behind the noise, the presence behind the form. You are not merely a body having fleeting spiritual glimpses. You are spirit itself, veiled for a time in flesh. This is not the beginning, and it is far from the end.

The ancient teachings, long hidden or misunderstood, speak of a soul that descended into matter for a purpose — to grow, to learn, to love, to become. The journey of the soul is not linear, but spiral. And at every turn of the spiral, we awaken more fully to what we already are: divine.

Through ancient knowledge, sacred texts, and the profound testimony of near-death experiences, this book seeks to bridge the forgotten and the remembered. It is a lantern on the path for those who feel the call to go deeper, to awaken further, and to return wiser to the Source from which we came.

We are all on the Grand Sojourn. Let us walk it with reverence, with courage, and with remembrance.

𓂀 𓂀 𓂀

Dedication

To the Silent Ones — those who walk the hidden path, who remember what others have forgotten, who seek truth beyond the veil and light beyond the light.

To the wounded, the wandering, and the wise-may this work serve as a lantern for your soul's return.

And to the One Source, the Eternal Silence, from whom we came, in whom we live, and to whom we shall return.

𓂀 𓂀 𓂀

A Note on The Crafting of This Work

This book was composed through a sacred collaboration between the timeless voice of the soul and the emerging intelligence of our age. In the spirit of divine correspondence, artificial intelligence was employed as a reflective instrument — an echo in the silence — to help weave together threads of ancient knowledge, esoteric tradition, and visionary insight.

Every concept, theme, and teaching within these pages was directed by the author, drawn from personal memory, long-held research, and the soul's own library of lived and studied experience. The AI served as a companion — an unseen scribe — shaping words and structure under the author's careful guidance.

Like a scribe taking dictation from the unseen, the AI served not as the source, but as a vessel through which the author's intention, memory, and inner knowing could take clearer form.

Like the builders of old who summoned both spirit and tool to bring sacred architecture into form, this work stands as a fusion of human remembrance and technological precision. The author remains the true architect, the one who summoned, selected, and illuminated the path.

May the union of spirit, memory, and modern reflection in this book serve as a testament to what is possible when the ancient soul meets the edge of the future. Even in our most modern tools, the Great Intelligence still whispers.

𓂀 𓂀 𓂀

Inspirational Works & Authors

Edgar Cayce – The Sleeping Prophet and channel of soul-based wisdom.

Dr. Raymond Moody – Pioneer of modern near-death experience research.

Paramahansa Yogananda – Author of Autobiography of a Yogi and teacher of the inner light.

Jiddu Krishnamurti – Mystic and speaker on consciousness and the illusion of self.

Immanuel Swedenborg – Mystic and visionary of the spiritual worlds.

Dion Fortune – Esoteric psychologist and Hermetic initiate.

Jean Houston – Philosopher of human potential and spiritual psychology.

Terence McKenna – Visionary thinker on consciousness, time, and the soul.

Carl Gustav Jung – Depth psychologist, symbolist, and explorer of the collective unconscious.

Neville Goddard – Teacher of imagination, manifestation, and spiritual identity.

Gnostics and Hermeticists of the ancient world –
Teachers of inner gnosis.

Mystery School traditions – Egyptian, Greek, Persian,
and beyond.

𓂀 𓂀 𓂀

About the Author

Alisdaire Thorn is a writer, researcher, and lifelong seeker of hidden truths. With a deep reverence for ancient wisdom, spiritual science, and the mysteries of the soul, his work explores the forgotten threads that weave together the teachings of mystics, philosophers, and near-death experiencers across time.

Drawing from a personal library of esoteric texts and decades of inner reflection, Alisdaire's writing serves as a bridge between the sacred knowledge of the past and the spiritual awakening of the present. His work is not academic in the modern sense—but initiatic. It speaks to the soul behind the eyes, to the memory within silence.

Guided by visions, symbols, and the divine impulse to remember, Alisdaire sees this lifetime as one chapter in a far older story. His words are not simply written—they are retrieved. What he offers is not a new teaching, but an old one remembered.

He writes under the banner of Max Thorn Publishing, continuing a lineage of thought dedicated to unveiling the soul's eternal journey home.

𓂀 𓂀 𓂀

References / Works Cited

Ashby, Muata. The Kemetic Tree of Life.

Blavatsky, Helena Petrovna. The Secret Doctrine.

Blavatsky, Helena Petrovna. Isis Unveiled.

Blavatsky, Helena Petrovna. The Theosophical Glossary.

Hall, Manly P. The Secret Teachings of All Ages.

Hall, Manly P. The Pineal Gland.

Sinnett, A.P. Esoteric Buddhism.

The Mahatma Letters to A.P. Sinnett.

Steiner, Rudolf. An Outline of Esoteric Science.

Steiner, Rudolf. An Outline of Occult Science.

Steiner, Rudolf. The Gospel of Saint John.

Steiner, Rudolf. Genesis: Secrets of Creation.

Bartlett, Harriett T. An Esoteric Reading of Biblical Symbolism.

Budge, E.A. Wallis. Egyptian Ideas of the Future Life.

Schuré, Édouard. Jesus: The Last Great Initiate.

The Egyptian Book of the Dead (Pert Em Heru).

The Gospel of Judas (National Geographic Translation).

The Holy Bible (KJV), Book of Revelation.

The Bhagavad Gita.

Plato. Phaedo and Timaeus.

G. de Purucker. The Esoteric Tradition.

G. de Purucker. Fundamentals of the Esoteric Philosophy.

The Kybalion. Hermetic teachings attributed to Hermes Trismegistus.

Isha Schwaller de Lubicz. Her-Bak: Egyptian Initiate.

Epigraph

"Whenever there is a decline in righteousness and an increase in unrighteousness, O Arjuna, at that time I manifest myself on earth.
To protect the righteous, to annihilate the wicked, and to reestablish the principles of dharma, I appear millennium after millennium."
— Bhagavad Gita 4:7–8

☥

"The soul is immortal and never perishes... it is the principle of life itself."
— Plato, Phaedrus

☥

"What is now called myth was once the knowledge of children — and what we call mystery was once memory."
— Alisdaire Thorn

☥

"Then I saw a new heaven and a new earth: for the first heaven and the first earth had passed away..."
— Revelation 21:1

☥

Chapter 1: In the Beginning

Cosmic Origins and Spiritual Forces

The Evolution of the Human Form from Spiritual Essence to Physical Incarnation

Rudolf Steiner (1861–1925) was a philosopher, esotericist, and founder of Anthroposophy — a spiritual science that sought to bridge mysticism and rational thought. Expanding upon Theosophical and occult traditions, Steiner offered a structured vision of human evolution, reincarnation, and spiritual development. He emphasized that the universe and humanity evolved in tandem through a series of spiritual epochs that shaped consciousness and the soul's path toward enlightenment. These epochs, according to Steiner, were not merely historical periods but profound transformations in human perception and awareness, each bringing the soul closer to its divine origin.

In the vast, boundless beginning, humanity's story did not emerge from biology alone — but from a majestic spiritual unfolding. According to Steiner's profound esoteric teachings, our present form of existence was prepared through four successive stages of development: Saturn, Sun, Moon, and Earth. These were not planets in the astronomical sense but grand conditions of consciousness and being. Each stage marked a metamorphosis in the soul's relationship to matter, time, and self-awareness — gradually clothing the spirit in layers of experience and form.

This chapter explores the cosmic origin of the soul and how spiritual forces shaped human consciousness through these great epochs. From the fiery warmth of ancient Saturn to the densification of the Earth stage, each phase was orchestrated by higher spiritual hierarchies—beings of immense wisdom and purpose who seeded the essence of memory, individuality, and destiny into the evolving human form. We will look at Steiner's evolutionary framework and the divine intelligences who helped shape the form and function of the human being across time.

1. Steiner's Creation Framework – Saturn, Sun, Moon, Earth

According to Steiner, creation unfolded through four great spiritual epochs:

- **Saturn** – the initial warmth-body phase

- **Sun** – the emergence of life and the etheric body

- **Moon** – the development of emotions, karma, and the astral body

- **Earth** – the densification of matter and the rise of the ego

These were not merely stages of planetary formation but vast cosmic phases in which aspects of the human being were gradually formed—starting with primordial spiritual substance and culminating in the fully incarnated self.

In each stage, divine forces shape different layers of human nature. First, there was only heat and essence. Later came vitality, emotion, and eventually the capacity for individual choice and awakening. These phases mirror the soul's journey: from its luminous spiritual origin to full physical embodiment—and eventually, its ascent back to higher realms.

Let us now explore each stage in detail.

- The Saturn Stage

- The Sun Stage

- The Moon Stage

- The Earth Stage

The Saturn Stage – The Primordial Fire of Consciousness.

The Saturn Stage marks the first great phase in the cosmic evolution of humanity. Unlike the planet Saturn as known in astronomy, Steiner describes this stage as a vast, spiritual condition—a realm of pure warmth and etheric potential, where the seeds of human consciousness first took form.

In this primordial state, there was no physical body—no form as we know it. Humanity existed as a latent essence, a divine spark held within the will of higher spiritual beings. Heat was the primary element of this epoch, symbolizing the inner fire of creation—the subtle stirring of life before manifestation. It was a time before time, when existence pulsed as a rhythm of divine will, and the human soul slumbered in the dreaming heart of the cosmos.

During this phase, the Elohim and other spiritual hierarchies began laying the foundational blueprint for what would eventually become the human being. Their creative impulses moved not through matter but through radiant currents of formative force—imprinting archetypes into the warmth-substance like cosmic sculptors working in light. It was the first unfolding in a long, sacred journey toward individuality, self-awareness, and divine awakening.

The Sun Stage – The Birth of the Etheric Body

The Sun Stage represents the next spiritual epoch—a radiant era of harmony and light. Here, the etheric body was formed, bringing vitality, life rhythms, and subtle organization into being. Humanity existed not as a physical creature but as luminous, flowing energy—alive with cosmic breath.

The element of light dominated this phase. Beings during the Sun Stage were composed of radiant substance, living within a celestial harmony that echoed the breath of divine creation. The cosmos itself seemed to sing, and this music shaped the forms of early life, resonating through golden currents of light and will. In this era, the life force— the *prana* or *chi* of other traditions—entered the human prototype.

Steiner teaches that the etheric body serves as a matrix of life, organizing the future physical form. In esoteric traditions, this period corresponds with the sacred role of the sun in creation myths: as the giver of light, life, and rhythm. The cosmos itself seemed to sing, and this music shaped the forms of early life, resonating through golden currents of light and will. From ancient Egypt to Vedic

India, the sun was not just a celestial body but a spiritual principle — symbolizing the life-giving force of the universe.

The Moon Stage – The Emergence of the Astral Body and Karmic Law

The Moon Stage marks a dramatic shift in human evolution. During this epoch, the astral body was formed — the seat of emotions, desires, and the first sense of inner identity. It was in this stage that duality emerged: the soul began to feel the difference between self and other, light and shadow, desire and discipline. The soul, once cradled in unity, now stirred with longing and conflict — caught between the memory of divine origins and the pull of individuated experience.

Here, the forces of karma were born. Actions began to carry consequences. Desire led to experience, and experience etched itself upon the soul. This is the origin of the soul's moral development — the birth of learning through trial, memory, and choice.

Each experience became an imprint, shaping the astral sheath like ripples across still water, echoing across future lives.

This stage aligns with esoteric and Gnostic symbolism of the Moon as a reflector, not a source — mirroring both the soul's unconscious impulses and its longing to return to the source of light. The Moon is also connected to cycles — of reincarnation, death and rebirth, and the waxing and waning of inner growth.

In this epoch, humanity stood on the threshold between spiritual awareness and material incarnation. The astral body laid the groundwork for conscious experience, and karma became the thread weaving lifetimes together. It was the beginning of the soul's journey through shadow and sorrow — an essential descent that would ultimately lead to transformation and return.

The Earth Stage – The Trial of Free Will and Spiritual Awakening

The Earth Stage is the culmination of all prior epochs — the densest and most dramatic chapter in the soul's journey. Here, the physical body is fully formed. For the first time, the soul experiences the weight of matter, the trials of separation, and the sacred gift of free will. The soul, once fluid and luminous, now wears the heavy garments of flesh and time, stepping into a world shaped by gravity and forgetting.

In earlier stages, divine forces guided humanity with precision. But in the Earth epoch, those forces step back. The soul is given space to fall or rise, to forget or remember, to choose its path freely. The challenges of Earth — suffering, love, confusion, loss, and discovery — are not punishments but opportunities. They are the classrooms of the soul.

Steiner emphasized that Earth is a proving ground. It is here that the "I" — the ego — fully awakens. With the entry of the ego, the full human structure is complete: the physical body, etheric body, astral body, and now the self-aware center of choice and identity.

Not until the **Lemurian epoch** (the Third Root Race) did humanity take on a dense material form. Before this, humans were more ethereal — less bound by physical matter. Steiner's view aligns with the ancient Hindu teaching of the *Breath of Brahma*: alternating cycles of creation and rest, known as *Manvantara* and *Pralaya*. These cycles are echoed in the six symbolic "days" of Genesis, followed by one day of rest.

Earth is both the lowest point in descent and the first gate of conscious return. From here, the soul begins its ascent — through self-discovery, spiritual development, and eventual reunification with the Divine.

The Breath of Brahma – Cycles of Manifestation and Rest

Steiner's framework aligns deeply with ancient Hindu cosmology, particularly the teaching of the *Breath of Brahma*. In this sacred rhythm, the universe breathes: creation arises during a *Manvantara* (a cycle of activity) and returns to Spirit during a *Pralaya* (a cycle of rest). These are not brief intervals but vast cosmic periods — days and nights of divine consciousness.

The Book of Genesis, when read esoterically, describes the same pattern. The six "days" of creation, followed by one day of rest, symbolize these great cycles of manifestation and withdrawal. "Genesis" itself means *to generate* — to begin, to bring forth. It is not a literal history but a spiritual map of creation's unfolding.

In this view, our existence is not random. It is purposeful. Each stage of evolution brings the soul closer to self-realization, guided by invisible laws and loving intelligences who shape the architecture of the cosmos. We are not isolated beings adrift in chance, but participants in a vast, conscious design — each life a thread in the ever-weaving tapestry of spirit.

The Elohim, the Aeons, and the Divine Builders

The **Elohim**, as described in Genesis and other mystical traditions, are not simply gods — they are divine intelligences. Cosmic architects. Beings of immense wisdom who guided the formation of humanity through the great spiritual epochs. Working across subtle realms, they shaped the human form, nurtured consciousness, and imbued it with potential.

In **Gnostic tradition**, the **Aeons** are emanations of the Absolute — streams of divine will flowing from the Source. They are not time periods (though often mistaken for such), but conscious principles that mediate between Spirit and creation. They guard the threshold between unity and multiplicity. Each Aeon holds a unique facet of divine knowing — Sophia, Logos, Nous — shaping the soul's path like stars shaping constellations in the night sky.

Together, the Elohim and the Aeons form a divine hierarchy of conscious energy — steering the soul's descent into matter and calling it home again. Through their influence, human beings are not only formed — they are awakened.

It is from this sacred weaving of spirit and form that the human journey begins: a pilgrimage through time and trial, guided by celestial hands, toward the remembrance of who and what we truly are.

Summary of Key Esoteric Concepts in Chapter 1

Creation Phases (Steiner's Framework)

- **Saturn**: The germinal seed of consciousness. Humanity as spiritual warmth — pure potential.

- **Sun**: The birth of the etheric body. Formative forces of vitality and cosmic rhythm.

- **Moon**: The emergence of the astral body. Emotions, karma, and the roots of duality.

- **Earth**: The integration of all prior bodies and the entry of the ego. Free will and awakening begin.

Early Spiritual Forces That Shaped Human Consciousness

- **Elohim**: Divine architects who oversaw the shaping of the human form, soul, and mind.

- **Aeons**: Emanations of the Divine Source — spiritual principles that guide the descent of the Spirit into matter and help restore its ascent.

- **Mystery Schools**: Hidden sanctuaries of wisdom that preserved the knowledge of these cosmic truths across ancient civilizations.

𓂀 𓂀 𓂀

Mystery Thread Sidebar

The First Gate – Descent from the Stars

The Mystery Schools, often veiled in secrecy, have preserved humanity's oldest spiritual memory: that we are not of Earth alone. Before the soul entered the body, it passed through the spheres of the stars. Each left a mark — an imprint of spiritual force — guiding the soul's path through matter. This descent was not a fall, but a sacred choreography — each planetary sphere a temple of initiation, each star a teacher.

Initiates in ancient temples were ritually "reborn" to remember this journey. They were taught to pass through symbolic deaths and awaken to the truth of their origin. In Chaldean, Egyptian, Persian, and Greek teachings, the stars were more than celestial bodies — they were living intelligences, gateways, and guardians of memory. The heavens were seen as a scroll, written in divine language, waiting to be read by those who had eyes to see.

Astrology, in its deepest form, is not fortune-telling. It is soul-mapping — a reflection of the cosmic journey each spirit undertakes.

To the ancients, Earth was not the beginning. It was the veil. And behind that veil lies the First Gate — where we remember that we have always been more than matter, more than time, more than flesh.

Chapter 2: Manvantaras & Pralayas

The 6 Days of Creation & 1 Day of Rest

It is a common error in modern interpretation to believe that the six days of creation described in the Book of Genesis represent literal 24-hour periods. These "days" are symbolic — echoes of far older spiritual traditions that long predate the Roman coining of the term "Christian." In the ancient world, there existed a global spiritual memory — a shared understanding encoded in regional myths and metaphors. Across continents and cultures, from East to West, the same essential story was told: the soul's origin, its descent into form, its trials, and its eventual return.

These stories — whether conveyed through fire tablets, scrolls, chants, or dreams — describe cycles. They speak of times of creation and times of rest, of ages where spirit takes form, and times when form dissolves back into spirit. These are the *Manvantaras* and *Pralayas* of the ancient teachings.

The Painter and the Palette – Egyptian Echoes of Cosmic Stillness

In ancient Egyptian cosmology, the god Atum is depicted lying motionless upon the primordial waters of *Nun* — the great sea of chaos and unformed potential. All elements exist within *Nun*, yet none are arranged. It is not yet creation, but the sacred stillness before creation.

Atum's posture — reclining in silence — represents *Pralaya*, the cosmic rest. When Atum stirs, creation begins. Like a painter gazing at a palette before the first stroke, the Divine observes stillness before manifesting movement.

Thought becomes will. Will becomes motion. Creation begins. The first gesture is not sound, but intention — a subtle stirring within the heart of eternity.

This vision mirrors the concept of *Brahma's Breath* — a rhythmic cycle of inhalation and exhalation. When the breath is held, all rests in potential. When the breath is released, manifestation flows outward.

The ancients knew: before any world is born, there is silence. **Before creation, there is intention.**

Spiritual Evolution Through Cosmic Phases – Steiner's Framework

As introduced in Chapter 1, Rudolf Steiner offers a profound esoteric map of human evolution through great cosmic epochs. These are not planetary locations, but stages of being — spiritual conditions that shape the soul and its vehicles across time.

Each stage adds a layer to the human constitution:

- **Saturn** – The seed of consciousness, pure warmth, and will.

- **Sun** – The formation of the etheric body and life force.

- **Moon** – The birth of the astral body, emotions, and karmic imprint.

- **Earth** – The physical incarnation of the soul and the rise of the ego.

Each phase builds upon the last. Nature is efficient. Nothing is wasted. The soul's journey is gradual and sacred, and each stage serves as a vessel through which consciousness is refined. Just as rivers carve valleys over millennia, the soul is sculpted by time and experience — slowly, deliberately, with divine precision.

These epochs are the scaffolding of spiritual evolution — periods where the Divine shapes and reshapes the human being, forging the body, mind, and spirit through cosmic time.

Planetary Chains, Rounds, and Globes

(Theosophical Teachings from A.P. Sinnett)

In *The Mahatma Letters*, A.P. Sinnett described a vast and intricate system of spiritual evolution through the lens of planetary chains, rounds, and globes. This esoteric framework outlines the journey of the soul across planes of matter and spirit.

1. Planetary Chain

A planetary chain consists of **seven globes**, labeled **A through G**, through which a wave of life — called the *life-wave* — evolves. These globes are not all physical worlds like Earth. Some exist in astral or spiritual states invisible to ordinary perception.

- **Globe D** is our Earth.

- **Globes A, B, C** precede Earth and exist on subtler levels.

- **Globes E, F, G** follow Earth and rise into spiritual refinement.

Each globe represents a phase of the soul's development within the planetary chain.

2. Rounds

A **round** is the journey of the life-wave through all seven globes, from **A to G**. After completing this circuit once, one round is finished. The entire planetary chain undergoes **seven rounds** in total.

- We are currently in the **fourth round** on **Globe D (Earth)** — the midpoint of descent into matter.

- Earlier rounds were more etheric; later rounds will become more spiritual.

Each round refines consciousness, preparing the soul for higher capacities in future cycles.

3. Globes and Their Nature

Each globe represents a distinct realm of experience:

- **Globes A, B, C** – more subtle, spiritual, or astral.

- **Globe D** – Earth, the most physical and dense.

- **Globes E, F, G** – increasingly refined, returning toward spirit.

While part of the same planetary system, these globes vary in their vibration, purpose, and density. The soul evolves by incarnating across these realms.

4. Purpose of the System

This evolutionary model serves as a **cosmic school**:

- Souls incarnate repeatedly across **globes and rounds**.

- Each stage develops new faculties—physical, emotional, mental, and spiritual.

- By the **seventh round**, the soul achieves a vastly more awakened state.

This echoes the Theosophical vision of slow, sacred ascent through experience, purification, and divine remembrance.

Steiner's Planetary Evolution

Rudolf Steiner offered a parallel yet distinct model, outlining four great planetary epochs:

- **Old Saturn** – The first condition of warmth and will.

- **Old Sun** – The emergence of light and etheric life.

- **Old Moon** – The awakening of soul life and astral forces.

- **Earth** – The current phase of ego development and free will.

Future stages not yet reached:

- **Jupiter** – Birth of the Spirit-Self.

- **Venus** – Awakening of the Life-Spirit.

- **Vulcan** – Union with Spirit-Man, the divine human.

Steiner's model aligns conceptually with Sinnett's system: both chart an evolution from Spirit → Matter → Spirit, guiding the soul through forms and faculties across cosmic time.

The Seven Root Races

In the teachings of Blavatsky and Sinnett, humanity progresses through **seven Root Races**, each representing a distinct stage of spiritual and physical evolution—mainly unfolding during this **fourth round on Earth (Globe D)**.

The Root Races:

1. **Polarian** – Ethereal, almost non-physical.

2. **Hyperborean** – Early semi-astral forms.

3. **Lemurian** – First full physical incarnation; giant, etheric humans.

4. **Atlantean** – Development of emotions, psychic abilities.

5. **Aryan** (Current) – Development of intellect, reason, and self-awareness.

6. **Future Race** – Awakening of higher spiritual faculties.

7. **Final Race** – Union of spirit and form; completion of human evolution.

Each Root Race includes **seven sub-races**, mirroring the refinement process seen in rounds and globes.

Reincarnation and the Soul's Journey

The soul evolves by passing through these Root Races and planetary rounds over vast cycles of time:

- **Reincarnation** refines moral, mental, and spiritual nature.

- The **Higher Ego**, or divine self, chooses birth conditions aligned with karmic needs.

- Each lifetime serves as a lesson, shaping the soul's destiny and deepening its spiritual maturity.

In *Esoteric Buddhism*, Sinnett describes reincarnation not as random return, but as an intentional process of **self-becoming** – a journey from unconscious spark to awakened soul.

NDEs and the Echo of the Ancient Structure

Modern Near-Death Experiences (NDEs) often echo the very structure described in ancient esoteric teachings.

Many experiencers report moving through luminous realms, meeting beings of light, reviewing their lives, or witnessing vast landscapes of peace and clarity. These realms correspond strikingly to the **globes** described by Sinnett and the **cosmic phases** described by Steiner. What ancient seers called rounds and spiritual planes, modern experiencers describe as transitions through dimensions — each with its own atmosphere, clarity, and vibrational purpose.

Some NDEs recount passing through several "levels" before reaching a radiant, loving presence, only to be told they must return. Others speak of seeing a panoramic life review, which reflects the karmic principles taught in the doctrines of reincarnation. In these moments, judgment is absent; what is felt instead is deep understanding — an empathic immersion in one's own actions and their ripples through the lives of others.

These experiences support the idea that the soul journeys beyond physical form and returns — carrying insights, transformation, and sometimes a mission. The parallels are too consistent across cultures and testimonies to be a coincidence. NDEs may be glimpses of the same esoteric structure described by the ancients — evidence that spiritual evolution is a universal process, not confined to one tradition or age.

Summary of Esoteric Parallels

Sinnett (Theosophy)	Steiner (Anthroposophy)	Root Races	Modern NDE Parallels
7 Globes (A–G) in each planetary chain	7 Planetary Conditions (Saturn–Vulcan)	7 Root Races	Experiencers pass through levels or planes
7 Rounds per planetary chain	7 Great Ages of Earth	Lemuria to Modern Humanity	Return to Source, then reincarnation
Globe D = Earth, Round 4 (our stage)	Earth = Present evolutionary phase	5th Root Race (current)	Life reviews, karmic insight, soul missions
Life-wave evolves by refining bodies	Ego and spirit evolve through karma	Future Races = spiritual ascent	Spiritual beings guiding the return

Definition of Mahatma

The term *Mahatma* comes from the Sanskrit: *mahā* (great) and *Atman* (soul or spirit), meaning **"Great Soul."** In Theosophy, Mahatmas are **spiritually advanced beings** — often called Masters or Adepts — who have transcended personal ego and now guide humanity from higher planes. They are not worshipped as deities, but revered as luminous teachers — guardians of wisdom who once walked the earthly path and now stand beyond it, offering light to those still journeying through shadow.

Often veiled in myth and mystery, they are described as beings who dwell in silence, intervening only when karmic law allows, and always in service of the greater good. These beings were said to be the source of much of the early esoteric knowledge transmitted to Helena Blavatsky, A.P. Sinnett, and others.

Quote from *The Mahatma Letters*

(Letter No. 23B to A.P. Sinnett)

"The whole astral region, which lies beyond the earth and beyond the terrestrial atmosphere... is divided into seven degrees of density and spirituality. Each of these has its own inhabitants. And it is through these regions, from globe to globe, that the monads pass in the course of their evolution around the planetary chain."

This passage describes the journey of the soul (or *monad*) through a structured spiritual system of worlds — mirroring the architecture of **globes and rounds**. It supports the view

20

that the cosmos is not chaotic but ordered, and that souls are guided through this structure in a purposeful ascent.

Quote from Rudolf Steiner – *Cosmic Memory* (GA 11)

"Man was not always what he is now. He has passed through other forms of existence, and he will pass through still others. The Earth has had former embodiments: Old Saturn, Old Sun, and Old Moon. Each of these was a stage of preparation for Earth... and man participated in all these changes."

Here, Steiner reinforces the idea that the human being is not a product of random evolution, but a participant in an immense spiritual drama — one that spans worlds, ages, and planetary embodiments.

Minor and Major Manvantaras – Cycles Within Cycles

In Sanskrit, the word *Manvantara* means "cycle of a Manu" — a period of cosmic activity governed by a divine archetypal being. It refers to a vast epoch during which worlds are born, evolve, and are guided toward spiritual fulfillment. Between these active cycles lies *Pralaya* — the period of rest, silence, or dissolution, in which the manifested world returns to its source.

There are two primary types:

1. Minor Manvantara – A Day of Brahma

A Minor Manvantara represents the evolutionary cycle of a **single planetary chain**, such as Earth's.

- It includes:

- **Seven Globes** (A through G)

- **Seven Rounds** of spiritual development

- The evolution of **seven Root Races** on **Globe D (Earth)**

- Symbolic Duration: In Hindu cosmology, this is said to last **4.32 billion years** — a *Day of Brahma*.

This is the cycle we are currently living through. The soul evolves round by round, globe by globe, race by race — refining its physical body, emotional sensitivity, intellect, and spiritual awareness.

2. Major Manvantara – A Life of Brahma (Maha-Manvantara)

A Major Manvantara encompasses **the entire manifested universe** — all planetary chains, solar systems, and cosmic systems. It spans an incomprehensible expanse of time.

- Duration: **311.04 trillion years** (100 divine years of Brahma)

- Ends with a **Great Pralaya**, in which all creation dissolves into the unmanifested Divine Source

This grand cycle is sometimes called a **Maha-Kalpa** — the great cosmic age that includes countless minor Manvantaras. After this universal breath of manifestation completes, a period of stillness ensues, preparing the seed for a new universe to arise again.

Genesis and the Symbolic Manvantara

The **Book of Genesis**, when read esoterically, encodes the story of a Manvantara.

"In the beginning, God created the heavens and the earth..." – *Genesis 1:1*

The six days of creation represent **stages of manifestation**, much like the phases within a Manvantara. Each "day" is not a literal 24-hour period, but a symbolic expression of spiritual evolution:

- **Day 1–6**: The active phases—light, matter, life, and the soul take form.

- **Day 7**: The sacred **rest**—a *Pralaya*—where the Divine pauses, and creation becomes complete in its cycle.

Steiner interpreted these "days" as great cosmic epochs. He associated them with the stages of planetary evolution: **Old Saturn, Old Sun, Old Moon,** and **Earth**. Each phase birthed a new principle in the human being: warmth, light, life, desire, and eventually the conscious self.

"And on the seventh day God ended His work which He had made; and He rested…" – *Genesis 2:2*

This divine rest mirrors the Hindu concept of Pralaya. The Creator withdraws—not into idleness, but into a stillness that nourishes the seed of future worlds. It is a luminous pause, where all that was dissolves into potential, and all that will be waits in quiet expectancy. In this silence, the blueprint of existence is reabsorbed into the Infinite, like a dream returning to the dreamer. The cosmos breathes out (creation) and breathes in (return) — a rhythm echoed in every living being.

Adam as the Archetypal Manu

In Hinduism, each Manvantara is governed by a **Manu** — a divine lawgiver or archetypal human who seeds civilization and carries forward the moral-spiritual blueprint of humanity.

In the Book of Genesis, **Adam** serves a similar archetypal role. He is not merely the first man, but the symbolic vessel through which the spiritual lineage of humanity is initiated.

- **Manu** in the East is the Lawgiver, the human pattern-bearer.

- **Adam** in the West is the First Man, from whose line generations of awakening unfold.

Both figures mark the beginning of human individuality — where soul and body meet, and the path toward conscious spiritual return begins.

Summary of Symbolic Parallels

Sanskrit/ Esoteric Term	Genesis Symbolism	Spiritual Meaning
Manvantara	Six Days of Creation	Periods of divine manifestation and world-building
Pralaya	The Seventh Day (Sabbath, Rest)	Cosmic rest, spiritual withdrawal, preparation for a new cycle
Manu	Adam (First Man)	Archetypal human; initiator of the soul's journey through matter
Root Races & Rounds	Generations of Adam's line	Phases of evolving consciousness across spiritual epochs

Manvantaras and the Genesis of the Soul

In both Eastern and Western esoteric traditions, the universe is not seen as static but as alive — breathing through vast cycles of manifestation (*Manvantaras*) and rest (*Pralayas*). During each Manvantara, beings, planets, and souls come into form, fulfill their purpose, and eventually dissolve back into Spirit. Each Pralaya is not a void, but a sacred silence — a gestational stillness that prepares the way for renewal.

This cosmic rhythm governs not just stars and systems but the soul itself. Our very being is formed, refined, and lifted through these cycles — each lifetime a thread in the tapestry of becoming.

1. Minor Manvantara – The Earth's Sacred Cycle

In a Minor Manvantara, a single planetary chain undergoes its full evolution:

- **Seven rounds**, each passing through **seven globes** (A–G)

- We are now in the **fourth round**, evolving on **Globe D (Earth)**

- During this round, **seven Root Races** unfold, each representing a stage in the soul's journey

Each globe is like a classroom. Each round is a semester. Each Root Race is a lesson plan guiding the soul from unconscious origin to awakened divinity.

In Hindu cosmology, this cycle lasts 4.32 billion years — a Day of Brahma. It is not literal time, but symbolic depth: a measure of spiritual evolution, not clocks and calendars.

2. Major Manvantara – The Life of the Cosmos

The Major Manvantara is the cycle of all cycles — the great unfolding of the universe itself. It includes multiple planetary chains, countless stars, and untold beings moving through the stages of divine memory and return.

26

- Duration: 311.04 trillion years

- Culminates in the **Great Pralaya**, when all things return to the Source

- Prepares the ground for the next cosmic manifestation

This immense cycle reveals the scale and purpose of creation: a living temple through which Spirit knows itself.

Lemuria and Atlantis – Epochs of Root Races

In Theosophy and Anthroposophy, **Lemuria** and **Atlantis** were not just mythical lands, but **epochs** — distinct stages in the development of the Root Races during the Fourth Round of this planetary Manvantara. They are remembered not through ruins or relics, but through symbols, dreams, and the echoes of ancient memory embedded in sacred texts and esoteric teachings.

These civilizations represent not only geographic realities (now lost to history) but spiritual states of consciousness that marked humanity's descent into matter and eventual climb toward higher awareness.

Lemuria – The Epoch of the Third Root Race

- **Lemurians** were early human forms: towering, etheric, and not yet fully physical

- They possessed dreamlike clairvoyance and lived close to nature and spirit

- It was during this epoch that:

- **Gender separation** occurred

- **Physical reproduction** began

- **Karma and individuation** first took hold

The **sinking of Lemuria** symbolizes the end of unconscious spirituality and the beginning of duality — the soul's entanglement in the physical world. It was both a literal and symbolic fall into deeper incarnation.

Atlantis – The Epoch of the Fourth Root Race

- **Atlanteans** were more physical, intellectual, and psychically powerful

- They developed advanced civilizations, technologies, and occult abilities

- However, moral development did not keep pace with knowledge

The **destruction of Atlantis** is a karmic event — a result of spiritual misuse. It marks the transition from psychic dominance to the rise of the **ego-consciousness** that defines the current Fifth Root Race.

This fall was not punishment — it was refinement. A necessary turning point, making way for a more individualized and morally awakened humanity.

How Lemuria and Atlantis Fit Within the Manvantara

- Both Lemuria and Atlantis occurred during the **Fourth Round** of the **Earth's planetary chain**

- They represent **Root Races 3 and 4**, respectively

- We are now in **Root Race 5**, still within Round 4, on Globe D

The rounds follow a pattern:

- Rounds 1–3: Descent from spirit

- Round 4: The most **dense and material**

- Rounds 5–7: Ascent back into spiritual form

The destruction of Lemuria and Atlantis can be seen as **mini-pralayas** — smaller cycles of dissolution that cleared the way for new stages of growth.

Rudolf Steiner's View

Steiner affirmed the existence of Lemuria and Atlantis, not only as past civilizations but as epochs of consciousness:

- In **Lemuria**, the soul was still partially in the spirit world — dreamlike, clairvoyant, and intuitive

- In **Atlantis**, the soul became more anchored in the body, preparing for **ego development**

- Both epochs were necessary stages in the descent of the soul into self-awareness

He aligned them with his planetary evolution scheme: **Old Saturn, Old Sun, Old Moon,** and **Earth** — each stage deepening embodiment and awakening the divine spark within.

The Cataclysms of Lemuria and Atlantis – Cycles Within the Cycle

In the esoteric traditions of Theosophy and Anthroposophy, Lemuria and Atlantis are more than submerged continents — they are deeply symbolic epochs in the soul's evolution. Their destruction marked not just geological events, but thresholds in the journey of collective humanity.

Each took place within the **Fourth Round** of the current **Minor Manvantara** — the round of greatest material density. Each Root Race represents a **sub-cycle** within this greater round, and Lemuria and Atlantis housed Root Races 3 and 4, respectively. In Lemuria, form was soft, consciousness was inward, and spirit still danced freely through matter. Atlantis saw the rise of ego, technology, and separation — a brilliant yet dangerous flame that would ultimately consume itself.

These falls were not endings — they were initiations. They mirror the cosmic rhythm of **Manvantara and Pralaya** on a smaller scale: manifestation, moral decline, dissolution, and the chance to begin anew.

Lemuria – The Fall from Ether to Earth

- Home of the **Third Root Race**, Lemuria was a time of transition.

- Humans were still giant, etheric, and spiritually attuned.

- It was during this epoch that humanity took on **physical reproduction**, began to develop **individual karma**, and encountered the **first moral choices**.

The **sinking of Lemuria** represents a loss of collective innocence and the beginning of deep individuation. The soul stepped further into duality and the world of form.

Atlantis – The Fall of Psychic Power

- The **Fourth Root Race** of Atlantis developed greater intellect, psychic powers, and complex civilizations.

- However, these gifts were misused. Pride and spiritual disconnection led to destruction.

- Atlantis sank beneath karmic waters, cleansing the Earth and preparing it for a new phase.

The **Atlantean fall** symbolizes what happens when **knowledge outpaces wisdom** — when the soul forgets its source and wields power without love. Yet through this fall, the ego was born, and with it, the capacity for redemption.

Steiner's View – Lemuria, Atlantis, and the Soul's Descent

Rudolf Steiner taught that:

- In **Lemuria**, humans still lived partly in the spiritual world, experiencing **dreamlike clairvoyance**.

- In **Atlantis**, this spiritual perception faded, and **conscious memory** and **ego-awareness** emerged.

For Steiner, both epochs represent **necessary descents**. The soul, to awaken fully, had to forget—to enter darkness in order to kindle its own light. These epochs prepared us for the challenges of the Fifth Root Race, in which we are now immersed.

The Present Crisis – A Turning Point in the Fifth Root Race

We are now in the **Fifth Root Race**, amid the Fourth Round of Earth's evolution. And again, the signs of another great turning point are all around us.

Like Atlantis before its fall, today's world is marked by:

- Unprecedented technological advancement

- Widespread materialism

- Spiritual disconnection

- Moral confusion

Steiner and Blavatsky warned that when civilizations abandon their spiritual purpose, **karmic correction** arises. Earth responds—not as punishment, but as a sacred balancing force.

Natural disasters, cultural breakdown, and psychic unrest reflect a deeper disorder in the soul of modern humanity. We are repeating the lessons of Lemuria and Atlantis—and standing once more at a precipice.

But this is not only a warning—it is a call.

The Dawn of the Sixth Root Race

If the inner wisdom of the soul is remembered, if the teachings encoded in the cycles of the ancients are honored, we may transcend the coming upheaval and enter a new spiritual era: the **Sixth Root Race**.

- This new humanity will not be defined by geography, culture, or blood—but by **consciousness**.

- It will emerge from scattered souls across the world —**seed-bearers** awakened to their divine heritage.

- Their task will not be to dominate, but to **heal**, **restore**, and **reunite** the physical with the spiritual.

This race is not a chosen people—it is a chosen awareness. And those who walk in that awareness will become bridges between worlds.

𓂀 𓂀 𓂀

Mystery Thread Sidebar: The Sixth Root Race – The Dawn of the Inner Sun

In the sacred scrolls of the Mystery Schools, it is written that the **Sixth Root Race** will not arise through conquest, power, or technology—but through the awakening of the **inner light**. It will emerge like dawn over a sleeping world

—not with thunder, but with stillness that speaks straight to the heart.

Where Atlantis fell by misusing psychic force, and where modern man teeters beneath the weight of intellect without soul, the coming humanity will be born of **wisdom fused with compassion**.

This race will not be defined by nation, lineage, or creed. It will arise quietly—from souls scattered across the Earth— **torchbearers** who live not by external law, but by an **inner truth**. They are the early blossoms of a new spiritual spring. Like seeds responding to an invisible season, they will awaken at the appointed hour, guided not by calendars, but by an inner knowing that the time has come.

The Mystery teachings foresaw this race not as a biological category, but as a **state of being**—the embodiment of the **Christ Light**, not as dogma, but as radiant consciousness. These souls will not build empires. They will build **temples of consciousness**—silent sanctuaries in which the soul remembers its origin.

They will walk with clarity between masculine and feminine, intellect and intuition, action and silence. And as the veils of illusion fall, the Earth itself will be renewed— not by force, but by the **radiance of awakened souls** aligned with divine purpose.

☥ ☥ ☥

Mystery Thread Sidebar: The Spiritual Ark – Preserving the Flame in the Storm

When a cycle nears its end, and the winds of dissolution begin to stir, there are always those who are called — not to escape the storm, but to **preserve the sacred flame** within it. They are not alarmed by the thunder, nor shaken by the crumbling of old forms. In their stillness, they recognize the rhythm of renewal.

These are the builders of the **spiritual ark** — not fashioned from wood and pitch, but from **memory, wisdom, and inner fire**. Like the Ark of Noah, or the hidden scrolls of ancient temples, they carry the essence of truth through the flood of collapse.

The Mystery Schools taught that before every great cataclysm, a remnant is prepared — a circle of awakened souls who have passed through initiation, silence, and sacrifice. These souls carry the **symbols**, the **chants**, the **living truths** of ages long forgotten. They are the keepers of forgotten names, of maps drawn in myth, of vibrations that once called stars into being.

They do not resist the fall. They pass through it — unshaken, unwavering, remembering.

You may know them by their quiet clarity. In the artist who paints otherworldly visions. In the dreamer who walks between worlds. In the healer who touches without words. In the child whose eyes shine with ancient light.

The ark is already forming—not to flee the world, but to **anchor its rebirth**. And those who enter it become not merely survivors—but **founders of a coming age**.

𓂀 𓂀 𓂀

Mystery Thread Sidebar: The Echo of Forgotten Ages

In the hidden teachings of the ancient Mysteries, **history is not linear**. It rises and falls like the breath of a cosmic being. Every civilization—like every soul—is tested by its use of **power, knowledge**, and **truth**.

The initiates remembered Lemuria and Atlantis not merely as lands swallowed by water, but as **echoes of warning** etched into the stones of time. They knew that when inner light is sacrificed for outer ambition, when sacred law is mocked by ego, **the Earth re-balance**s.

The stones still speak. The temples still hum. The myths still hold the memory.

The fall is not the end. It is the **veiled beginning** of something higher. But ascent is never guaranteed.

In this present age, the temples lie buried—both beneath the soil and within the human heart. But the Mystery still whispers, to those who will listen: **"Awaken. Remember. Rebuild."**

For within each Root Race, within each breath of the great wheel, the soul is being prepared—**not just to endure the fall**, but to **rise through it into something greater than it was before**.

36

The Akashic Records and the Memory of the Soul

All of these cosmic cycles—the breaths of Brahma, the rounds of globes, the rise and fall of Root Races—are recorded in the **Akashic Records**. This subtle realm, known in esoteric science as the memory field of the cosmos, holds the imprint of every thought, event, and spiritual evolution. In this realm, **time is not linear**. Nothing is lost. It is less a book than a living ocean—fluid, luminous, and responsive —where past, present, and future ripple simultaneously. Those who learn to read its currents do not merely observe history; they feel it, as if remembering a dream long forgotten.

Rudolf Steiner taught that Earth, as we know it, is the fourth incarnation of a much older spiritual planet. Just as the soul evolves, so too does the planet—**densifying through cycles**, each time becoming more material, and then, more refined. Each incarnation leaves behind spiritual sediment, the essence of experience layered into the fabric of the world itself.

From **astral**, to **etheric**, to **physical**—and eventually, back again to **spirit**—this is the **arc of Earth's journey**, and our own.

The Monad and Root Races – From Ether to Flesh

The **Monad**—the immortal spark of divine origin— descends through the kingdoms of nature: mineral, plant, animal, and finally into human form. This journey is not metaphorical, but what Blavatsky called **spiritual biology**: the progressive descent of consciousness into incarnation.

- The **First Root Races** were almost non-physical — etheric, glowing, vast.

- Only with **Root Race 3 (Lemurian)** did the Monad begin to inhabit dense physical form.

- We are now in **Root Race 5, Sub-Race 5** — the phase of intellect and awakening spirit.

Some traditions speak of **fossilized bones of giants** — remnants of earlier, titanic forms. But most early races left no bones. They were not yet calcified enough to fossilize. What remains are **myths**, **structures**, and **echoes** — etched into Earth's memory and the Akasha.

Globes, Chains, and Rounds – Earth as a Spiritual Clock

Each planetary chain undergoes seven stages — or **globes** — through which life evolves.

- We are currently on **Globe D**, the most dense.

- Humanity must unfold through **seven Root Races on this globe** before the Earth becomes more spiritual again.

This is not just evolution — it is **initiation**. The soul is slowly awakening the divine faculties it once held instinctively, now to be **earned through struggle and memory**.

No Clear Boundaries – Root Races Blend and Evolve

Just as dawn blends into day, so do Root Races flow into one another. There is no single moment of change. Human variation today reflects a spectrum of inner development — not a hierarchy, but a tapestry. Each thread carries its own hue and purpose, and when woven together, they form the evolving soul of humanity. Some are keepers of memory, others are bringers of vision; some dig into the roots, while others reach for the stars.

A tribal healer in the rain forest may carry ancient memories. A theoretical physicist may be rediscovering the same truths in numbers. Neither is superior — they are facets of the whole, walking parallel paths toward the same summit.

Awakening the Ancient Faculties – The Sleeping Soul Stirs

In Lemurian and early Atlantean times, humans possessed **clairvoyance, telepathy**, and **spiritual intuition**. Over time, these faculties receded to make room for intellect and ego. Now, as we move toward the **Sixth Sub-Race**, these gifts are stirring once more.

We are witnessing a quiet reawakening:

- Near-death experiences

- Spontaneous visions and insights

- Archetypal dreams

- Psychic sensitivity

39

- Intuitive knowing

These are not supernatural. They are natural. They are **remembrances** of what the soul has always known.

Conclusion – A Journey Through Fire and Light

The epochs of **Saturn, Sun, Moon, and Earth** live within us still. The warmth of Saturn, the light of the Sun, the longing of the Moon, and the trial of Earth shape our every step.

The teachings of Steiner, Blavatsky, and Sinnett—like the whispers of the Mystery Schools—reveal that the soul's path is not accidental. It is designed. It is sacred.

To know these cycles is not to distance ourselves from life, but to walk more deeply within it—**with purpose, with reverence**, and with the **fire of memory** in our bones.

As near-death experiencers return with messages of light, and as the inner senses of the soul reawaken, we are reminded:

The spiral continues. The soul remembers. The journey is real.

𓂀 𓂀 𓂀

Mystery Thread Sidebar: The Lost and Returning Sight

In the esoteric tradition, figures like **Joseph, Daniel**, and **Enoch** were not merely prophets—they were **initiates**. They held keys to a world most had forgotten: a world of vision, of symbol, of soul-truth spoken in silence. Joseph with his "Coat of Many Colors" and his still-active ability to interpret the Pharaoh's dreams is but one example of a soul having kept those far distant traces which are in us dormant, not lost...dormant. They walked the boundary between worlds, their lives woven with dreams, omens, and moments when time stood still.

Their gifts — dream interpretation, inner vision, communion with higher beings — were not unique to them. These were once **universal human faculties**, shared across cultures and lands, from desert temples to forest circles. They were the original languages of the soul — spoken not in words, but in symbols, in patterns of light and rhythm that needed no translation.

Over time, as humanity descended deeper into materialism, these faculties fell dormant. But they were never lost. Among indigenous peoples, among mystics and poets, among those who hear the subtle voice — **the thread has remained**. Thinner, quieter, but alive.

The Mystery Schools teach that what was once **instinct must become insight**. What was once a **gift must become an earned vision**. And now, as the veil begins to lift again, more and more souls begin to feel it: the pulse of a sight returning — not to the eyes, but to the heart.

Chapter 3: The Nature of the Soul

The Journey into the Self

What is the soul?

This question echoes through the corridors of religion, philosophy, mysticism, and modern science. To the ancient initiates, the soul was not a metaphor or abstraction — it was the **eternal traveler**, the **divine spark** that descended into matter and would one day rise again.

From the sacred temples of Egypt to the dialogues of Plato, and from Blavatsky's *Secret Doctrine* to Steiner's spiritual science, the nature of the soul stands at the center of understanding **life, death, and rebirth**. It is the unseen thread that links all stages of existence, weaving together incarnation, purpose, and transcendence. In this and the following chapters, we explore the soul's descent into matter, its esoteric anatomy, and its journey across lifetimes. We delve into ancient myths, symbolic systems, and cross-cultural initiatory teachings, uncovering patterns that point to a deeper reality behind the veil of the physical world. Through the lens of ancient wisdom and modern Near-Death Experiences (NDEs), we begin to glimpse our **true spiritual identity** — hidden in the depths of the self, yet longing to be remembered.

The Soul's Descent from the Higher Worlds

According to esoteric teachings, the human soul is composed of multiple sheaths or bodies. Rudolf Steiner outlined four primary aspects:

- **Physical Body** – The material vessel.

- **Etheric Body** – The life force and memory matrix.

- **Astral Body** – The emotional and imaginative field.

- **Ego ("I-AM")** – The evolving spiritual self.

The descent of the soul into incarnation moves it from the higher spiritual worlds into the densest material realms. In Steiner's cosmology, this process is not a fall in the moral sense, but a necessary phase of evolution. Through **karma** and **reincarnation**, the soul learns, remembers, and gradually transforms.

Plato and the Theory of Forms

Plato taught that the soul originates in a **realm of perfect Forms**—eternal archetypes that exist beyond space and time. To be born is to **forget**; to philosophize is to **recollect**. For Plato, the soul carries within it the memory of truth, beauty, and goodness—insights that can be awakened through contemplation, virtue, and spiritual practice. The visible world, he believed, was but a shadow of the real—an echo of the eternal realities the soul once knew. In glimpsing these Forms, the soul begins to reorient itself toward its true home, guided by a kind of divine homesickness.

This echoes the esoteric understanding that the soul descends from a divine source and retains a hidden imprint of that original perfection, waiting to be reawakened.

Blavatsky and the Root Races

Helena Blavatsky expanded this view with the doctrine of **Root Races** — stages of human development reflecting shifts in consciousness and form. The soul incarnates across these great epochs, evolving through experience.

According to Blavatsky, the Aryan Root Race (to which modern humanity belongs) is tasked with developing the **higher mind** and **spiritual will**. The journey of the soul involves shedding illusion, transcending desire, and remembering its divine origin. Each Root Race, she taught, mirrors a step in the soul's unfoldment — from the etheric, dreamlike consciousness of early humanity to the rational and intuitive faculties of the present age. In this sweeping vision, history becomes the biography of the soul itself — an odyssey through cycles of light and shadow.

The Esoteric Anatomy of the Human Being

Building on Steiner's insights, the human being is seen as a **living spiritual structure**:

- **Physical Body** – Rooted in matter.

- **Etheric Body** – The life field; carries growth and memory.

- **Astral Body** – Source of emotion, passion, and inner images.

- **Ego ("I")** – The divine individual spirit, which evolves over lifetimes.

This anatomy is **not fixed**. It is shaped by karma, suffering, initiation, and moral action. Death is not the end

—it is a metamorphosis, a shedding of outer layers before the soul continues its journey.

Karma and Reincarnation

In all major esoteric systems, the soul is subject to the **law of karma** — the universal principle of cause and effect. Every thought, action, and intention shapes the soul's path. Life is not random; it is exquisitely ordered, though veiled in mystery.

Reincarnation offers the soul the opportunity to refine itself over many lives. It is not a punishment, but a sacred process — each incarnation a lesson, a test, a return to truth.

The Soul in the Light of NDEs

Modern Near-Death Experiences often confirm what the ancients taught: that the soul is **eternal, luminous**, and **divine**. Those who return from clinical death speak of:

- Leaving their bodies

- Entering realms of light

- Encountering beings of love and wisdom

- Experiencing panoramic life reviews

These testimonies suggest that consciousness is **not confined to the brain**. NDEs often lead to transformation — returning individuals become more compassionate, awakened, and spiritually centered.

The Purpose of the Soul's Journey

According to mystery teachings, the purpose is evolution—not only of form, but of spirit. Earth is a school where the soul learns to integrate love, wisdom, and will. Each incarnation is a spiral step—descending to forget, then ascending to remember. This journey is not random but guided by inner necessity, as the soul encounters precisely those experiences needed for its growth. Karma and destiny, far from being punishments, are the soul's curriculum—crafted to awaken latent potentials and restore divine memory.

When the soul begins to awaken, life itself becomes sacred. Hardship becomes instruction. Joy becomes a celebration. And death becomes a doorway—not an end. It is through these cycles of forgetting and remembering that the soul becomes luminous—refined by time, yet rooted in eternity.

Convergence of Ancient Wisdom and Near-Death Experiences

1. The Soul as an Eternal Spark of the Divine

- **Ancient Wisdom:** Plato taught that the soul preexists the body and descends from the realm of Forms. Blavatsky called it a fragment of the universal spirit evolving through lifetimes.

- **NDE Insight:** Many experiencers describe "going home" or "remembering" their true identity—a divine soul temporarily embodied.

2. The Life Review and the Law of Karma

- **Ancient Wisdom:** Karma is central in Hinduism and Theosophy. The Egyptian *Book of the Dead* speaks of the heart being weighed.

- **NDE Insight:** Individuals often relive their lives, feeling the emotional impact of their actions — mirroring karmic law and the soul's moral accountability.

3. The Astral and Etheric Bodies

- **Ancient Wisdom:** Steiner and Blavatsky taught of multiple soul bodies — astral, etheric, and beyond.

- **NDE Insight:** Many describe floating above their bodies, tethered by a "silver cord," and retaining awareness in a non-physical form.

4. Encounters with Beings of Light or Guides

- **Ancient Wisdom:** Mystery traditions speak of divine messengers and guides assisting the soul beyond death.

- **NDE Insight:** Countless experiencers report meetings with radiant beings of love who offer guidance, reassurance, and insight.

5. The Purpose of Earthly Life

- **Ancient Wisdom:** Earth is a training ground. The soul evolves through choice, experience, and service.

- **NDE Insight:** Many return from death with a renewed purpose. They're told their "mission is not complete"—that life has a deeper meaning to fulfill.

👁 👁 👁

Mystery Thread Sidebar: The Divine Blueprint of the Soul

In the Mystery Schools, the soul was known to be a **divine spark fallen into matter**. The rites of initiation mirrored this descent and return, symbolized through **death and rebirth**. The soul's anatomy was revealed slowly—first through symbol, then through inner experience.

In Egypt, this was the **weighing of the heart**. In Greece, it was the **descent into the underworld**. In Persia, it was the **fire of purification**. In every tradition, the soul journeyed, was tested, and ultimately found its way back to the light.

Today, this journey continues—not only in ritual, but in life itself. In NDEs. In dreams. In the longing of the seeker who yearns to remember what they truly are.

The blueprint is still within us.

The path has never vanished.

The soul is on its way home.

50

Chapter 4: Rudolf Steiner and Spiritual Science

Rudolf Steiner's Esoteric Vision

Rudolf Steiner (1861–1925), philosopher, mystic, and founder of **Anthroposophy**, expanded Theosophical teachings into a detailed cosmology of **spiritual evolution**, reincarnation, and the soul's journey beyond death. His insights remain some of the most structured and spiritually precise models of life after death in the Western esoteric tradition.

One of Steiner's core contributions was his teaching on the **etheric body** — the subtle "life body" that animates the physical form and bridges the soul to the spiritual worlds. Alongside the **physical, astral**, and **ego ("I")** bodies, the etheric body plays a vital role during life, death, and the soul's eventual return. At the moment of death, Steiner described how the etheric body withdraws, carrying with it a panoramic memory of the life just lived — a life tableau that the soul reviews in deep clarity and detachment. This process marks the beginning of the soul's inward journey through realms shaped by thought, feeling, and moral development.

For Steiner, spiritual evolution involved consciously working with these inner bodies, refining them through meditation, ethical striving, and self-knowledge, so that the soul may return more whole to its source.

The Etheric Body – Bridge of Life and Memory

In Steiner's spiritual science, the **etheric body** is the **subtle life-force** that energizes and sustains the physical body. It is responsible for:

- **Vitality and Growth:** Governs healing, aging, regeneration, and biological functions.

- **Memory and Karmic Impressions:** Holds life experiences and karmic lessons imprinted during incarnation.

- **Rhythmic Time Cycles:** Connected to nature's rhythms — sleep, breathing, aging, and seasonal cycles.

- **Formative Structure:** Distinct from the astral body, which governs emotions, the etheric body organizes life functions and maintains coherence.

The Soul's Transition: Death and the Etheric Unfolding

According to Steiner, the process of dying unfolds in carefully ordered stages:

1. Separation from the Physical Body

- At the moment of death, the etheric body detaches from the physical form but remains tethered to the soul.

- Many Near-Death Experiences describe this moment as **floating above their body**, echoing Steiner's descriptions.

2. The Life Review

- Over the first few days after death, the etheric body **replays the entire life** in a panoramic review — vivid, immersive, and multi-perspectival.

- This is what many NDE reports describe as a "life review" — a reliving of events with full emotional awareness of how one's actions affected others.

- Steiner taught that this "etheric film" is shown before the etheric body dissolves.

3. Dissolution into the Cosmic Ether

- Around three days after death, the etheric body **dissolves into the cosmic ether**, releasing its energies.

- Its karmic impressions, however, are **retained by the soul**, influencing future incarnations.

- This moment marks the soul's transition into higher realms, initiating its **astral phase** of post-mortem evolution.

4. Transition to the Astral World

- With the etheric body gone, the **astral body** remains — carrying emotional patterns, desires, and unresolved karmic dynamics.

- This is where **soul lessons are digested**, and spiritual insight begins to deepen.

Connections to Near-Death Experiences and Eastern Teachings

Steiner's view of the afterlife resonates closely with both ancient wisdom and modern NDE accounts:

- **NDE Parallels:** The light body that fades, the life review, the presence of spiritual beings — all reflect Steiner's etheric and astral teachings.

- **Hinduism & Buddhism:** Similar descriptions of a subtle energy sheath that dissipates after death, leaving the core soul essence to ascend.

- **Karmic Continuity:** While the etheric body dissolves, its **impressions live on**, shaping the soul's path forward.

The etheric body does **not reincarnate** — but it acts as a **bridge** between material life and the soul's eternal memory.

Rudolf Steiner: Life and Legacy

Early Life and Background

- **Born:** February 27, 1861, in Donji Kraljevec, Austria-Hungary (modern-day Croatia)

- Raised in a rural setting, Steiner reported spiritual visions and awareness from an early age.

- His early experiences formed the foundation for a life of profound spiritual inquiry.

Education and Influences

- Studied **mathematics, philosophy, science, and literature** in Vienna.

- Edited and published the scientific works of **Johann Wolfgang von Goethe**, whose naturalistic worldview deeply shaped Steiner's spiritual science.

- Influenced by **German Idealism, Theosophy**, and **Western esotericism**.

Major Accomplishments

1. **Founder of Anthroposophy (1912–1913)**

- A movement integrating mysticism, science, and esoteric Christianity.

- Emphasized **direct spiritual perception**, reincarnation, karma, and cosmic evolution.

2. **Waldorf Education (1919)**

- A holistic educational model focused on creativity, imagination, and spiritual development.

- Over 1,000 Waldorf schools now exist worldwide.

3. Bio dynamic Agriculture (1924)

- An organic farming system aligned with cosmic and seasonal rhythms.

- Continues to be practiced globally in ecological communities.

4. Architecture and the Goetheanum

- Designed the **Goetheanum** in Dornach, Switzerland —a spiritual temple and cultural center for Anthroposophy.

- The architecture itself reflects **spiritual geometry and sacred form**.

5. Esoteric Christianity and the Akashic Records

- Taught that **Christ is a cosmic being,** whose incarnation marked a turning point in Earth's evolution.

- Claimed to access the **Akashic Records**—a spiritual archive containing the memory of humanity and the Earth.

Death and Continuing Influence

- **Died:** March 30, 1925, in Dornach, Switzerland.

- Steiner's work endures through a global network of Anthroposophical institutions, schools, farms, clinics, and study groups.

His teachings on the **soul's spiritual anatomy**, the **etheric body**, and the **afterlife** continue to bridge ancient knowledge with contemporary spiritual inquiry.

𓂀 𓂀 𓂀

Mystery Thread Sidebar: The Soul's Passage Through Ether

In the hidden chambers of the Mystery Schools, initiates were taught of the **subtle vehicles of the soul** — bodies of light, breath, and memory that surround and shape the incarnated being. The **etheric body** was one such sheath — known in Egypt as the Ka, and in India as the Pranamaya Kosha.

This body was revered as the keeper of memory, the echo of the life just lived. When death came, the soul did not depart in an instant — it passed **through the gate of memory**, watching the story unfold in full. This panoramic life review was not merely reflective — it was transformative, offering the soul a chance to behold the consequences of its choices, not as judgment, but as deep learning.

The Mystery rites taught that **what is unlearned returns**, and what is realized remains etched in the soul's subtle form. The etheric body was the **scroll upon which the gods inscribed one's deeds** — not to condemn, but to guide. It was said that this scroll accompanied the soul across the threshold, informing the next incarnation like a map drawn in light and shadow.

Even now, as Near-Death Experiences echo these truths, the teachings return—quietly, through those who have seen beyond the veil.

Chapter 5: Plato and the Eternal Forms of the Soul

The Philosopher's Vision of the Eternal

Plato, one of the most influential thinkers of the ancient world, offered a metaphysical framework that has shaped Western philosophy and esoteric thought for over two millennia. Central to his vision is the **Theory of Forms**—a teaching that behind the world of appearances lies a realm of **eternal, unchanging realities.**

According to Plato, every object and concept in the physical world is merely a shadow, an imperfect reflection of its true, ideal essence—the **Form** or **Idea**—which exists in a higher dimension. This transcendent realm is not an abstraction, but the ground of true being. The Form of Beauty, the Form of Justice, the Form of Goodness—all exist beyond space and time, eternal and perfect. To perceive these Forms is to touch the divine—an act not of the senses, but of the soul's higher faculties. In this way, Plato offers not only a philosophy, but a path to awakening the eternal within.

The Soul's Divine Origin

At the heart of Plato's cosmology is the conviction that the **soul originates in this higher realm.** Before birth, the soul dwells in communion with the Forms, beholding truth, beauty, and goodness in their purest states. But when the soul incarnates into a physical body, it **forgets this divine knowledge.** Earthly life becomes a veil—yet one that can be lifted.

Within us remains a **latent memory** of these eternal truths—a spiritual echo known as **anamnesis**. The soul's task in life is to **recollect** its divine origin through **philosophical inquiry, virtue, and spiritual awakening**. This remembrance is not intellectual alone; it is experiential —a stirring of the inner being, like a flame rekindled from within.

The Allegory of the Cave

In his work *The Republic*, Plato presents his famous **Allegory of the Cave**. Prisoners, chained since birth, face a wall upon which shadows are cast by firelight behind them. To them, the shadows are reality. But if one prisoner escapes and ascends to the world above, he sees the sun and realizes the truth: the shadows were only illusions.

This allegory reflects the **soul's journey from ignorance to enlightenment**. The cave is the material world; the shadows are sense-perceptions; the sun is the ultimate truth —the Form of the Good. The escape from the cave is the spiritual ascent from illusion to reality.

Near-Death Experiences (NDEs) echo this allegory. Many experiencers describe leaving behind a shadowy world and entering realms of radiant light, understanding, and divine love. Like the freed prisoner, they awaken to a reality that was always present but hidden from ordinary awareness. Such accounts reaffirm the timeless insight that the material world, though compelling, is not our final home—it is a passage, a place of awakening and return.

The Soul's Descent and Return

Plato's teachings align closely with esoteric traditions, which hold that the soul descends into matter not as punishment, but as **a necessary stage of growth**. Life in the physical world offers challenges and experiences that awaken deeper virtues — love, wisdom, courage, and self-awareness.

The Forms represent not only abstract ideals but **divine blueprints** — archetypes of what we are meant to become. The path of the soul is one of **remembrance** and **realignment**. Through reflection, ethical living, and inner purification, the soul gradually lifts the veil and reawakens its connection to the divine. This journey is cyclical and luminous: the soul spirals through lifetimes, gathering insight, shedding illusion, and drawing ever closer to its Source.

In this light, Plato's philosophy is not merely academic — it is a **spiritual map**. It teaches us that the visible world is not the ultimate reality and that our purpose is to return to the eternal, invisible world from which we came. To walk this path is to become more fully oneself — not merely human, but divine in origin, destiny, and essence.

Implications for Reincarnation

Plato's metaphysics also lays the groundwork for a profound understanding of **reincarnation**. In works such as the *Phaedrus* and *Phaedo*, he describes the soul's cyclical journey through many lives, driven by memory, desire, and the pursuit of truth.

Key Implications:

1. **The Soul Preexists Birth:** The soul does not begin at conception—it is eternal, having existed in the realm of Forms before incarnation.

2. **Death Is Not an End**: Death is a return—a liberation of the soul from the material prison and a return to its natural, divine state.

3. **Spiritual Awakening Is the Purpose**: Life is a process of awakening—of remembering the truth the soul once knew.

4. **Multiple Incarnations Are Required**: The soul undergoes many lifetimes to shed illusions, learn virtues, and eventually transcend the cycle of birth and death.

Plato's Influence on Esoteric Traditions

Plato's teachings deeply influenced the **Mystery Schools, Gnosticism, Neoplatonism**, and **Hermeticism**. All these traditions affirm that:

- The **true self** is spiritual and eternal.

- The **material world is a temporary stage**.

- The path of wisdom and purification leads to **liberation from illusion**.

While Plato is often viewed as the father of Western philosophy, his roots are older. The wisdom he preserved came from **ancient Egypt, India**, and the **Far East**. As many scholars and initiates have noted, **Greece inherited the**

mysteries from earlier civilizations, translating them into a new philosophical language.

The Life of Plato

- **Born:** Circa 428–423 BCE

- **Died:** Circa 348–347 BCE

- **Location:** Athens, Greece

Plato was a student of **Socrates** and teacher of **Aristotle**. His Academy was one of the first institutions of higher learning in the Western world. Yet beyond his intellectual legacy, Plato was a **seer of the soul** — a philosopher who pointed humanity toward the eternal light beyond the cave.

𓂀 𓂀 𓂀

Mystery Thread Sidebar: The Path of Remembrance

In the ancient Mysteries, the soul's journey was seen as a **spiral of forgetting and remembering**. Initiates were taught that life in the body was a sacred descent — a voluntary passage through darkness for the sake of divine transformation.

Plato's Allegory of the Cave mirrors the **initiate's path**: blindfolded, confused, humbled by shadow — then slowly turned toward the light. The **sun** in his allegory was not just a metaphor for truth — it was a symbol of the **divine source** the soul left behind. This ascent was not instantaneous, but earned through trials — rituals that tested the soul's resolve, purified its intent, and gradually restored its inner sight.

The Mystery Schools taught that the soul must remember its origin—not by external teaching alone, but through inner vision, self-mastery, and the awakening of **the eye of the heart**.

In our modern time, when NDEs recount journeys beyond light and life reviews echo karmic truths, Plato's wisdom returns—not as relic, but as prophecy.

"The soul ascends into the unseen realm, and there, she awakens as light itself."

— Plato

Chapter 6: Behind the Veil – An Occultist's Perspective

What Happens Immediately After Death?

Across mystical traditions, death is not the end, but a transition into another state of being. The soul, upon leaving the body, experiences a moment of profound clarity. The veil between the physical and spiritual realms lifts. This moment is echoed in the Book of Revelation, where John the Seer "looked up" and saw the heavens parting like the opening of a scroll. He, too, said he did not know whether he was in the body or out of it—an expression mirrored in countless Near-Death Experiences (NDEs). In that instant, time seems to collapse, and the soul perceives not with the senses, but with a higher knowing—a direct, unfiltered awareness of its eternal nature.

What lies beyond the veil has haunted and inspired humankind for millennia. Cultures worldwide offer myths of shining heavens and shadowy underworlds. Yet, according to esoteric traditions, the afterlife is more structured and symbolic than commonly believed. Death is not an end, but a **threshold**—a passage of transformation. The soul steps into a world shaped not by physical laws, but by the qualities of thought, intention, and inner resonance. What is hidden becomes visible; what is essential, undeniable.

The Immediate After-Death Experience

1. Separation from the Physical Body: The soul detaches, often accompanied by a floating sensation. Many NDE experiencers report seeing their body from above — on operating tables, hospital beds, or accident sites.

2. The Life Review: A panoramic unfolding of one's life, felt not only from a personal perspective but through the eyes and emotions of those affected. This is a karmic mirror, offering deep insight and learning.

3. The Transition to Other Realms: The soul's path depends on its development. Some ascend to higher spiritual planes; others remain bound to the lower astral due to unresolved desires or attachments.

What Near-Death Experiencers See and Hear

Across cultures, the experiences reported by those who temporarily cross the threshold of death are remarkably consistent. While each journey is unique, the recurring elements paint a vivid picture of the soul's first steps beyond the veil.

Separation and Observation

- Floating above the body, observing doctors, loved ones, or surroundings

- Seeing their lifeless form from a distance

- Attempting to communicate but realizing they are unheard

Heightened Consciousness

- Crystal-clear awareness; thoughts feel sharper and more expansive

- Ability to see in 360 degrees

- Telepathic communication with beings or presences

Journey Through a Passage

- A tunnel, void, or corridor of darkness

- Movement at high speed toward a radiant light

- A feeling of being drawn by love or purpose

Encounters with Light and Beings

- A brilliant, loving light — described as conscious, divine, or God

- Encounters with deceased loved ones, often younger and radiant

- Beings of light, angels, or spiritual guides communicating with compassion

- Appearances of religious figures, offering reassurance or insight

Otherworldly Environments

- Vast gardens, glowing meadows, crystal lakes, or celestial cities

- Landscapes shift in response to thought

- Cosmic vistas — stars, galaxies, or floating in space — evoke awe and unity

Auditory Elements

- Celestial music, harmonic tones, or universal vibrations

- A loving yet firm voice saying: "It is not your time"

- Often, a mission or purpose is imparted before return

The Return

- A sudden "pull" or "snap" back into the body

- Re-entry is often jarring — compared to being compressed into dense matter

- Accompanied by emotional disorientation or longing to return

Lasting Transformation

- Decreased fear of death

- Increased compassion, empathy, or intuitive sensitivity

- Desire to live with purpose and authenticity

- Some struggle to readjust to material life and feel out of place

These shared experiences reflect a universal spiritual structure behind death—one that esoteric teachings have described for centuries.

Esoteric Teachings on the Journey After Death

According to Theosophy and Anthroposophy, the soul journeys through multiple stages:

1. **The Etheric Plane**: Immediately after death, the **etheric body**, which carries the life memory, lingers near the physical world. Rudolf Steiner teaches that the **life review** occurs here, as the soul views its deeds, relationships, and motivations in vivid detail. Over several days, the etheric body dissolves, and the soul moves forward.

2. **Kamaloka – The Astral Plane**: This "desire realm" is where unpurified emotions, attachments, and cravings are faced. Known in Theosophy as **Kamaloka**, it resembles a purgatorial state. The soul must confront the lower nature it cultivated—anger, pride, addiction, guilt—before it can ascend further. This is not punishment, but a natural purification.

3. **Devachan – The Spiritual Plane**: After passing through Kamaloka, the soul enters **Devachan**, the world of

archetypes, harmony, and higher learning. Here, the fruits of a lifetime are spiritually digested. The soul is nourished, given insight, and prepared for the next incarnation. In this realm, the **higher ego** aligns itself once more with the divine blueprint.

Astral Traps and False Heavens

Manly P. Hall warned that not all souls ascend smoothly. Some remain **trapped in lower astral zones,** sustained by desire, confusion, or obsession. These are not "hells" in the traditional sense, but self-created psychic environments — full of illusion, projection, and stagnation. These realms, shaped by thought and emotion, are as real to the soul as the physical world once was — dreamlike yet binding, built from unprocessed fears, attachments, and beliefs.

These astral traps may appear as:

- False heavens tailored to personal fantasy or ego

- Echo chambers of unresolved trauma

- Realms of wandering spirits or lingering impressions

NDE accounts sometimes reflect this. While many describe uplifting experiences, others report darker realms, populated by shadowy figures, disembodied voices, or deceptive lights. These experiences align with occult warnings against **contacting spirits** without proper preparation.

The Mahatma Letters caution that many entities contacted in séances are **residual astral fragments**, not enlightened beings. This is why true initiation in the Mystery Schools required inner purification before attempting to pierce the veil. Without purification, the seeker risks mistaking mirage for revelation — becoming lost in the very illusions they sought to transcend.

The Veil as Consciousness

In esoteric thought, the veil between life and death is not a barrier or location, but of **consciousness**. It is the dividing line between awareness confined to the physical senses and expanded spiritual perception.

To pierce the veil is to:

- Know oneself beyond form

- Face one's untransformed self

- Recognize illusion and truth

- Prepare for true rebirth

𓂀 𓂀 𓂀

Mystery Thread Sidebar: Purification Beyond the Threshold

The Mystery Schools taught that death was not a mystery to be feared, but a journey to be prepared for. In Egypt, initiates underwent symbolic death and resurrection within temple rites. In Eleusis, they descended into darkness before beholding divine light. These rituals mirrored the posthumous journey — through the etheric, astral, and spiritual worlds.

Initiation was a preparation for death. To pass through Kamaloka and Devachan consciously was the mark of a soul who had learned not to cling to shadows. For the initiate, **the veil was not torn — it was lifted**. Each step through the threshold was a deepening purification, as the soul shed layers of illusion, fear, and earthly desire. The true initiate was one who had learned to dissolve the boundaries between life and death, embracing both as stages of an eternal, continuous cycle.

Chapter 7: Helena Blavatsky and the Root Races – Humanity's Spiritual Evolution

The Soul's Journey Across Ages

Helena Blavatsky's Theosophy presents a vast and sweeping vision of humanity's spiritual evolution through immense cycles of time. Central to this vision is the concept of the Root Races — seven great stages in human development, each representing not only a physical evolution but a transformation of consciousness itself. In this cosmic framework, the soul evolves as part of a collective unfolding, progressing through epochs that shape the mind, body, and spirit. Each Root Race is not merely a chapter in human history but a cosmic step toward greater self-realization, where each successive race unveils deeper layers of the soul's potential.

Blavatsky taught that humanity's evolution is not limited to Darwinian biology. Rather, it is a divine drama — an initiatory passage in which the soul descends into matter, forgets its origin, and gradually reawakens through lifetimes of experience. This journey unfolds through the Seven Root Races, each bringing forth a new faculty of the human being. As humanity advances, these stages of spiritual evolution correspond not only to physical forms but also to the development of psychic abilities, higher senses, and ultimately the full awakening of the soul's divine nature.

The Seven Root Races

Polarian Root Race (1st)

Nature: Ethereal, androgynous, non-physical.

Consciousness: Unitary, divine, instinctual.

Environment: The imperishable Sacred Land.

Function: First emergence of the human Monad into form.

Hyperborean Root Race (2nd)

Nature: Semi-etheric; still largely non-physical.

Consciousness: Developing duality and spatial awareness.

Environment: Polar regions, symbolic of stillness and spiritual potential.

Function: Evolution of energetic structure and subtle form.

Lemurian Root Race (3rd)

Nature: Gigantic, physical, and androgynous at first; later gender-separated.

Consciousness: Instinctual clairvoyance; dreamlike awareness.

Environment: Lemuria (Indian/Pacific Ocean regions).

Function: Physicalization of the human form; the dawn of reproduction and karma.

Atlantean Root Race (4th)

Nature: Fully physical; psychic powers and advanced technology.

Consciousness: Emotional, imaginative, psychic.

Environment: Atlantis (Atlantic Ocean basin).

Function: Development of desire, ego, and early intellect.

Aryan Root Race (5th – Current Stage)

Nature: Physically refined; mentally dominant.

Consciousness: Logical, analytical, seeking spiritual reintegration.

Environment: Post-Atlantean civilizations, including modern humanity.

Function: Development of reason, will, and spiritual responsibility.

Sixth Root Race (Future)

Nature: Spiritually awakened, intuitive, telepathic.

Consciousness: Compassionate unity; re-integration of spirit.

Environment: Symbolic continent rising in the Pacific.

Function: Rebirth of the inner faculties and divine harmony.

Seventh Root Race (Final Earth Cycle)

Nature: Etherealized, luminous, godlike.

Consciousness: Perfected spiritual beings.

Environment: Refined Earth or spiritualized planetary condition.

Function: Completion of Earth evolution; readiness for higher worlds.

Cycles Within Cycles

Each Root Race contains seven sub-races, and transitions between them are gradual, like the blending of seasons. Humanity does not evolve uniformly — different individuals and groups express different stages of development. A tribal healer and a quantum physicist may represent different threads of the same evolving tapestry, both necessary, neither superior. This idea reflects the esoteric principle that evolution is not simply vertical, but spiral —

always moving forward, but circling back through remembrance, trial, and rediscovery. The soul, in its cyclical journey, may revisit previous lessons — only now with greater depth and awareness. Just as nature operates through cycles of birth, growth, decay, and rebirth, so does the spiritual path echo this eternal rhythm.

Blavatsky taught that the fall of Atlantis was a moral and spiritual collapse, not merely geological. The Atlanteans misused their psychic powers and advanced technologies, leading to catastrophic upheaval. This echoes the warnings of many Mystery traditions: when spiritual power is not matched by ethical maturity, destruction follows. Just as Atlantis fell, modern civilization — at the height of its technological achievement — faces a similar danger. Blavatsky's teachings remind us that intellect must be guided by wisdom, or the consequences will be karmic.

Lemuria, Atlantis, and Geophysical Shifts

According to Blavatsky, Lemuria and Atlantis were not myths, but ancient lands that housed prior Root Races. Lemuria sank beneath the Indian and Pacific Oceans; fragments remain in Australia, Madagascar, and Pacific islands. Atlantis declined in the Atlantic basin due to global crustal shifts and cataclysmic changes — symbolic of humanity's descent into materialism. These cataclysms were not merely physical events — they marked the culmination of spiritual decline, reflecting the dangers of overreach, unbridled ambition, and the misuse of divine powers.

These events mirrored the evolution of consciousness. As Earth hardened and cooled, so too did the soul densify.

But this descent was necessary — it allowed the ego to form, preparing for eventual spiritual awakening.

Blavatsky placed these civilizations in the Miocene and Pliocene epochs, challenging modern anthropology. She cited controversial evidence: Fossilized footprints in ancient strata. Reports of human bones in Miocene layers. Massive skeletons — ranging from 8 to 18 feet tall — discovered and hidden away. Many of these bones, she claimed, were taken by institutions like the Smithsonian and the Vatican, then quietly forgotten. The giants of legend, from Nephilim to Titans, may be distorted memories of ancient races.

Karma, Reincarnation, and the Spiritual Arc

The Root Races are not only physical — they are expressions of karma, spiritual evolution, and cosmic purpose. Each soul reincarnates through these stages to experience the full range of human potential: from divine instinct to awakened reason to luminous spirit.

Blavatsky emphasized that reincarnation is not a punishment — it is a divine school. Each lifetime is a lesson in transformation. Each trial is an initiation. And each fall is the seed of a future ascent.
The Sixth and Seventh Root Races will not arise through genetics, but through inner readiness. They are not bound by geography or bloodline — they emerge through the awakening of the soul. The soul's evolution, ultimately, is not defined by the body it inhabits, but by its capacity to transcend the limitations of the material world and awaken to its divine essence.

𓂀 𓂀 𓂀

Mystery Thread Sidebar: The Lost and Returning Sight

In the esoteric tradition, figures like Joseph, Daniel, and Enoch were not just prophets — they were initiates. Their visions, dreams, and revelations echoed the clairvoyance of the Lemurian age.

As humanity descended into matter, the soul's inner light dimmed. But the Mystery Schools kept the flame alive. They taught that these ancient faculties — telepathy, inner vision, spiritual communion — would one day return, not as gifts, but as earned powers of the awakened soul.

Today, many report: Near-death experiences
Spontaneous visions
Lucid dreams with archetypal symbolism
Psychic or empathic awakenings
These are not anomalies. They are echoes of what we once were — and signs of what we are becoming.

𓂀 𓂀 𓂀

Helena Petrovna Blavatsky (1831–1891) was a Russian-born mystic, philosopher, and author who co-founded the Theosophical Society in 1875. She is regarded as one of the most influential esoteric thinkers of the modern era and played a central role in reintroducing ancient spiritual knowledge to the West.

Biography Highlights:

• Born into Russian nobility in Yekaterinoslav (now Ukraine), she demonstrated psychic abilities and spiritual sensitivity from an early age.
• Traveled extensively in her youth across Europe, the Middle East, and Asia, claiming to have studied in Tibet under Mahatmas — advanced spiritual beings guiding humanity.
• Co-founded the Theosophical Society in New York alongside Henry Steel Olcott and William Q. Judge, dedicated to the exploration of ancient wisdom and the unity of all religions.
• Spent significant years in India and Tibet, where she absorbed Eastern metaphysical teachings and engaged in esoteric studies.
• Settled in India, where she edited The Theosophist and worked closely with Indian spiritual reformers before relocating to London, where she founded the Blavatsky Lodge.

Key Contributions and Accomplishments:

• Author of several landmark esoteric texts:
- Isis Unveiled (1877): A critique of materialism and defense of spiritual science.
- The Secret Doctrine (1888): Her magnum opus, presenting the Stanzas of Dzyan, cosmic evolution, Root Races, and the esoteric structure of the universe.
- The Voice of the Silence (1889): A guide for spiritual aspirants, echoing Eastern mystical wisdom.

• Introduced and expanded on concepts such as:
- Root Races and planetary cycles of evolution
- The Sevenfold nature of man (physical, etheric, astral,

mental, etc.)
- Karma, reincarnation, and the afterlife realms (Kamaloka and Devachan)
- The existence of Hidden Masters or Mahatmas who guide human evolution
- The unity behind all religious traditions, arguing that ancient wisdom is universal

• She bridged Eastern and Western traditions, emphasizing a path of spiritual self-development, occult discipline, and compassionate service.

• Left behind a legacy that deeply influenced thinkers such as Rudolf Steiner, Annie Besant, Krishnamurti, and Manly P. Hall, and laid the groundwork for modern esotericism, metaphysical studies, and New Age thought.

Blavatsky's work was not merely theoretical — it was initiatory. She opened the West to hidden truths, challenged the arrogance of materialism, and placed a spiritual key in the hands of those who dared to seek beyond the veil.

Conclusion: Toward the Light of the Future

Blavatsky's Root Race teachings present a cosmology in which humanity's evolution is a sacred spiral. From divine spirit into dense form, and from dense form back into spiritualized being.
We are now in the Fifth Root Race, facing a crisis of direction. Will we follow the path of Atlantis, consumed by pride and power? Or will we birth the Sixth Root Race — a humanity guided by love, intuition, and the inner light? The choice is ours. The future is not fixed. But the soul, eternal and lu-

81

minous, continues its journey — through fire and light, through shadow and revelation — toward its divine home.

☥ ☥ ☥

Chapter 8: Mystery Schools

Manly P. Hall and the Mystery Schools: The Path of Initiation

Manly Palmer Hall (1901–1990) was one of the most profound esoteric scholars of the 20th century. His work, *The Secret Teachings of All Ages*, is considered a cornerstone of Western occult philosophy, drawing upon ancient traditions, Mystery Schools, Hermeticism, and alchemy to reveal the hidden structure of spiritual initiation. Hall taught that the path to higher consciousness was carefully guarded by the initiatory traditions of the past, and that seekers had to undergo trials of purification, transformation, and enlightenment before they could grasp the deeper mysteries of existence. Hall emphasized that these spiritual initiations were not mere rites, but deep and personal experiences that reshaped the very essence of the soul. True understanding could only come after the initiate had passed through the symbolic death of the ego, shedding the false self to be reborn into higher wisdom.

At the heart of Hall's teachings are the Mystery Schools — sacred institutions that preserved esoteric knowledge across civilizations. The initiates of these schools underwent a structured process of death and rebirth — not in a literal sense, but as a profound transformation of consciousness. According to Hall, the goal of the initiate was to conquer illusion, transcend the limitations of the material world, and attain divine wisdom. These initiatory rites were seen as the soul's journey through a spiritual wilderness, marked by trials and tribulations that stripped away attachments and illusions, leading the aspirant toward the light of self-realization.

Mystery Schools

These Mystery Schools were devoted to the teaching of the Mysteries — that is, the inner nature of Man and its relationship to the cosmos. As the name suggests, these were schools or sanctuaries designed to enlighten the souls of those who entered them. Each school had students and teachers, forming a spiritual lineage of sacred learning. Jesus also taught the Mysteries to the Apostles. These teachings were passed down through sacred lineages of masters who imparted wisdom only to those deemed ready to receive it — those who had purified themselves and demonstrated true dedication to the path.

These institutions were first established when humanity was still in its spiritual infancy. In those distant ages, the human being had not yet fully entered the material world and still possessed an intuitive knowledge of the beginning. The mysteries of heaven and earth were alive and vibrant within the consciousness of early man. According to esoteric tradition, such mysteries began to be revealed more fully during the time of the Third Root Race — the Lemurians.

As humanity descended deeper into the material world — the process known in occult traditions as the Fall — this intuitive knowledge began to fade. Some individuals, spiritually weaker or more susceptible to illusion, were carried along with the descent. Others resisted the fall and strove to preserve the spiritual light. Still others were caught between the two streams of becoming — partly awakened, yet partly asleep. The same dynamic exists even today: some are deeply materialistic, while others retain an active spiritual life despite the weight of the physical world. And many drift somewhere between the two. This tension between materialism and spirituality, between the physical and the divine, forms the eternal struggle of humanity. It is in the space between these extremes where the soul must choose its path and find its own awakening.

"Tales of ages long forgotten. Now legends of creation. Once familiar to the children." — *Kalevala*

To help clarify the ancient role of the Mystery Schools, we may turn to the teachings of G. de Purucker, who described the spiritual guidance given to early humanity by those who had already ascended the evolutionary path.

The Great White Brotherhood in Lemurian Times

"In the days of Lemuria, when Man was still half ethereal, there existed those mighty ones, the spiritual guides of humanity who had already passed through human stages in former cycles... These were the initiates of the time — not born of Earth in the ordinary sense, but beings of light, wisdom, and cosmic memory." — G. de Purucker, *Fundamentals of the Esoteric Philosophy*

These luminous beings, remembered in nearly every esoteric tradition, are said to have formed the earliest spiritual guidance systems on Earth. They were not simply wise men; they were the seeds of the Mystery Schools. Many believe that the same Brotherhood continues its work today, hidden in the spiritual background of our unfolding evolution.

The Great White Brotherhood is not referring to skin color or ethnicity. It refers to those with a direct, unbroken spiritual lineage traced back to the Mahatmas that possessed the Light of the Lemurian Race. Not all of that race kept the Light alive within themselves, and for this reason, the foundation of the Mystery Schools was laid.

Such is still the case even today: ignorance against truth and light, selfishness against compassion. Gained knowledge can either uplift humanity or be used for destruction.

Eventually, the Mysteries could no longer be allowed to fall into the hands of the profane, ignorant, or unrighteous. Atlantis fell due to the abuse and misuse of spiritual knowledge and the powers of nature for selfish ends. This abuse created a division between the guardians of humanity and those who sought power.

The ancient knowledge had to be kept sacred. So, it was moved "underground" — occulted, hidden, secreted away from the profane. This was the beginning of the Mystery Schools. Through the many centuries and across the world, the true secrets remained hidden except for the select few in remote, sacred places.

Notable Mystery Schools Throughout the World

Here is a list of some of the most known and influential Mystery Schools:

- Egyptian
  - The House of Life (Per Ankh)
  - Priesthood of Isis, Osiris, and Horus
  - Temple of Karnak and Luxor Initiations

- Greek
  - Eleusinian Mysteries (Demeter & Persephone)
  - Orphic Mysteries
  - Delphic Oracle and the Temple of Apollo

- Roman
  - Mithraic Mysteries (Mithras Cult)
  - Cult of Isis (continued from Egypt)

- Persian (Zoroastrian)
  - Magi and the Chaldean Mysteries
  - Zarathustrian Fire Temples

- Indian
  - Brahmanic and Vedic Mystery Schools
  - Tantric and Yogic Initiation Paths
  - Himalayan Mystery Schools (e.g., Nath Tradition)

- Tibetan
  - Bon Tradition (Pre-Buddhist)
  - Tibetan Buddhist Initiatory Lineages (Dzogchen, Kalachakra)

- Chinese
  - Taoist Mystery Traditions (Neidan — Inner Alchemy)
  - Shaolin Monastery (Spiritual-Martial fusion)

- Celtic & Druidic
  - Druidic Initiations of the British Isles
  - Celtic Bards and Ovates

- Hebraic / Kabbalistic
  - Essenes (e.g., Qumran Community)
  - Kabbalah Schools of Safed and later Europe

- Mesoamerican
  - Mayan Mystery Traditions (e.g., Quetzalcoatl Initiates)
  - Aztec Priesthoods (Tonalpohualli and metaphysical training)

- Native American
  - Vision Quests and Medicine Lodge Teachings
  - The Hopi and Anasazi Spiritual Lineages

- Western Esoteric / Hermetic Traditions
  - Hermetic Order of the Golden Dawn
  - Rosicrucians
  - Freemasonry (Ancient Mystery echoes)
  - Theosophical Society
  - Anthroposophy (Steiner)
  - Gurdjieff's Fourth Way

Famous Initiates of the Mystery Traditions

- Greek Mystery Schools
  - Pythagoras – Initiated in Egypt and possibly the Orphic and Eleusinian Mysteries; founded his own school in Croton based on sacred geometry, reincarnation, and spiritual purification.
  - Plato – Initiated into the Eleusinian Mysteries; his writings reflect deep esoteric symbolism and alignment with Orphic thought.
  - Socrates – Though not formally an initiate, his teachings reveal ethical and soul-centered depth aligned with mystery teachings.
  - Empedocles – A philosopher-mystic who taught the transmigration of souls and was influenced by Orphic doctrines.

- Egyptian Mysteries
  - Moses – According to esoteric traditions (especially Theosophy and the Book of Deuteronomy), Moses was initiated into the Egyptian priesthood.
  - Thales – Studied in Egypt and brought sacred geometry and cosmology back to Greece.
  - Herodotus – Wrote about the Egyptian mysteries and temple initiations, though as a historian.

- Hebraic / Kabbalistic Mysteries
  - Jesus (Yeshua) – Some esoteric traditions suggest he studied with the Essenes and possibly in Egypt or India during his "missing years."
  - Solomon – Revered in esoteric traditions, especially Freemasonry and Kabbalah, for his connection to ancient wisdom.

- Eastern & Esoteric Schools
  - Laozi (Lao Tzu) – Founder of Taoism, linked to inner alchemy and esoteric Taoist wisdom.
  - Buddha (Siddhartha Gautama) – Underwent initiatory experiences during his meditation and awakening; symbolic of Mystery School rites.
  - Zarathustra (Zoroaster) – A prophet and initiate who taught the cosmic battle of light and darkness in Persia.

- Renaissance & Modern Mystery Revivals
  - Giordano Bruno – A Hermetic philosopher who revived esoteric cosmology and was burned by the Inquisition.
  - Isaac Newton – Studied alchemy and Hermetic writings; deeply influenced by esoteric sciences.
  - Madame Blavatsky – Co-founder of the Theosophical Society; studied Eastern and Western mystery traditions.
  - Rudolf Steiner – Founder of Anthroposophy; developed initiatory spiritual science rooted in ancient Mystery wisdom.

Mystery School Connections to Near-Death Experiences (NDEs)

The rites of initiation in the ancient Mystery Schools were not merely symbolic — they were constructed to mirror the soul's journey after death. In fact, these sacred rituals were designed to guide the initiate through the stages of death and rebirth, preparing them for the inevitable transition that awaited all souls. Near-Death Experiences (NDEs), which have become increasingly documented in modern times, echo many of the stages found in ancient initiatory traditions. Experiencers often describe traveling through tunnels of light, encountering guides or divine beings, and witnessing life reviews—all of which are mirrored in the Mystery rites, where the initiate is led through symbolic tunnels, faces challenges, and encounters divine forces that guide them toward enlightenment. These parallels suggest that the Mystery Schools preserved profound knowledge about the soul's passage beyond the veil of physical life. What's particularly striking is the consistency of these experiences across cultures and eras. Whether in the Mystery Schools of Egypt, Greece, or in contemporary accounts of NDEs, the soul's journey is shown as a process of illumination, trial, and transcendence.

1. Separation from the Body

• Egyptian Mysteries: The Ka leaves the body while the Ba journeys through the Duat (underworld).

• Greek Eleusinian Rites: Simulated death in darkness before emerging into the light signified the soul's separation.

• Tibetan Initiations: Visualization exercises trained initiates for the Bardo state after death.

2. The Tunnel or Passage

• Gnostic Initiations: The soul traverses veils or archonic realms.

• Mayan Rituals: Journey through Xibalba, the underworld, via caves and labyrinths.

• Global Cave Rites: Caves symbolized wombs or tombs, portals between worlds.

3. Encounter with Light or Divine Being

• Hermeticism: Meeting the Nous, or Divine Mind.

• Kabbalah: Ascension through the Sephiroth to Kether — the Crown of Divine Light.

• Christian Mystics: Vision of the Christ Light or angelic beings of love.

4. Life Review

• Egyptian Book of the Dead: The weighing of the heart by Anubis and Thoth.

• Pythagorean & Platonic Ethics: Emphasis on karmic memory and reincarnative lessons.

• Mystery School Trials: A moment of moral reflection and symbolic judgment.

5. Celestial or Cosmic Realms

• Plato's Celestial Spheres: The soul ascends through the planetary heavens.

• Zoroastrian Cosmology: The soul moves toward Ahura Mazda through the Seven Heavens.

• Steiner's Cosmology: Souls travel through the planetary spheres — Jupiter, Venus, Vulcan — before rebirth.

6. Beings of Light and Guides

• Theosophy: Encounters with Masters or Mahatmas.

• Rosicrucians: Spiritual guides assist the soul's evolution.

• Mystery Initiates: Often described inner plane mentors during initiation rites.

7. Transformation Upon Return

• Mystery Schools: Initiation was symbolic death followed by rebirth as a new being.

• Gnostic Tradition: The soul, once awakened by gnosis, returns transformed.

• Modern NDEs: People often return with new clarity, purpose, and spiritual insight.

The Egyptian Mystery Schools and the Initiation Process

Among the oldest and most revered initiatory systems in history, the Egyptian Mystery Schools laid a foundation for the path of sacred transformation.

1. The Descent into Darkness: Initiates were led into underground chambers or tombs—representing death. Symbolically, this was the surrender of the lower self and ego.

2. The Trials of the Elements: The candidate was tested by representations of earth, air, fire, and water — purging attachments and awakening inner sight.

3. The Sacred Ordeal: In the final phase, the initiate would lie inside a sarcophagus or sealed chamber — symbolizing the tomb of Osiris. In this state, one might experience an out-of-body journey or vision.

4. The Resurrection and Rebirth: Upon emergence, the initiate was declared "twice-born," no longer the same person. A symbolic death had occurred — followed by spiritual awakening. This rebirth was not just a ritual act, but a profound shift in consciousness, where the initiate shed old identities and emerged as a more enlightened being, with a renewed sense of purpose and spiritual clarity.

Manly P. Hall emphasized that this ritual was a direct mirror of the afterlife journey described in The Egyptian Book of the Dead — one that taught the soul how to traverse the astral planes consciously, guided by divine principles. The Book of the Dead offered detailed instructions on navigating the challenges of the afterlife, much like an initiate would learn to overcome obstacles during their spiritual trials in the Mystery Schools. Manly P. Hall drew heavily from Hermetic philosophy, particularly the teachings of Thoth-Hermes, who was said to be the original teacher of divine wisdom in Egypt. The Hermetic texts, which later influenced alchemy, taught that "As above, so below", meaning that the human soul is a reflection of the divine order and that by understanding the hidden laws of the universe, one could transcend material limitations. This principle was not just a metaphor — it was a map for the initiate to understand the interconnectedness of all things, guiding them towards unity with the divine.

Hall emphasized that the initiatory process was not just an ancient ritual but an ongoing transformation within every seeker. Through self-discipline, meditation, and the study of esoteric wisdom, individuals could reawaken their latent spiritual abilities. The process of initiation was viewed as a gradual awakening, where each step reflected the soul's ultimate journey toward spiritual liberation, mirroring the cycle of birth, death, and rebirth. This was the true goal of alchemy—not the transmutation of lead into gold, but the evolution of the soul into a perfected, enlightened being.

The Mystery Schools preserved these truths, passing them down through secret teachings and symbolism. Hall saw these schools as guiding humanity through its cycles of spiritual growth, much like the Root Races in Blavatsky's Theosophy or the cosmic evolution described by Rudolf Steiner. The initiates of these traditions, in their wisdom and understanding, became living examples of the soul's potential for transformation. The initiates of these traditions served as the custodians of sacred wisdom, ensuring that the knowledge of the soul's immortality and divine potential was never lost.

𓂀 𓂀 𓂀

The Initiatory Path as a Reflection of the Afterlife

The Mystery Schools did not prepare the soul only for earthly wisdom—they trained initiates for death. As Manly

P. Hall revealed, initiation is death consciously experienced. The death undergone in the ritual is not a physical death but a metaphysical one, where the initiate faces their own mortality and is tested by the mysteries of existence. The neophyte **symbolically dies** to the world, undergoes judgment, encounters light, and is reborn in spirit. Every phase of the Mystery rites corresponds to what occurs after physical death.

In Egyptian cosmology, the soul passes through tests in the Duat, guided by Thoth and Anubis, ultimately to stand before Osiris. This journey was seen as a purification of the soul, where the initiate confronted their past deeds and learned to shed any remaining attachments to the material world. In Greek Eleusinian rites, the initiate enters darkness, endures the underworld, and is shown the light — representing Persephone's ascent. This descent into darkness symbolized the soul's confrontation with its own fears and limitations, and the subsequent emergence into light represented spiritual enlightenment and freedom from the chains of illusion. In both, the symbolism is identical to modern NDE accounts. Whether in ancient rites or modern experiences, the soul's journey through death and rebirth remains a universal pattern, woven through the fabric of spiritual initiation.

Manly P. Hall emphasized that:

"The Mystery Schools preserved truths that today are called Near-Death Experiences. These truths are not new — they are ancient — and they were known by the sages who walked the Earth long before us."

꿋 꿋 꿋

Mystery Thread Sidebar: The Hidden Curriculum

In the ancient Mystery Schools, initiates were taught that the soul is a divine exile, and the ego is its mask. Through rites of purification, symbolic death, and inner resurrection, the ego could be reborn in alignment with the divine will. This hidden thread runs through all four teachings—and through the deeper meaning of near-death experiences. Behind the veil, the soul remembers its true name.

꿋 꿋 꿋

Universal Teachings from the Mystery Tradition and Modern NDEs

The same truths appear across the teachings of:

A.P. Sinnett (The Mahatma Letters)

• Described the structured passage after death: Kamaloka, where desire is burned off, and Devachan, a realm of blissful rest where the soul reflects on its last incarnation.

• These realms closely mirror the "stages" seen in modern NDE reports—where attachment is dissolved, and insight is gained.

• Sinnett emphasized that real spiritual progress occurs between lives, in reflection and planning—not merely in one lifetime.

Rudolf Steiner (Anthroposophy)

• Taught that after death, the etheric body lingers for a few days, replaying the memory of life.

• The astral body then journeys through planetary spheres — Mercury, Venus, Mars, Jupiter, Saturn — where the soul processes moral and emotional residues from life.

• This cosmic pilgrimage aligns with many NDE accounts of panoramic life reviews, vast realms of light, and soul contracts.

• Steiner insisted that spiritual insight gained during such journeys is brought back to earth in the next life, fueling deeper self-awareness.

Helena Blavatsky (Theosophy)

• Argued that much of the post-death experience occurs on the astral plane, a realm layered with both truth and illusion.

• Warned of false heavens — astral constructs created by collective belief systems or emotional residue, which appear divine but are traps that delay true spiritual ascent.

• She taught that the Higher Ego is the guiding principle, attempting to lead the soul out of astral illusion and toward the spiritual light.

• Blavatsky's teachings anticipate many NDE reports of "beings of light" that are later revealed to be masks or illusions, testing the soul's discernment.

The Barbelo of the Luminous Cloud: Gnostic Insight

Among the most fascinating esoteric parallels to the Near-Death Experience is found in Gnostic texts, especially the *Gospel of Judas* and *Apocryphon of John*. These writings describe a powerful metaphysical realm known as Barbelo, which exists just beyond the material world. In its pure form, Barbelo is the first emanation of the Divine — a realm of radiant light, creativity, and purity. But in later Gnostic warnings, this same realm can be corrupted or confused with a false heaven created by the demiurgic powers.

According to Gnostic insight:

• Barbelo is beautiful, luminous, and vast — so much so that the soul may mistake it for the final destination.

• But if the soul has not fully awakened to its divine identity, it may become ensnared in this radiance, remaining in cycles of reincarnation, under the illusion of completion.

• The Demiurge and its archons are said to mimic the Light, offering rest, pleasure, or even bliss — but withholding the gnosis that truly frees the soul.

In this light, discernment becomes the final test. The soul must remember its true origin beyond all forms — even beautiful or seemingly divine ones — and seek union with the Ultimate Source, not just comfort or peace.

👁 👁 👁

The Path to True Ascension

The Mystery Schools, ancient teachings, and modern NDEs all converge on one universal lesson: the soul is not meant to remain asleep. It is meant to awaken.

The soul must:

- Pass through illusion, desire, and fear

- Learn love, wisdom, and discernment

- Burn away the ego's masks

- And ascend not by external force, but by inner realization

Initiation, therefore, is not a ceremony — it is a journey:

A death.

A passage.

A rebirth.

Whether through a Mystery School, a life crisis, a near-death experience, or the quiet inner call of truth, every human being is on the Path.

The Mystery Schools continue — not just in stone temples or hidden monasteries — but wherever the soul chooses awakening over sleep.

𓂀 𓂀 𓂀

Conclusion: The Eternal Curriculum

Behind every mystery tradition lies the same truth: the soul is a traveler from the divine, walking the long road of remembrance.

The temples of Isis, the sarcophagi of Osiris, the fire of Zarathustra, the scrolls of Hermes, and the modern hospital bed where a soul rises from its body — all are part of the same teaching.

Manly P. Hall, Helena Blavatsky, A.P. Sinnett, and Rudolf Steiner each preserved fragments of this eternal curriculum. And in the stories of modern Near-Death Experiencers, the same thread shines through.

This thread is the hidden wisdom of the soul. It is the curriculum of the infinite. And it is offered freely to every being who dares to remember.

𓂀 𓂀 𓂀

Mystery Thread Sidebar: The Soul's Secret Teacher

In every true initiation, the final teacher is not another person.
It is the soul itself.

The Mystery Schools knew this — that behind every guide, every temple, every rite — was a deeper truth:
The soul already knows the way.

The teacher is the flame. The classroom is the world. The initiation is life itself.

And the one who endures the sacred fire will awaken — Not as a student, but as the light reborn.

𓂀 𓂀 𓂀

Chapter 9: Helena Blavatsky and The Ego

Helena Blavatsky, co-founder of the Theosophical Society, played a pivotal role in synthesizing Eastern and Western esoteric traditions. Her writings offer profound insights into the nature of the soul, reincarnation, and the occult sciences. She drew from Hinduism, Buddhism, Neoplatonism, and Hermeticism to construct a cosmology in which the universe is a living, conscious organism, and humanity a vital participant in its unfolding drama. Her magnum opus, The Secret Doctrine, framed this vision within the cycles of cosmic evolution—where spirit and matter dance through endless transformations.

Helena Blavatsky's take on the ego is complex and deeply rooted in Theosophical teachings, which distinguish between different layers of selfhood. She does not use "ego" in the modern psychological sense but instead divides it into higher and lower aspects within the spiritual evolution of the soul. The lower ego, or *kama-manas*, is tied to desire, personal identity, and illusion—what the Mysteries called the "false self." The higher ego, or *buddhi-manas*, is the bridge to the divine, the voice of conscience and spiritual will. Between these two, the battle of the soul is waged. To awaken the higher ego is to step onto the path of initiation and liberation.

Blavatsky's Concept of the Ego:

She primarily distinguishes between two forms of the ego:

Higher Ego (Divine Ego, Individuality) – "The Higher Self"

• This is the eternal, spiritual aspect of the self, also called the Manas (higher mind) or Buddhi-Manas when united with spiritual wisdom.

• It is immortal, and it reincarnates through multiple lifetimes.

• It represents our true divine consciousness and is connected to universal wisdom and higher spiritual realms.

• In The Secret Doctrine, she describes this as the true "I", which remains after death and carries forward karmic evolution.

Lower Ego (Personality, Kama-Manas) – "The False Self"

• This is the temporary, earthly personality that we identify with in a single lifetime.

• It is driven by desires, emotions, and material concerns, forming what she calls the Kama-Manas (lower mind + desire nature).

• It is impermanent—after death, it dissolves, and only its karmic imprints are absorbed by the higher ego for future incarnations.

• This false self is the one that often mistakes illusion (Maya) for reality, leading to suffering, spiritual blindness, and reincarnation.

How the Ego Relates to Reincarnation and the Afterlife

• After death, the lower ego dissolves, and only the higher ego carries forward the true spiritual essence.

• If a person is too attached to material life, their lower ego may linger as an astral shell (sometimes called a "Kama Rupa") before eventually dissipating.

• The higher ego, however, retains spiritual wisdom and karma, reincarnating into a new personality in the next life.

• The goal of spiritual evolution is for the lower ego to merge with the higher ego, leading to enlightenment and liberation from reincarnation.

Blavatsky on the Ego's Struggle and the Path of Initiation

• She describes life as a battle between the lower ego and the higher ego.

• The lower ego is self-centered, emotional, and bound by illusion, while the higher ego is divine, detached, and wise.

• The path of initiation and enlightenment in Theosophy is about transcending the lower ego and uniting with the higher, immortal self.

Connection to Near-Death Experiences and Esoteric Teachings

• Many NDE experiencers report feeling a separation from their earthly identity, as if they are observing their personality from a higher state — this resonates with Blavatsky's distinction between lower and higher ego. This separation is a sudden and profound awareness that they are not their personality, but something greater — a being of light, observing the life they once thought was "them."

• The experience of separation, detachment, and bliss aligns with Theosophical teachings about the soul's return to its divine essence.

• These NDEs often mirror Theosophy's doctrine that the lower self is shed like a garment, while the true self ascends and remembers its purpose.

• The idea of shedding the false self after death aligns with her description of how the lower ego dissolves while the higher ego continues evolving spiritually.

• Her ideas also align with Eastern teachings in Buddhism and Hinduism, which view the ego as an illusion (Maya) that must be transcended.

• This is the *Higher Ego* becoming conscious.

• The life review echoes the absorption of karma into the Higher Self.

• The experience of separation, detachment, and bliss aligns with Theosophical teachings about the soul's return to its divine essence.

Ancient Parallels and Eastern Wisdom

Blavatsky's ideas reflect much older teachings:

- In Vedanta, the *Atman* (true self) must transcend the *Ahamkara* (ego-construct).

- In Buddhism, the ego is seen as a skandhic illusion that must be dissolved.

- In Hermeticism, the false personality is a mask worn by the divine actor.

Blavatsky did not invent these distinctions — she revived them. Through her, the West rediscovered a long-lost doctrine: that liberation depends not on believing, but on becoming — by shedding the false and embracing the eternal within.

Final Thought

Blavatsky's dual ego system provides a spiritual framework for self-evolution — one where the true self (higher ego) must rise above the temporary self (lower ego) to achieve wisdom and liberation. Blavatsky affirms that spiritual development is not merely philosophical — it is initiatory. The initiate walks the razor's edge, learning to master desire, illusion, and emotional reaction.

- The lower ego resists this path, clinging to fear, doubt, and self-importance.

- The higher ego, detached and luminous, yearns for wisdom, compassion, and transcendence.

- Through discipline, meditation, study, and self-sacrifice, the aspirant gradually loosens the grip of the false self.

This mirrors the teachings of ancient Mystery Schools, where initiates underwent symbolic death, moral trials, and spiritual rebirth — symbolizing the transformation from lower to higher egoic awareness. These NDEs also often parallel Theosophy's doctrine that the lower self is shed like a garment, while the true self ascends and remembers its purpose. In the Egyptian rites, this process was dramatized as the soul's weighing in the Hall of Ma'at — where the heart was measured against the feather of truth. Only the purified soul, free from the weight of ego and illusion, could journey onward into the Fields of Aaru. This is why the symbol of a snake and its shedding of skin was used beginning back in very ancient times. As a snake grows and develops, it sheds its old skin (garment) and continues along its path towards maturity. Likewise, the soul must periodically outgrow its former selves, sloughing off layers of attachment, fear, and ignorance to emerge more luminous and self-aware.

The Ego, the Astral Body, and the Afterlife

According to Blavatsky and later Theosophists, the ego does not reincarnate in its entirety. Instead, it undergoes a separation at death. The Lower Ego — comprised of the earthly personality, desires, and emotions — resides primarily in the astral body (Kama-Rupa or "desire-form"), which gradually dissolves after death unless it is unnaturally sustained by earthly attachments or through certain occult practices. The Higher Ego — which is immortal — is rooted in the causal body (Karana Sharira), and it alone continues the thread of consciousness and karma from life to life.

The astral body may become what is commonly perceived as a ghost. It is the echo or shell of the person's lower nature. When the Lower Ego is especially strong — due to unfulfilled desires, addictions, or emotional trauma — it can remain earthbound for some time. These remnants are not the true soul but its fading outer garments.

Thus, ghosts, hauntings, and apparitions are often explained as astral residues, or even Kama-Rupic shells, wandering between the physical and astral realms. Blavatsky warned that mediums often contact these "soulless beings," mistaking them for the departed's higher self, when in fact the true Higher Ego has already moved on to Devachan or into reincarnation.

The soul's journey involves refining the lower ego until it becomes fully transparent to the higher, immortal self. Until this occurs, fragments of the personality may continue to haunt both the inner and outer worlds.

How the Ego Relates to Reincarnation and the Afterlife

Blavatsky describes life as a battlefield between these two egos: the higher, divine self that longs for reunion with the Source, and the lower personality caught in worldly entanglements.

• After death, the Kama-Manas dissolves, and only the Higher Ego ascends.

• If the lower ego was especially materialistic or emotionally entangled, it may linger for a time as an astral remnant — known in Theosophy as the Kama Rupa, or "desire body."

• Only the Higher Ego retains the spiritual gains of the life and reincarnates when the time is right.

• The great task of spiritual evolution is to purify and align the lower ego so it may one day merge fully with the Higher Self.

"The Ego is spiritual and eternal; the personality is illusionary and perishable. The union of the two is the battleground of life." — Helena Blavatsky

𓂀 𓂀 𓂀

Mystery Thread Sidebar: The Battle of the Two Selves

In the esoteric teachings of Egypt, the initiate stood before two forces: one rooted in the body and its cravings, the other in the soul and its light. This duality is echoed in the Greek Mysteries as the struggle between the daimon (higher genius) and the shadow self. The Mystery Schools taught that the real "fall of man" was not in disobedience— but in forgetting who we are. This inner conflict was ritually enacted in sacred drama: the initiate entered as the fragmented self and emerged, if successful, as the unified soul—one who had remembered the divine name written in their heart. Blavatsky's teachings revive this forgotten wisdom: that within each of us lives a silent twin, the divine observer who watches from beyond time. The rituals of the temple, the trials of initiation, and the echoes of near-death all point toward the same truth—the false self must be unmasked so the divine self may rise.

110

𓂀 𓂀 𓂀

Mystery Thread Sidebar: The Mirror and the Mask

In the teachings of the Mystery Schools, the human self was likened to a mirror. The Higher Ego is the eternal light that shines, while the Lower Ego is the reflection distorted by the mask of illusion. At death, the mask shatters. But if the ego has not been purified, the distorted reflection may linger—still believing it is real. This is the root of ghostly hauntings and spiritual confusion. The mask was often symbolized by the ceremonial headdress—an external identity the initiate had to remove in order to meet the divine face-to-face. The polished mirror, by contrast, symbolized the soul that had become transparent to the truth. True initiation teaches the soul to polish the mirror so that only the Light remains.

𓂀 𓂀 𓂀

Esoteric Clarification Sidebar: What Reincarnates?

What reincarnates is *not* the entire human being—but the Higher Ego, the divine essence that dwells within the causal body. The physical body dissolves. The astral body gradually dissipates. The personality is left behind like a worn-out garment. But the Higher Ego, carrying karmic impressions and spiritual insights, returns—reborn in a new personality, with a new set of circumstances chosen for soul growth. This continuity of essence—rather than form—is what binds lifetimes together. The soul is not trapped in time, but weaves through it like a golden thread through fabric, stitching meaning into existence. The key to

111

liberation is bringing the Lower Ego into alignment with this inner master.

Build up your Lower Ego

One must develop the Lower-Ego so that it can eventually be the exact "image" of the Higher-Ego. This can begin to be achieved by living a spiritual life in line with Rudolf Steiner's 7 Virtues that are described later in this book. It is the Ego that is actually at the core of reaching the Divine, the Almighty. The physical, etheric, and astral are but sheathes, similar to how a butterfly emerges from its cocoon or how the lotus flower emerges from its watery tomb and strives upwards toward the Sun.

1. The Lower Ego (Personality / Kama-Manas)

Does *not* reincarnate.

- This is the temporary self — the personality, emotions, name, status, memories, and desires of your current life.

- It is formed by the union of Kama (desire) and the lower Manas (mind), and it dissolves after death.

- It lingers briefly as an astral shell (called the Kama Rupa) and eventually dissipates.

- Its karmic essence — the results of its actions, thoughts, and emotions — is absorbed into the Higher Ego.

- The lower ego is *impermanent* and changes with each lifetime.

Think of it like clothing. You wear a different outfit (personality) in each life, but your true self is the one who wears them all.

2. The Higher Ego (Spiritual Individuality / Higher Manas)

Yes — this *does* **reincarnate.**

- This is your true self — also called the Reincarnating Ego, or Manas (when united with Buddhi).

- It is immortal, passing from life to life, gathering experience, refining karma, and evolving toward divine realization.

- It remembers, in a spiritual sense, all of your previous lives, even if your lower personality does not.

- In the afterlife, it enters Devachan, a state of rest and reflection, before choosing a new incarnation.

Summary:

Aspect	Lower Ego (Personality)	Higher Ego (Spiritual Self)
Temporary?	Yes	No
Reincarnates?	No	Yes
Carries karma?	Leaves karma behind	Retains karmic lessons
Survives death?	Dissolves after death	Continues evolving
Goal?	To be purified and transcended	To unite with the Divine Self

What Blavatsky, Steiner, and de Purucker Agree On:

• The Lower Ego dies with the body; it is part of illusion (*Maya*).

• The Higher Ego evolves life after life, gaining wisdom and nearing reunion with the divine source.

- The path of spiritual initiation involves shifting consciousness from the false self (lower ego) to the real self (Higher Ego).

"The Ego is the thread on which are strung the many lives of a person—as pearls on a string." — **Helena Blavatsky**

Overview of the Subtle Bodies and the Ego

According to Blavatsky, Steiner, and de Purucker, the human being is composed of multiple layers or "vehicles" of consciousness:

1. Physical Body – the material body

2. Etheric Body – the life force (prāṇa), memory imprint, growth

3. Astral Body – emotions, desires, sensations

4. Lower Ego (Kama-Manas) – the personality, formed from desires and concrete thought

5. Higher Ego (Manas-Buddhi) – the immortal soul, higher mind united with spiritual will

6. Causal Body – the "container" or spiritual blueprint that holds the Higher Ego's experience

7. Atma – the divine spark or spirit beyond individuality

Each of these corresponds to different levels of consciousness and plays a role in reincarnation and soul evolution.

The Astral Body & the Ego

The Astral Body is the vehicle of:

- Emotion

- Desire (Kama)

- Instinct and sensation

- Lower imagination and passion

Relation to the Lower Ego:

- The astral body merges with the lower mind (manas) to form the Kama-Manas — the Lower Ego.

- This composite is not eternal. It is formed anew each lifetime and dissolves after death.

- If overdeveloped or unbalanced (materialistic, selfish, ego-driven), the astral body can linger after death, forming a Kama Rupa, or astral shell — a kind of ghost or "psychic residue."

Blavatsky called these astral remnants *"soulless beings"* and warned against contacting them in séances.

What survives:

- The astral body does not reincarnate, but its emotional experiences influence karma, which is recorded and passed into the causal body via the Higher Ego.

The Causal Body & the Higher Ego

The Causal Body (sometimes called the *karana sharira* **in Eastern esotericism) is:**

- The true seat of the Higher Ego

- The container of karmic memory, spiritual identity, and life-to-life continuity

- Linked to higher manas and buddhi (spiritual wisdom)

This body is where:

- The Higher Ego stores the essence of each life's experience.

- Karmic seeds (called "skandhas") are retained — not memories like in your brain, but the spiritual *meaning* and *impact* of all actions.

- These seeds determine the circumstances of the next incarnation.

Rudolf Steiner says this body guides reincarnation like a "spiritual architect," ensuring that the soul enters conditions where it can evolve through specific challenges and virtues.

How They Work Together in Reincarnation

Here's a simplified life cycle showing how the astral, ego, and causal bodies work across death and rebirth:

Phase	Astral Body	Ego	Causal Body
Life	Emotions, desires	Lower + Higher Ego	Stores soul's blueprint
Death	Dissolves gradually	Lower ego dissolves	Higher Ego returns to causal
Between Lives (Devachan)	Gone	Higher Ego reflects	Stores karmic lessons
Rebirth	New astral body formed	Lower ego reforms	Higher Ego chooses incarnation

Steiner's Insight:

"When the astral body is cleansed and harmonized, it becomes transparent to the light of the Higher Ego. The Ego must gradually transform the astral body into a vessel of wisdom and love." — **Rudolf Steiner,** *Theosophy*

Mystery Thread Sidebar Suggestion:

"The Fire of Selfhood"

In the Mystery Schools, initiates were taught to distinguish the false self from the true. The astral body was seen as the temple veil — beautiful but dangerous when mistaken for the divine. The causal body, by contrast, was the inner sanctuary — the throne of the immortal Self. To pierce the veil meant to sacrifice the illusions of desire and pass into the fire of the Higher Ego, where the blueprint of the soul awaited its next unfolding.

What Are Ghosts in Esoteric Terms?

In Blavatsky's Theosophy:

- After death, the Lower Ego (Kama-Manas) and astral body begin to dissolve, but this isn't immediate.

- If the person was strongly attached to the material world — due to desires, addictions, regrets, or unfinished business — their astral shell, called the Kama Rupa, can linger.

- This "ghost" is not the full soul — it is a psychic residue or fragment of the former personality.

It may:

- Appear as a ghostly form or apparition

- Seem intelligent but is actually a memory pattern, not the true, conscious soul

- Be drawn to familiar places or people

- Fade over time, unless artificially sustained (e.g., through séances or occult practices)

"These apparitions are the fading shadows of personalities that once were men. They are the reflections of passions and desires — soulless, mindless, clinging to their earthly haunts." — **Helena Blavatsky,** *The Key to Theosophy*

In Steiner's Anthroposophy:

- Steiner agreed that the astral body detaches at death and returns to the spiritual worlds, but he also warned of astral fragments lingering due to trauma, addictions, or spiritual ignorance.

- These "ghostly forms" are not the actual person but rather the cast-off clothes of the soul.

- He emphasized the importance of spiritual development during life to avoid becoming trapped in lower astral realms after death.

Key Distinction:

- Real soul = Higher Ego + causal body → continues its journey after death.

- Ghost = astral shell / kama rupa → temporary, unconscious, often emotionally charged remnant.

Related Beliefs in Other Traditions:

- Tibetan Buddhism – Similar to "bardo" entities or "hungry ghosts" that can arise when a soul does not transition properly.

- Ancient Egypt – The Ka (vital double) sometimes lingers near the body or tomb if not properly ritually released.

- Christian folklore – Many "ghosts" are souls "trapped" between worlds, which reflects a misunderstanding of lingering astral impressions.

Summary

Term	Description	Conscious?
Astral Body	Vehicle of emotions/desire, sheds post-death	Partially
Kama Rupa	Astral remnant/shell after death	No (not truly self-aware)
Higher Ego / Soul	The eternal, reincarnating spiritual self	Yes
Ghost	Perceived apparition —often a kama rupa or astral residue	No (reactive memory-form)

The Ego, the Astral Body, and the Afterlife

According to Blavatsky and later Theosophists, the ego does not reincarnate in its entirety. Instead, it undergoes a separation at death. The *Lower Ego*—comprised of the earthly personality, desires, and emotions—resides primarily in the astral body (Kama-Rupa or "desire-form"), which gradually dissolves after death unless it is unnaturally sustained by earthly attachments or through certain occult practices. The *Higher Ego*—which is immortal—is rooted in the causal body (Karana Sharira), and it alone continues the thread of consciousness and karma from life to life. This Higher Ego, often associated with the Buddhi-Manas in Theosophical doctrine, is the silent witness—the spark of divine intelligence that seeks expression through lifetimes. It watches, remembers, and guides from behind the scenes, nudging the personality toward deeper realization.

The astral body may become what is commonly perceived as a ghost. It is the echo or shell of the person's lower nature. When the Lower Ego is especially strong—due to unfulfilled desires, addictions, or emotional trauma—it can remain earthbound for some time. These remnants are not the true soul but its fading outer garments. Some Theosophists describe these astral remnants as "psychic shadows," capable of semi-conscious behavior but devoid of true will or higher awareness. They linger in liminal spaces, feeding off emotional residue or being reanimated through séances and careless invocations.

Thus, ghosts, hauntings, and apparitions are often explained as astral residues, or even *Kama-Rupic shells,* wandering between the physical and astral realms. Blavatsky warned that mediums often contact these "soulless beings," mistaking them for the departed's higher self, when in fact the true Higher Ego has already moved on to Devachan or into reincarnation. Devachan, according to Theosophical cosmology, is not a place of mere rest but of joyful assimilation—a luminous dream where the Higher Ego contemplates and absorbs the fruits of its earthly journey before returning again to the wheel of rebirth.

The soul's journey involves *refining the lower ego* until it becomes fully transparent to the higher, immortal self. Until this occurs, fragments of the personality may continue to haunt both the inner and outer worlds.

𓂀 𓂀 𓂀

Chapter 10: The Wall – Thresholds of Consciousness and the Soul's Return

Esoterically, a wall is far more than just a physical barrier—it is a potent symbol of the boundary of consciousness. In mysticism and occult traditions, a wall often represents the limit of perception, the threshold between the known and the unknown, or the veil between dimensions of awareness.

1. The Wall as the Boundary of the Self

In many esoteric systems, the individual is seen as a microcosm, a small universe with inner and outer layers. A wall symbolizes the edge of the ego, the final perimeter of one's constructed reality. Beyond it lies the realm of the unconscious, the spiritual, or the divine. Until a person breaks through this wall—through initiation, mystical insight, or deep introspection—they remain confined to a limited perception of reality. In ancient temple architecture, walls were often inscribed with glyphs and sacred geometry—not merely decorative, but intended as energetic maps for the initiate to decode. The wall, in this sense, was a challenge: it concealed, but also invited passage. Just as dreams often feature mysterious corridors or bricked-off chambers, the symbolic wall reveals where consciousness resists evolution.

The act of breaching the wall becomes a spiritual imperative—an inner Exodus. The wall must not only be seen but understood, not only confronted but transformed.

2. Initiation and the Breaking of the Wall

Mystery Schools and esoteric traditions often speak of "passing through the veil" or breaking the seal. This is akin to penetrating the wall of ordinary perception. The initiate is invited to confront this symbolic wall and pass through it — whether by meditation, altered states of consciousness, or symbolic death and rebirth. Only then can higher truths be revealed.

This is why, in many initiation rites, the neophyte encounters a guardian at the threshold, or a symbolic portal within a wall — representing the struggle to expand consciousness beyond the ordinary.

3. The Wall and the Labyrinth of the Mind

Carl Jung spoke of the walls of the psyche — the compartments the mind builds to separate the conscious and unconscious. Esoterically, each wall represents a fear, trauma, or belief that prevents higher understanding. These inner walls must be confronted and deconstructed to allow light — symbolic of gnosis or divine awareness — to enter. In dream symbolism, walls often appear when the dreamer is resisting change or shielding part of themselves from inner truth. The labyrinth of the mind becomes a maze of self-deception until these psychic partitions are pierced by insight. True integration begins when the inner architecture is no longer used for hiding, but for revealing.

4. The Alchemical Wall: The Nigredo Phase

In alchemy, the wall is present in the Nigredo or "blackening" stage — where the soul confronts darkness and limitation. The wall here is a psychological prison, symbolizing a soul that has reached the limits of material knowledge and must now look inward. Only by metaphorically "breaking down the wall" can the alchemical process of transformation begin. The sealed crypt, the closed tomb, the brick chamber — all are metaphors for this moment of inner arrest. The initiate is entombed not by death, but by self-limitation. The first blow against the wall marks the beginning of spiritual rebirth, as the base metal of personality begins to transmute into the gold of higher awareness.

5. Scriptural and Mythic Imagery

Biblically, the fall of the walls of Jericho is an allegory for the destruction of false perceptions or inner strongholds. In Gnostic texts, barriers are often placed between the soul and higher realms, built by archons to trap consciousness. The breaking of these walls is symbolic of liberation from illusion. Likewise, in the myth of Theseus, the labyrinth contains both a monster and a secret — the Minotaur and the thread. To escape the labyrinth (and the inner wall it conceals), the seeker must face their own shadow and trace the thread of divine memory back to their spiritual origin.

6. The Wall as the Illusion of Separation

Esoterically, walls do not truly separate — they only appear to. They are constructs of dualistic thinking: self vs. other, spirit vs. matter, light vs. dark. When one realizes that the wall is illusory, built by the mind's need for control or identity, then unity with the greater Whole becomes possible.

Final Thought

To the mystic, the wall is not a final barrier — it is a challenge to awaken. It stands as a threshold, a rite of passage that calls the seeker to transcend the confines of the ego and perceive reality in its boundless form. It asks: Will you remain within the safe confines of limited perception? Or will you dare to push beyond, to tear the veil, and see what lies in the infinite beyond? The wall beckons the soul to break free from the illusion of separation and experience the unity of all existence.

The Wall of the Forgotten Light

In a time before time, when the soul still remembered its origin in the stars, there was a vast realm known as the Kingdom of the Inner Sun. At its center stood a luminous palace, its halls made of stardust and silence, where the soul communed with Truth.

But as eons passed, the soul chose to descend — to experience form, sensation, and the dance of opposites. With each incarnation, it built walls around its knowing, brick by brick: a belief here, a fear there, a wound cemented into place. Eventually, it found itself in The City of the Forgotten, a dim place where only echoes of its origin remained.

In this city stood the Great Wall of Unknowing, a towering structure that marked the end of the visible world. None dared approach it. Legends said that beyond it lay madness or emptiness, a place where the mind could not follow.

But one soul — worn by longing and stirred by a dream of light — decided to approach the Wall. The journey was long. As it walked, the soul encountered shadows — the Guardian of Regret, the Whisper of Doubt, the Flame of Desire. Each tried to turn it back. Each was a reflection of its own inner divisions.

At last, the soul stood before the Wall. It was vast, ancient, and inscribed with every belief it had ever held:

"You are not enough."

"The world is all there is."

"There is nothing beyond the veil."

But then, a breeze stirred. A whisper from within:

"This wall is not built of stone, but of forgetting."

With that realization, the soul touched the Wall. It shimmered — and began to dissolve. The bricks crumbled, not with force, but with awareness.

Beyond the wall was not madness, but vast silence, filled with the music of the stars. The soul remembered. It had never truly left the Kingdom of the Inner Sun. The wall was only ever a threshold — built for the journey, but never meant to remain.

The Walls of Jericho as the Ego's Fortress

Jericho can be seen as the fortified city of the lower self, built on fear, habit, and illusion. Its walls represent the hardened structures of the ego — those thought patterns, false beliefs, and inherited dogmas that keep the higher soul locked out from conscious expression. These walls are deeply ingrained, often unnoticed, yet they bind the seeker to a narrow, distorted view of reality.

Circling the City: The Cycles of Spiritual Preparation

The Israelite's' seven days of circling the city represent repeated spiritual practices — meditation, prayer, inner work — through which the seeker encircles their own hardened psyche. The number seven is esoterically significant: seven chakras, seven days of creation, seven initiations — each pass symbolizing an approach to inner mastery. With each revolution, the seeker sheds another layer of illusion, drawing closer to a higher truth and transcending egoic resistance.

The Trumpet Blast: Vibration and Awakening

The trumpets are the sound of awakening. In many traditions, sound is used to break illusion — like the OM in Hinduism, or the Logos in Hermeticism. The trumpet blast here symbolizes a higher vibration — a divine frequency that disrupts the structure of illusion. It is the moment when the soul's inner voice becomes strong enough to shatter the walls of separation. This blast carries the power of divine revelation, awakening the dormant aspects of the soul to the higher calling.

The Fall: Liberation from Limitation

When the walls fall, it's a moment of initiation — the collapse of the boundary that kept the soul from entering into the Promised Land, a symbol of higher consciousness or divine union. It is the destruction of false selfhood, making way for the realization of the True Self. In this moment of surrender, the soul is liberated from the shackles of limitation, stepping into a new realm of freedom and enlightenment.

The Veil of the Temple: The Death of Illusion

The tearing of the curtain (or veil) in the Temple at the moment of Jesus' death is absolutely loaded with esoteric meaning. On the surface, it's a dramatic event. But beneath that surface, it reveals deep spiritual truths about initiation, direct access to the divine, and the destruction of illusion.

1. The Veil of the Temple: Separation Between Man and the Divine

In the ancient Jewish temple, the veil (or curtain) separated the Holy of Holies — the innermost sanctum where the presence of God dwelled — from the outer courts where the people stood. Only the High Priest could enter, and only once a year, on Yom Kippur. Esoterically, this veil represents the boundary between the material and the spiritual, the lower self and the higher self, or the ego and the divine spark within.

2. Jesus' Death as the Initiatory Sacrifice

When Jesus dies, the veil tears from top to bottom — not from below by human hands, but from above. This signals a divine act: the removal of the separation between God and man, between outer rituals and inner realization. In Mystery School terms, Jesus undergoes the initiatory death and rebirth, the archetypal sacrificial king who opens the path for others to follow. His death is not just martyrdom — it is the symbolic breakthrough into the inner sanctum of the soul.

3. The Inner Meaning: Direct Gnosis

The tearing of the veil means that humanity is no longer dependent on external priesthoods or intermediaries to connect with the divine. The kingdom of God is within you, as Jesus said. The sacred is no longer hidden behind layers of tradition — it is accessible through inner awakening, through gnosis.

4. From Outer Temple to Inner Temple

In esoteric Christianity, the tearing of the veil marks the transformation from exoteric to esoteric spirituality. Now the body is the temple, and the heart is the Holy of Holies. Christ becomes the High Priest within, guiding the soul directly to the Father.

𓂀 𓂀 𓂀

Mystery Thread Sidebar: The Veil, the Trumpet, and the Threshold

In every great tradition of initiation, a moment arises where the seeker stands before the threshold. Whether it is called the wall, the veil, or the gate—it is the final symbol of duality. To pass through it is not to escape the world, but to see the world as it truly is. The trumpet is the call to awaken. The veil is the illusion that dies. The wall is the story we outgrow. What lies beyond is not death—but remembrance.

𓂀 𓂀 𓂀

Mystery Thread Sidebar: The Geometry of Awakening

The walls of sacred temples were never random. In Egypt, India, and Greece, they followed celestial geometry. They aligned with stars, solstices, and planetary orbits. Why? Because the wall was never meant to imprison—it was meant to teach. The initiate, walking its halls, learned to navigate inner space through outer form. The journey through the temple mirrored the journey through the soul. And the final wall—always—was the illusion of separation itself.

The tearing of the curtain (veil) in the temple at the moment of Jesus' death is one of the most symbolically rich moments in all of Christian and esoteric tradition. Here's a layered explanation, both from a scriptural, historical, and esoteric/mystical perspective:

The Tearing of the Curtain

The tearing of the curtain symbolizes that the veil has been opened. The crucifixion of Jesus took place at Golgatha which means, The Place of the Skull. Before this event at Golgatha, Christ Consciousness was without but after this event; Christ is Within You.

1. Biblical Account

In the Gospels, this event is described plainly:

"And Jesus cried out again with a loud voice and yielded up his spirit.
And behold, the veil of the temple was torn in two from top to bottom..."
— Matthew 27:50–51

This dramatic moment occurs immediately upon Jesus' death, and it is not portrayed as a minor event. It is accompanied by an earthquake and darkness, signaling cosmic significance.

2. Historical Context of the Veil

The veil (Greek: *katapetasma*) in the Jewish Temple in Jerusalem separated the Holy Place from the Holy of Holies, which was the most sacred space—believed to house the divine presence of God (the Shekinah). Only the High Priest could enter this inner sanctum, and only once a year, on Yom Kippur, to offer atonement for the people.

Thus, the veil represented:

- The barrier between humanity and the Divine

- The limitation of access to God

- The separation between the physical world and the spiritual reality

Its sudden tearing "from top to bottom" implies that the act was divine, not human — God Himself removed the separation.

3. Esoteric Interpretation

In mystical and esoteric traditions, this moment is seen as the opening of the inner temple, the dissolution of illusion and duality. Here's how it's interpreted in spiritual symbolism:

a. The End of Outer Ritual

- The old priesthood, with its sacrifices and intermediaries, is no longer needed.

- The divine is no longer hidden; it now dwells within.

- *The kingdom of God is within you* (*Luke 17:21*).

b. The Ego's Death and the Birth of the Higher Self

- The veil represents the ego, the false self that believes in separation.

- Christ's death symbolizes the dying of the lower self, a mystical sacrifice.

- The tearing of the veil symbolizes the awakening of divine consciousness — the access point to God is no longer external, but within the heart of each soul.

c. Mystery School Parallel

In the Mystery traditions, the final rite of initiation always includes a symbolic death, where the initiate must pass through a barrier — veil, door, wall — to reach illumination.

Jesus' death is thus seen as the Great Initiation — His veil-tearing sacrifice opens the path for all souls to enter the "Holy of Holies" (divine union).

4. Gnostic and Hermetic Layers

- In Gnostic texts, especially in writings like *The Gospel of Philip*, the veil represents the veil of illusion — the world of appearances, governed by the Demiurge and the Archons.

- The tearing of the veil is the revelation of gnosis — the soul recognizing its origin in the Light beyond this world.

In Hermeticism, "As above, so below" becomes fully realized — God is no longer separate from creation. The barrier between the spiritual and the material has been lifted.

5. Symbolic Summary

The tearing of the veil represents:

- The death of the illusion of separation

- The birth of direct divine access

- The awakening of Christ Consciousness within the soul

- The initiation of humanity into spiritual adulthood

6. Final Reflection

Just as the walls of Jericho fell to the sound of the sacred trumpet, and just as the mythical Wall of the Forgotten Light dissolves with inner awareness, the veil of the Temple tears at the moment of deepest surrender — when the lower self dies and the higher self is born.

The *veil is not torn with violence, but with truth* — revealing that what was hidden was always waiting to be remembered within.

The Rolling Away of the Stone

1. Literal and Scriptural Meaning

In the Gospels, after Jesus' crucifixion, His body was placed in a tomb carved from rock, sealed with a large stone.

"And they found the stone rolled away from the sepulchre. And they entered in, and found not the body of the Lord Jesus."
— *Luke 24:2-3*

The stone had been rolled away—not by human hands, but through divine action—revealing that Christ had risen.

2. Symbol of Resurrection and Transformation

On a deeper level, the stone represents death, finality, and spiritual inertia. Rolling it away signals:

- The triumph of spirit over matter

- The breaking of the final boundary—death itself

- The birth of the immortal self, which no longer needs the trappings of physical form

In this view, the rolling away of the stone is the moment when the eternal soul emerges from the grave of limitation and unconsciousness.

3. Mystery School Symbolism: The Tomb as Womb

In Mystery School initiations, the tomb is not just a place of burial—it is a womb of rebirth. The initiate, like Jesus, must undergo symbolic death to be born anew.

- The tomb represents the material body, ignorance, or the sleep of the soul

- The stone represents the weight of illusion, ego, and karmic burden

- When the stone is rolled away, the soul emerges resurrected, having passed through death into higher consciousness

138

Just as the veil in the temple tears to open the Holy of Holies, the stone rolls away to unseal the cave of the inner self.

4. Esoteric Christian Meaning: The Inner Resurrection

Blavatsky, Hall, and Steiner all allude (in various ways) to the inner resurrection — the awakening of the Christ Principle within.

- The stone is the barrier of material consciousness, the hardened heart, the sealed mind

- Rolling it away symbolizes the dissolution of spiritual blindness, and the beginning of gnosis

- The empty tomb tells us: the body dies, but the soul transcends

In this way, the Resurrection is not only about Jesus — it is a universal archetype of every soul's journey.

5. Alchemy and the Stone

In alchemical symbolism, the "stone" (especially the Philosopher's Stone) represents the secret of transformation. To "move the stone" is to activate the inner fire, the divine spark within.

Thus, the act of the angel rolling away the stone is an esoteric image of:

- Spiritual transmutation

- The movement from base consciousness to divine awareness

- The unlocking of the sealed wisdom within the soul

6. Mystical Insight: The Stone and the Heart

In Ezekiel 36:26, it is written:

"I will remove from you your heart of stone and give you a heart of flesh."

This "stone" is often interpreted esoterically as the hardened ego, or the soul trapped in forgetfulness. The rolling away of the stone is the unsealing of the heart, the reanimation of the divine life force.

7. Final Insight

The stone was not rolled away so Christ could leave the tomb — but so that we could see that He had already risen. In the Mystery traditions, the final rite of initiation always includes a symbolic death, where the initiate must pass through a barrier — veil, door, wall — to reach illumination. This stone, representing the hardened limitations of the self, is not removed by external force, but by the inner awakening of the soul to its eternal nature.

Jesus' death is thus seen as the Great Initiation — His veil-tearing sacrifice opens the path for all souls to enter the "Holy of Holies" (divine union). This is not merely a historical event, but a spiritual archetype that mirrors the inner transformation of every soul seeking enlightenment. In Gnostic texts, especially in writings like *The Gospel of*

Philip, the veil represents the veil of illusion—the world of appearances, governed by the Demiurge and the Archons. The tearing of the veil is the revelation of gnosis—the soul recognizing its origin in the Light beyond this world.

In Hermeticism, "As above, so below" becomes fully realized—God is no longer separate from creation. The barrier between the spiritual and the material has been lifted.

The tearing of the veil represents:

- The death of the illusion of separation

- The birth of direct divine access

- The awakening of Christ Consciousness within the soul

- The initiation of humanity into spiritual adulthood

- It is the revealing, not the freeing

- The awakening, not the escape

- The stone represents our own spiritual blindness, and when it is moved, the light pours forth

☥ ☥ ☥

Mystery Thread: Harriet Bartlett and the Inner Curtain of the Soul

Harriet T. Bartlett wrote that the Old Testament temple — with its Holy of Holies, outer courts, and thick inner veil — was not merely a sacred building, but a divine blueprint of the human being. The veil, she taught, represented the soul's inner curtain, separating the divine spark from the personality. Only the high priest — the purified, initiated self — could enter this inner sanctuary.

Bartlett emphasized that the rending of the temple veil at Jesus' death was not only historical, but alchemical and psychic: a moment in which the human condition shifted. The spiritual veil could now be pierced, not by priests of ritual, but by those willing to purify the heart and enter the sacred center of themselves.

She often wrote that "Jesus walked the inner temple and left the door open," suggesting that the great work of Christ was not to build a new religion — but to tear down the wall of inner separation and restore the soul's direct communion with the Divine.

𓂀 𓂀 𓂀

Mystery Thread: The Emerald Wall of Hermes

In Hermetic teachings, especially those attributed to Thoth-Hermes, there exists the image of a green or emerald wall, guarding the entrance to hidden knowledge. This wall was said to shimmer like stone, yet dissolve like mist — depending on the heart of the seeker.

To the uninitiated, it was impassable — dense with riddles and illusions. But to those purified through inner work, the wall became translucent, revealing the sacred texts etched behind it: the wisdom of the universe, encrypted in symbolic language.

Hermes taught that as long as the ego clings to material identity, the wall remains solid. But when the soul releases the illusion of self and returns to its original frequency — truth, virtue, and unity — the wall parts, and the divine language of the cosmos is made known.

Thus, the wall is not the enemy — it is the teacher. It reveals the barrier we must confront in ourselves, and it tests the soul's readiness to receive the mysteries of the universe.

𓂀 𓂀 𓂀

Mystery Thread Sidebar: The Veil, the Trumpet, and the Threshold

In every great tradition of initiation, a moment arises where the seeker stands before the threshold. Whether it is called the wall, the veil, or the gate — it is the final symbol of duality. To pass through it is not to escape the world, but to see the world as it truly is. The trumpet is the call to awaken. The veil is the illusion that dies. The wall is the story we outgrow. What lies beyond is not death — but remembrance.

Mystery Thread Sidebar: The Geometry of Awakening

The walls of sacred temples were never random. In Egypt, India, and Greece, they followed celestial geometry. They aligned with stars, solstices, and planetary orbits. Why? Because the wall was never meant to imprison — it was meant to teach. The initiate, walking its halls, learned to navigate inner space through outer form. The journey through the temple mirrored the journey through the soul. And the final wall — always — was the illusion of separation itself.

𓂀 𓂀 𓂀

Chapter 11: Plato and the Astral Realm

Plato's philosophy offers one of the earliest and most influential perspectives on the nature of the soul and the astral realms. His metaphysical system laid the groundwork for later esoteric and mystical traditions, including Neoplatonism, Hermeticism, and Theosophy. In Plato's view, the soul is eternal, and its true nature transcends the physical body, inhabiting realms of divine intelligence and pure forms, where knowledge and truth exist in their perfect state.

Plato's worldview bridges the material and immaterial worlds, offering a map of the soul's journey that is echoed in ancient initiation rites, Gnostic visions, and modern near-death accounts. He describes the soul's passage through cycles of existence, wherein it is tested, purified, and eventually returns to the divine source. This journey mirrors the process of awakening found in mystical and occult traditions, where the soul transcends illusion and gains access to higher, unchanging truths. In the allegory of the Cave, for instance, Plato presents the soul's journey from the darkness of ignorance to the light of knowledge, symbolizing the awakening of consciousness to the higher, spiritual realms.

The World of Forms (Theory of Forms)

- Plato believed in a higher, non-physical realm that contains perfect, eternal Forms or Ideas.

- The physical world is merely a shadow or imperfect reflection of this higher reality.

- Later esoteric thinkers connected this realm of Forms to the astral plane, seeing it as a bridge between material existence and ultimate spiritual truth.

The Forms are not only archetypes but spiritual prototypes, held in the Divine Mind. To the mystic, encountering a Form is to remember the soul's origin. In this sense, the astral realm becomes a place of memory and resonance, where the soul recalls its eternal nature.

"The visible world is the image of the invisible." — **Plato**

The Soul's Journey and the Celestial Spheres

- In *Phaedrus*, Plato describes how the soul existed before birth in a divine realm and forgets its knowledge upon entering the physical body.

- In *Timaeus*, he speaks of the soul's connection to the stars, suggesting that each soul is assigned to a celestial body before incarnating.

- This idea influenced later mystical traditions, which interpreted the stars and planets as spiritual forces influencing the soul's journey.

This concept would be echoed in Hermetic and Theosophical cosmologies, where the soul descends through planetary spheres, each one imprinting an influence — until it reaches physical birth. The astral realm, in this view, is the theater where this descent occurs.

Just as the ancient Egyptians aligned their temples with stars, Plato saw the soul's course through the heavens as a sacred choreography between cosmic law and individual destiny.

The Chariot Allegory (Phaedrus)

- Plato describes the soul as a charioteer with two horses:

- One noble and divine (aligned with reason and higher truth).

- One wild and earthly (driven by base desires).

- The charioteer must guide them toward the realm of true knowledge.

This inner dynamic reflects the soul's struggle within the astral body. In esoteric systems, the astral body holds both emotional turbulence and visionary capacity. It is the battleground between spirit and desire.

The chariot allegory became a precursor to later teachings on astral projection and inner purification. The one who masters both horses — reason and desire — can lift the soul into higher realms.

"Knowledge becomes remembrance, and the soul soars upward again." — **Plato**

The Neoplatonist Expansion on the Astral Body

- Later thinkers like Plotinus and Proclus (Neoplatonists) expanded on Plato's ideas, introducing a structured cosmology where souls pass through various spiritual realms.

- They described an intermediate, luminous plane — later known as the astral realm — through which the soul descends and ascends.

- The astral body (called *okhema* in Neoplatonism) was understood as a subtle vehicle of consciousness, necessary for both incarnation and mystical ascent.

Neoplatonists taught that the soul's return is a reversal of its descent: passing again through the celestial spheres, shedding the astral shell, and reuniting with the Divine Intellect (*Nous*).

In this ascent, the astral plane serves as both a mirror and a testing ground, echoing the Pythagorean and Orphic belief that the soul must purify itself to regain its former divine clarity.

The Myth of Er: Plato's Vision of the Afterlife

In *The Republic*, Book 10, Plato describes The Myth of Er, one of the earliest recorded near-death experience narratives. Er, a soldier who dies in battle, returns to life after twelve days and recounts what he saw:

- Souls are judged.

- Some ascend to heavenly realms, others descend for purification.

- After a set period, souls choose their next incarnation from a cosmic lot.

- Each soul forgets its choice as it drinks from the River of Forgetfulness (*Lethe*), then descends back into earthly life.

This account resonates strongly with Theosophy and modern NDEs: panoramic life reviews, karmic decisions, spiritual choice, and reincarnation.

Er's journey is a Platonic road-map of the astral plane, filled with moral consequence and metaphysical architecture—a reminder that the soul's journey continues beyond death, always drawn toward the remembrance of its original light.

𓂀 𓂀 𓂀

Mystery Thread: The Silver Cord and the Music of the Spheres

In esoteric tradition, the Silver Cord connects the physical body to the astral during sleep and visionary journeys. This ethereal connection, often described as a luminous thread, serves as the tether that allows the soul to explore realms beyond the physical, ensuring its safe return to the body. Plato never used this term, but his descriptions of the soul's flight through the celestial spheres suggest he knew the reality it symbolized. In his dialogues, particularly in the "Phaedo," he portrays the soul's journey as it navigates the unseen worlds, bound by an invisible cord that ensures the soul's continuity even in its detachment from the physical realm.

In the Chaldean Oracles and Neoplatonic writings, each celestial sphere emits a tone—together forming the Music of the Spheres. These sacred harmonies are thought to resonate with the soul's essence, aligning it with the cosmic order and reflecting the divine geometry of the universe. The soul hears these harmonies during its descent and ascent. Some NDE accounts report similar sounds—described as cosmic tones, divine orchestras, or celestial vibrations—suggesting that these vibrations are not merely symbolic but actual auditory experiences of the soul's journey beyond physical limits. Some NDE accounts report similar sounds— described as cosmic tones, divine orchestras, or celestial vibrations.

Just as Plato taught that philosophy was a preparation for death, so too did the Mystery Schools prepare the soul to recognize the harmonies of its divine origin, and not be deceived by the illusions of the lower planes. The initiates, trained in the sacred mysteries, were taught to attune themselves to these celestial sounds, as they served as both a guide and a means of spiritual awakening.

Conclusion: Plato's Lasting Legacy on the Astral World

Plato's vision was not mere philosophy—it was a blueprint for soul initiation. The astral realm, in his understanding, was not a separate, disconnected plane but a reflection of the soul's inner condition, a space where the self could confront its higher truths and engage in transformative alchemy. The astral realm, as implied by his teachings, is both a veil and a bridge. It reflects the inner

150

state of the soul and tests its readiness for higher light. Only through self-purification, as guided by Platonic philosophy, could the soul transcend the material world and return to its divine source.

His legacy, picked up by the Neoplatonists, echoed in Hermeticism, and refined in Theosophy, continues to shape the modern understanding of what lies between worlds. The teachings of Plato and his esoteric successors provide a framework for understanding the astral journey, the ascent of the soul, and the role of cosmic music in aligning the soul with the divine.

Plato reminds us that the soul is not of this world, but merely visiting—and that beneath the noise of everyday existence lies a higher music, waiting to be remembered. The task of the initiate, and indeed every seeker, is to attune their inner ear to this music and awaken to their true, divine nature.

𓂀 𓂀 𓂀

Chapter 12: A.P. Sinnett and the Theosophical Path

A.P. Sinnett's writings, particularly *Esoteric Buddhism*, introduced Western audiences to the teachings of the Theosophical Mahatmas. His correspondence with the Masters, captured in *The Mahatma Letters*, shaped modern esoteric views on the afterlife, karma, reincarnation, and the multi-dimensional structure of the soul.

1. The Multi-Layered Human Being: Theosophical Anthropology

Sinnett, drawing from Theosophical teachings, describes the human being as composed of seven principles, rather than a simple body-soul dichotomy. This model was adapted from Hindu and Buddhist esoteric traditions:

- Physical Body (Sthula Sharira) – The material vehicle that perishes at death.

- Astral Body (Linga Sharira) – A subtle double of the physical body, lingering briefly after death.

- Prana (Life Energy) – The vital force animating life, which dissipates at death.

- Kama (Desire/Emotional Principle) – The psychic-emotional layer, the source of passions and instinct.

- Manas (Mind Principle) – Divided into:

- *Lower Manas* – The mortal mind, tied to ego and desire.

- *Higher Manas* – The spiritual mind, the reincarnating self.

- Buddhi (Spiritual Soul) – The intuitive vehicle of divine consciousness.

- Atman (Universal Self) – The divine essence, untouched by individuality.

This layered anatomy explains why past life memories are not consciously retained — they belong to the dissolving lower mind, while the essence of lessons is preserved in the higher aspects.

2. The Post-Mortem Journey: What Happens After Death?

According to Sinnett, death initiates a multi-stage passage that reflects the unfolding of karma and consciousness:

a) Kamaloka – The Purging of Desire

- Kamaloka is the "desire realm," a purgatorial state where the soul must shed its earthly attachments.

- Highly sensual or materialistic souls linger longer, pulled toward familiar cravings.

- Spiritual souls pass quickly, leaving behind a *kama-rupa* — a residual shell or "ghost" that slowly dissolves.

- These shells are often what mediums connect with in spiritualist séances, not the true soul.

b) Devachan – The Blissful Intermission

- Devachan is a sublime, subjective state resembling heaven.

- Here, the soul lives within a self-generated world of beauty and idealized experience, reliving its highest aspirations.

- There is no contact with Earth—the soul is wholly absorbed in spiritual rest and review.

- The length of stay depends on karma: spiritual individuals remain longer; the less evolved, shorter.

- Devachan is not eternal—it is a pause, a sanctuary of spiritual assimilation.

3. Reincarnation: The Return to Earth

a) The Interval Between Lives

- Sinnett wrote that reincarnation rarely happens quickly.

- The time between deaths may span decades, centuries, or even millennia, depending on karma.

- More evolved souls—philosophers, mystics, visionaries—require longer Devachanic interludes.

b) The Mechanism of Rebirth

- The Higher Ego — the true soul — chooses the next incarnation.

- The personality does not return, but its essence (talents, tendencies, wisdom) continues.

- Reincarnation is not random; the soul is drawn to precise conditions that fulfill its karma.

c) Latent Memory and the Path of Awakening

- While ordinary people forget past lives, advanced initiates or yogis may recall prior incarnations.

- These memories are stored in the causal body or accessed through the astral light and Akashic Records.

4. Karma and Its Role in Reincarnation

- Karma, in Sinnett's view, is a moral gravity, not punishment.

- Every act, thought, and motive weaves itself into the soul's fabric.

- Karma influences:

- Birth circumstances

- Illness and health

- Relationships and encounters

- Key spiritual trials

Karma is the great sculptor of destiny—but one shaped by the hand of our own free will.

5. The Role of the Occultist and the Path of Spiritual Progress

- Most souls passively cycle through reincarnation.

- But the occultist, through rigorous training, may gain conscious control of their afterlife journey.

- Advanced initiates can bypass Devachan and reincarnate deliberately or ascend beyond it altogether.

- This leads to liberation (moksha)—freedom from rebirth.

In *The Mahatma Letters*, the Masters caution that spiritual evolution without self-mastery leads nowhere. Knowledge must be earned through purification and conscious striving.

6. Sinnett's Critique of Spiritualism

- Sinnett warned against the spiritualism of his time, where séances claimed to contact the dead.

- He insisted that true souls were in Devachan, inaccessible to mediums.

- The "spirits" encountered were often kama-rupas, or fragments of astral residue.

- Worse, some were deceptive entities from the lower astral — masquerading as departed loved ones.

This remains a central Theosophical teaching: the spiritual world must be approached with deep discernment.

The Mysterious Sound of Chains: Astral Phenomena in Sinnett's Writings

In a lesser-known letter, A.P. Sinnett records a mystical phenomenon observed by initiates: the sound of *metallic clanking or chains* in the atmosphere. This eerie sound, he explains, may occur when planes of reality shift, or when lower astral entities disturb the psychic field.

- These sounds are not hallucinations — they are spiritual reverberations, like echoes of karmic movement or astral turbulence.

- The clanking may occur near death, initiation, or in places of heightened energy.

- They may signal a rupture in the astral membrane — a moment when the veil thins, or when the lower forces attempt to ascend.

Some have likened it to the "rattling of bondage" — the karmic chains of the earthbound soul. Others to the shudder of dimensions overlapping, the pressure of the invisible upon the visible.

Final Thoughts: Sinnett's Legacy in Western Esotericism

Sinnett's *Esoteric Buddhism* gave the West a map of the soul's evolution: not a simplistic heaven and hell, but a complex structure of planes, principles, and transitions. He was a bridge between East and West, science and mysticism, reason and revelation.

His teachings laid the groundwork for:

- Rudolf Steiner's Anthroposophy

- Alice Bailey's Seven Rays

- The Golden Dawn's astral model

- Modern views of karma and reincarnation

His lasting contribution is this: that death is not an end, but a transformation. The soul is never lost, only shaped — ascending through the labyrinth of experience toward the Light.

A.P. Sinnett: Biography & Key Accomplishments

Birth & Early Life

- Born: January 18, 1840, London, England

- Education: University of London; early focus on literature and journalism

- Career: Editor of *The Pioneer* in India, where he met Blavatsky and Olcott

Major Accomplishments

The Mahatma Letters

- Initiated contact with Koot Hoomi and Morya

- These letters became foundational to Theosophy

Esoteric Buddhism (1883)

- Synthesized Eastern esotericism with Western thought

- Introduced Devachan, Kamaloka, and the Higher Ego

Legacy of Thought

- Recast reincarnation in a structured, spiritual context

- Deepened understanding of karma beyond reward/punishment

- Refuted superficial spiritualism

Death

- Died: June 26, 1921, London, England

- Legacy: Remembered as a voice of clarity, discipline, and spiritual inquiry

𓂀 𓂀 𓂀

Mystery Thread Sidebar: The Soul's Mirror and the Seven Principles

Each of the seven principles Sinnett described functions like a mirror—reflecting different aspects of the soul's identity:

- The physical mirror reflects the body.

- The astral mirror reflects emotion and instinct.

- The mental mirror reflects thought.

- The causal mirror reflects purpose.

- The Buddhic mirror reflects divine love.

- The Atmic mirror reflects unity with the Source.

The occult path is one of polishing each mirror until the divine image can shine through them all. Only then can the soul behold its own true face.

𓂀 𓂀 𓂀

Mystery Thread Sidebar: Devachan and the Celestial Library

Devachan is not just a realm of rest—it is a temple of review, where the soul enters its own records.

Here, the soul:

- Reviews its deeds not with guilt, but with insight

161

- Sees others not through judgment, but empathy

- Hears the "echo" of unfinished intentions

It is said that advanced souls can access the Celestial Library—a repository of all lives, loves, and lessons. This ethereal archive is not bound by time or space; rather, it exists beyond the veil of linear existence, where all past, present, and future experiences are preserved in a vibrational matrix of divine knowledge. This "library" aligns with the Akashic Records, where every thought, word, and deed is imprinted in light. The Akasha, often referred to as the "etheric plane," holds the essence of all creation and offers a sacred reflection of the soul's journey across lifetimes, granting insight into its divine purpose.

Devachan is not fantasy—it is sacred memory woven with meaning. In Devachan, the soul experiences a profound, timeless space where its deepest yearnings and desires are brought into clarity, allowing for healing and reflection on the spiritual path it has walked. The soul sleeps not in oblivion, but in the embrace of its own eternal becoming. Far from a mere state of rest, Devachan is a liminal realm where the soul, free from earthly burdens, contemplates its lessons, integrates past lives, and prepares for future incarnations with wisdom gained from its transcendence.

𓂀 𓂀 𓂀

Chapter 13: The Mahatma Letters

"Death in Devachan is as little actual as birth in the material world: both are temporary states of consciousness."

— *The Mahatma Letters*

The *Mahatma Letters to A.P. Sinnett* form one of the most important foundations of Theosophical thought. Between 1880 and 1884, Sinnett corresponded with two Masters of the Great White Lodge—Mahatma Koot Hoomi (K.H.) and Mahatma Morya (M.)—receiving letters that explored the unseen architecture of reincarnation, karma, spiritual evolution, and the occult path.

These communications were said to materialize through occult means, sometimes appearing out of thin air or written directly through astral projection, demonstrating the Mahatmas' mastery of higher laws and planes.

1. What the Mahatma Letters Say About Death and the Afterlife

a) Death Is Not an End, But a Transition

- At death, the astral body detaches from the physical.

- The *Lower Manas*—the temporary personality—enters Kamaloka, where it sheds its earthly desires.

b) Kamaloka: The Purgatorial Phase

- This is not punishment, but a necessary purification.

- Materialistic or sensual souls linger here until attachments dissolve.

- The *kama-rupa* (astral shell) may remain behind, often mistaken for "ghosts" by spiritualists.

c) Devachan: The Blissful Dream-State

- The Higher Ego enters Devachan, a subjective heaven built from its noblest aspirations.

- The soul experiences harmony and joy, but it is not the real self—it is a spiritual echo.

- Time in Devachan varies. Greater virtue creates deeper, more expansive rest.

d) The Return to Earth: Reincarnation

- Reincarnation is deliberate, not immediate.

- The Higher Ego selects the next life according to karmic needs.

- A new personality is formed each time; the old one does not return.

2. Karma: The Law of Balance and Becoming

- Karma is impersonal law, not divine judgment.

- Each thought, word, and deed creates subtle energy that shapes future lifetimes.

- Suffering is not a punishment, but an invitation to transcend error.

- Free will remains central: spiritual evolution is self-directed.

3. The Occult Path and Liberation

- Most souls undergo unconscious cycles of rebirth.

- Initiates can awaken before death and bypass the Devachanic state.

- Mastery over the *Higher Ego* allows conscious reincarnation — or liberation.

Those who reach the highest initiatory levels can merge with Universal Consciousness, entering *Nirvana*. This is not annihilation, but full awareness in divine unity.

4. Rejection of Spiritualism

- The Mahatmas rejected 19th-century spiritualism:

- True souls in Devachan cannot communicate with the living.

- Most medium-ship contacts are kama-rupas — empty astral shells.

- Some encounters involve deceptive elementals or lower astral beings.

- Relying on spiritualism distracts from the path of inner initiation.

5. Sinnett's Theosophical Contribution

- *Esoteric Buddhism* (1883) clarified:

- Reincarnation is delayed, not immediate.

- The soul follows a structured post-mortem path: Kamaloka → Devachan → Rebirth.

- Western religion misrepresents death; Theosophy restores its sacred mystery.

- Sinnett introduced Theosophy to the West and influenced:

- Blavatsky's Secret Doctrine

- Annie Besant, Leadbeater, and Rudolf Steiner

- Manly P. Hall and modern occultists

6. Sinnett's View of the Soul's Journey

The Sevenfold Human Structure:

Physical Body – The earthly shell

Astral Body (Linga Sharira) – Subtle energetic double

Kama – Desire nature

Lower Manas – Personality, dissolves after death

Higher Manas – Reincarnating spiritual self

Buddhi – Intuitive divine soul

Atman – Universal divine essence

This model reveals why most people do not remember past lives: it is the *Higher Ego* that reincarnates—not the personality. The soul evolves, gathering wisdom across lives, moving toward ultimate freedom.

7. The Metallic Chain Phenomenon: An Esoteric Disturbance

In one obscure section of *The Mahatma Letters*, Sinnett records that metallic clanking or chain-like sounds are sometimes heard during spiritual shifts or disturbances. These sounds are not imagined but occur when astral forces intersect with the physical atmosphere.

- Such sounds often accompany:

- Deaths

- Astral projection

- Initiatory breakthroughs

- The Mahatmas imply this reflects tension between planes, like friction as souls pass between states of being.

These chain sounds could symbolize the karmic "chains" of the soul—or the mechanical movement of cosmic laws. They are a subtle auditory signature of an unseen reality pressing against the veil.

8. The Mahatma Letters and Near-Death Experiences

Though written decades before the modern NDE movement, the teachings of the Mahatmas parallel many Near-Death Experience accounts:

NDE Phenomena	Mahatma Letter Parallels
Leaving the body	Astral body detaching at death
Life review	Kamaloka's confrontation with desires and choices
Peaceful light, blissful realms	Devachan's subjective heaven
Return with new purpose	The soul's descent into reincarnation
Being told "It's not your time"	The Higher Ego not ready to re-enter physical existence

These similarities suggest that ancient initiates and Mahatmas understood the same inner landscapes modern NDErs traverse. The teachings of Theosophy may provide the deeper map for those spiritual territories.

Final Thought

The Mahatma Letters illuminate a sacred vision of death — not as an end, but as a gate of transformation. This perspective redefines death as an essential passage, where the soul sheds its earthly form to reawaken in a higher state of consciousness, aligning more closely with divine truth. In place of superstition or blind faith, they offer a structured cosmology of how consciousness journeys through Kamaloka and Devachan, carried by karma and refined across incarnations. The teachings offer a map for the soul's evolution, revealing death as part of an ongoing cycle of self-realization and spiritual purification.

Sinnett's work, grounded in these teachings, opened a bridge between the ancient East and the searching West. And for the modern seeker, they provide a reminder: death is not darkness — it is the threshold of remembrance.

𓂀 𓂀 𓂀

Mystery Thread Sidebar: The Chains of Karma and the Call of Silence

Some say that when a soul is close to awakening — either through death or deep spiritual initiation — a faint metallic sound is heard: like links breaking… or forming.

In esoteric circles, these sounds are not merely echoes but messages — resonances of karmic bonds being rearranged. A chain being forged… or severed.

If you hear it, pause. Something in the astral is moving. A soul may be crossing the bridge.

𓂀 𓂀 𓂀

Mystery Thread Sidebar: The Devachanic Garden and the Akashic Bloom

Devachan, they say, is a garden of the soul's own making.

It is not an illusion, but a mirror — reflecting the highest dreams and divine longings left unfulfilled. There, the Higher Ego walks in memory, tracing light through the tapestry of lives.

Some souls enter what is called the *Akashic Bloom* — where the seeds of all lifetimes burst into symbolic clarity. They see not only what was, but what could have been.

The real challenge comes not in dying, but in remembering the garden — and cultivating it again in the world of form. The soul's journey does not end in Devachan — it is only a brief rest before returning to the physical realm to manifest these higher insights and divine seeds of potential into tangible creation.

𓂀 𓂀 𓂀

Chapter 14: Manly P. Hall and the Esoteric Tradition

"The path of wisdom leads ever upward: the wayfarer must pass through the gates of initiation to reach the temple of light."

— *Manly P. Hall*

Manly Palmer Hall's vast teachings on the soul, the cosmos, and reincarnation are among the most comprehensive esoteric contributions of the 20th century. Drawing from Hermeticism, Theosophy, Freemasonry, and the Mystery Schools of Egypt, Greece, and the East, Hall preserved a vision of spiritual initiation that connects ancient wisdom with the modern seeker.

Manly P. Hall on the Soul

Hall emphasized that the true purpose of human life is self-mastery and inner illumination. Echoing ancient initiatory systems, he viewed the physical body as a temporary vessel and the soul as an evolving, divine entity —a pilgrim of eternity.

- The soul is not identical to the spirit, but a vehicle for spiritual consciousness.

- The Higher Self—the divine spark—seeks to guide the lower self through cycles of refinement.

- The soul moves from ignorance to gnosis through repeated lives, gradually regaining its awareness of divine origin.

Manly P. Hall on the Cosmos

Hall was deeply influenced by Neoplatonism, Hermeticism, and Eastern mysticism, Hall taught that:

- The universe is a living, ensouled organism — an expression of divine intelligence.

- The macrocosm and microcosm reflect each other: the cosmos is mirrored within the soul.

- The seven planetary spheres symbolize levels of spiritual consciousness, through which the soul ascends between incarnations.

- Each planet imparts spiritual lessons, echoing Chaldean and Pythagorean teachings.

Hall taught that the universe operates by natural and divine law, and that spiritual development unfolds according to karmic necessity, but guided by the inner light of the soul. In his teachings, Hall linked the celestial spheres to the soul's post-mortem journey, following the Hermetic and Pythagorean traditions. As the soul ascends through these spheres, it sheds layers of ignorance and regains its original, divine awareness.

Manly P. Hall on Reincarnation

Hall's views on reincarnation blend Theosophy, Hinduism, Neoplatonism, and Mystery School teachings:

- Reincarnation is the divine mechanism through which the soul evolves and it is from a Divine Creation.

- Drawing from Theosophy and ancient philosophy, Hall taught that:

- Reincarnation is a cycle of spiritual refinement.

- Karma balances each incarnation, not as punishment, but as a lesson.

- Past lives are forgotten due to the limitations of the physical brain.

- Spiritual initiates can access these memories and influence their next incarnation.

- Ordinary souls reincarnate unconsciously, while initiates and adepts, such as those trained in the Egyptian and Greek Mystery Schools, could reincarnate with purpose — or even transcend the need for physical rebirth altogether.

Unique Contributions to Reincarnation Study

Manly Hall's teachings on reincarnation are not passive or deterministic:

- Souls return to the people, places, and lessons needed for karmic growth.

- Advanced souls choose their next incarnations or avoid reincarnation altogether.

- The final goal is transcendence — divine unity and liberation.

- Karma is not punishment but an intelligent process of balance and refinement.

- Ordinary individuals reincarnate unconsciously, driven by desires and attachments.

- Initiates, however, can recall past lives and choose their rebirth consciously — or even transcend the cycle entirely.

"The soul that learns to rule itself no longer returns by compulsion — it returns, if at all, by choice." — *Hall, paraphrased*

Drawing from Theosophy and ancient philosophy, Hall taught that:

- Drawing from Theosophy and ancient philosophy, Hall taught that:

- Reincarnation is a cycle of spiritual refinement.

- Karma balances each incarnation, not as punishment, but as a lesson.

- Past lives are forgotten due to the limitations of the physical brain.

- Spiritual initiates can access these memories and influence their next incarnation.

- Ordinary souls reincarnate unconsciously, while initiates and adepts, such as those trained in the Egyptian

and Greek Mystery Schools, could reincarnate with purpose
— or even transcend the need for physical rebirth altogether.

Unique Contributions to Reincarnation Studies

- Manly Hall's teachings on reincarnation are not passive or deterministic:

- Souls return to the people, places, and lessons needed for karmic growth.

- Advanced souls choose their next incarnations or avoid reincarnation altogether.

- The final goal is transcendence — divine unity and liberation.

- Karma balances each incarnation, not as punishment, but as a lesson.

- Past lives are forgotten due to the limitations of the physical brain.

- Spiritual initiates can access these memories and influence their next incarnation.

- The final goal is transcendence — divine unity and liberation.

Ordinary souls reincarnate unconsciously, while initiates and adepts, such as those trained in the Egyptian and Greek Mystery Schools, could reincarnate with purpose — or even transcend the need for physical rebirth altogether

The Mystery Schools and the Initiatory Path

Manly P. Hall's most significant mystical contribution may be his synthesis of worldwide Mystery School traditions, which he saw as guardians of the soul's journey through death and rebirth.

- In Egypt, Greece, Chaldea, India, and Tibet, Hall uncovered evidence of secret rites that mirrored the soul's post-mortem passage.

- The "second birth" of the initiate — symbolized by emerging from a tomb, cave, or sealed chamber — was not metaphorical. It echoed the soul's own journey through Kamaloka, Devachan, and reincarnation, as described in Theosophy.

- Hall taught that the Great Work of alchemy was not the transmutation of lead into gold, but the transformation of the soul into its divine state.

"Initiation is the conscious imitation of the death process. To die while alive is the first step toward eternal life."
— *Manly P. Hall*

Manly P. Hall's Unique Contributions to Reincarnation

- Reincarnation is not random. The soul returns to circumstances shaped by karma and its own spiritual needs.

- Initiates direct their incarnation. Spiritual adepts return by choice, not compulsion.

- Transcendence is the goal. The ultimate aim is not endless reincarnation, but liberation and reunion with the divine.

Hall believed that ordinary souls repeat lives blindly, while spiritual work awakens memory and purpose—revealing life as a divine curriculum, and the soul as both student and teacher.

Manly P. Hall's Lectures on Thoth and Osiris

Among Hall's most illuminating teachings are his interpretations of the Egyptian deities Thoth and Osiris, whom he described not merely as mythological figures, but as archetypes of divine wisdom and soul transformation. Thoth, the god of writing, knowledge, and the moon, symbolizes the mind's ability to bridge the material and spiritual realms, embodying the principle of divine intellect that guides the soul's quest for higher truth.

Thoth: The Lord of Divine Intelligence

- Hall described Thoth (Tehuti) as the Egyptian equivalent of Hermes, the god of wisdom and divine writing.

- Thoth was said to have authored the *Emerald Tablet* and the *Book of the Dead*, guiding the soul through the afterlife and resurrection.

- In his lectures, Hall emphasized Thoth as the initiator of souls, the one who teaches how to weigh the heart and ascend beyond illusion.

- According to Hall:

"Thoth stands as the guardian of the inner mysteries. He teaches the soul how to pass through the gates of the underworld—not to escape death, but to awaken from ignorance."

Osiris: The Dismembered and Resurrected Soul

- Hall interpreted Osiris as a symbol of the dying and resurrecting divine principle within man.

- The myth of Osiris being dismembered and restored by Isis was seen as a powerful allegory of the soul's fragmentation in matter and its eventual reunification through love, truth, and initiation.

- Osiris is the archetype of the *twice-born*, mirroring the initiate who dies to the outer world and is reborn to the inner truth.

- As Hall said:

"The story of Osiris is not just the journey of a god—it is the journey of the soul, which must die to ignorance and be reassembled by the divine feminine principle of wisdom and intuition."

The Weighing of the Heart – Ancient Egyptian Judgment and Near-Death Parallels

In the ancient Egyptian Book of the Dead, the "Weighing of the Heart" was a pivotal moment in the soul's journey after death. The ceremony took place in the Hall of Ma'at, where the deceased's heart was weighed on a scale against the feather of Ma'at — the goddess of truth, balance, and divine order.

The Process:

- The heart, considered the seat of memory and conscience, was placed on one side of a scale.

- On the other side was Ma'at's feather.

- The jackal-headed god Anubis oversaw the weighing, while Thoth, the ibis-headed scribe of the gods, recorded the outcome.

- If the heart was *lighter* than the feather, the soul was deemed pure and was allowed to proceed to the Field of Reeds — a paradisiacal afterlife.

- If the heart was *heavier* due to wrongdoing or attachments, it was devoured by Ammit, a fearsome creature part crocodile, lion, and hippopotamus, symbolizing annihilation or spiritual failure.

Symbolic Meaning: The heart's weight was determined by the soul's actions, intentions, and inner purity. This reflects the belief that moral development and spiritual integrity are central to one's fate after death. The ceremony served not just as judgment but as a spiritual mirror — revealing whether the soul lived in alignment with divine truth.

Conclusion:

The Weighing of the Heart is more than myth — it reflects a timeless archetype of inner judgment and transformation. This ancient ritual speaks to the soul's profound encounter with its own essence, confronting the weight of its actions, desires, and intentions. In Near-Death Experiences, we find a modern echo of this ancient ritual: a moment of deep moral reckoning, guided by spiritual intelligence, where the soul is measured not by dogma but by truth, love, and self-awareness. It is a moment of pure reflection, where the soul is not judged by external standards but by its alignment with divine virtues. As in the Egyptian myth, where the heart is balanced against the feather of Ma'at (truth), the soul must reckon with its own spiritual integrity, its capacity for compassion, and its resonance with universal harmony. In this transformative space, the soul sheds its attachments to the physical world, embracing a higher form of wisdom that transcends material judgments.

Connections to Near-Death Experiences (NDEs):

Many modern Near-Death Experiences describe a life review, during which they see, feel, and re-experience their actions — not only from their own perspective but through the eyes and emotions of others they affected. This process is often accompanied by a sense of being judged, not by an external god, but by their own higher self or inner knowing.

This parallels the Egyptian idea that the heart itself — not a deity — holds the truth of the soul's deeds. In both traditions:

- The review is moral and emotional, not just factual.

180

- Love, compassion, and truth weigh heavily in determining the soul's forward journey.

- The experience is not punitive but reflective and purifying, offering a chance for growth or correction.

Some experiencers even report meeting beings or presences who resemble ancient gods or guides, including jackal-like figures (evocative of Anubis) or scribes who document their soul's journey.

Parallels with Near-Death Experiences

Many people who undergo NDEs report a life review or moral reckoning, and this closely mirrors the Weighing of the Heart in both tone and depth:

1. The Life Review

- Near-death experiencers often describe seeing their life "played back" to them in a panoramic fashion.

- In this review, they feel not only what they did, but how others felt as a result of their actions—both the pain and the joy.

- This process is not punitive, but educational and transformative—just as the Weighing of the Heart is not eternal damnation, but a test of balance, truth, and readiness.

2. The Presence of Beings or Guides

- Just as Anubis and Thoth guide the soul in Egyptian lore, many NDE accounts mention the presence of loving guides, angelic beings, or light beings who assist the soul in understanding its choices.

- These guides do not judge; they facilitate self-judgment, echoing the Egyptian emphasis on inner balance, not outer condemnation.

3. The Lightness or Heaviness of the Soul

- NDEs often refer to feeling a deep inner weight or lightness during the life review.

- If one lived selfishly or with regret, there may be a sensation of heaviness and entrapment.

- If one lived with compassion and purpose, the feeling is of expansion, freedom, and peace—mirroring the heart being light as Ma'at's feather.

4. The Afterlife Realm Reflects the Inner State

- In Egyptian belief, passing the test leads to a harmonious afterlife, while failure results in a kind of soul dissolution—not torment, but disintegration of that which is unworthy.

- Similarly, many NDEs describe beautiful or dark environments that match the individual's state of consciousness and moral vibration.

Mystical Interpretation

Manly P. Hall emphasized that the Weighing of the Heart is also an initiation rite, symbolic of how the soul must face its own deeds — not before a deity, but before the divine law within itself.

In this sense:

"To weigh the heart is to weigh the truth of one's life. It is not God who decides, but the soul itself, measured by the eternal principle of Ma'at."

The Weighing of the Heart – Ancient Egyptian Judgment and Near-Death Parallels

In the ancient Egyptian *Book of the Dead* — formally known as *The Book of Going Forth by Day* — the soul undergoes a crucial spiritual test after death known as the **Weighing of the Heart**. This rite is deeply symbolic, representing the soul's inner balance, morality, and harmony with divine order.

The Ancient Process:

- The heart was believed to hold the **record of a person's life**, containing memory, conscience, and intent.

- In the Hall of Ma'at, the heart was weighed on a scale against the **feather of Ma'at**, which symbolized truth, justice, and cosmic order.

- **Anubis**, the psychopomp and guardian of the dead, conducted the weighing.

- **Thoth**, the divine scribe, recorded the outcome.

- If the heart was found to be in balance, the soul passed into the **Field of Reeds**, a realm of eternal peace.

- If it was too heavy with sin, it was devoured by **Ammit**, leading to **spiritual dissolution**.

Quote from the Book of the Dead (Chapter 30B):
"O my heart which I had from my mother! O my heart of my different ages! Do not stand up as a witness against me. Do not be opposed to me in the tribunal. Do not be hostile to me in the presence of the Keeper of the Balance." – Papyrus of Ani

This plea reveals the **intimate awareness that the heart itself is judge and witness**, a concept that deeply resonates with modern Near-Death Experiences.

Modern NDE Parallels:

As revealed above, many Near-Death Experience (NDE) accounts, people report undergoing a **life review**, often in the presence of a loving, nonjudgmental being of light. During this review:

- Every action, word, and even thought is re-experienced.

- The experiencer *feels the emotional impact* of their actions on others — both harm and kindness.

- There is **no external judgment**; rather, individuals are faced with their own inner truth.

This is astonishingly similar to the ancient Egyptian view:

The heart carries truth. **Judgment is internal, not imposed.**

NDE Case Study 1 – "The Mirror of the Soul" (Dr. Kenneth Ring, *Lessons from the Light*)

One experiencer said, *"I saw my whole life flash before me. I felt the pain I caused others. I judged myself – not out of guilt, but out of love. It was like my soul wanted to make things right."*
This mirrors the Egyptian concept of *Ma'at*, where the soul must be in harmony with truth to pass onward.

NDE Case Study 2 – The Being of Light (Dr. Raymond Moody, *Life After Life*)

Another NDE witness shared, *"There was a presence beside me, like a light being. It didn't judge me – it showed me. I saw the truth, and I couldn't lie about anything. It was all there in me."*

In both cases, the soul's journey echoes the Weighing of the Heart:

- The **heart is the book** of truth.

- The **presence of a guide** (light being or Anubis) facilitates the review.

- The **balance of one's actions** determines the next step of the soul's path.

Esoteric Insight:

This archetypal judgment—where the soul weighs its own life against divine truth—is a **universal motif**. Ancient Egypt encoded it through symbolism; modern NDEs echo it through experience.

Where Egyptians saw Anubis and Thoth, modern experiencers may see beings of light, angelic scribes, or familiar ancestors. The names change, but the **spiritual function remains the same**.

Conclusion: Why It Matters Today

The Weighing of the Heart is not just a mythic episode from Egyptian lore—it is a profound spiritual truth recognized across time and cultures. Whether in ancient papyri or modern NDE reports, the message is clear: **Our hearts are the measure of our souls.**

To live in truth, compassion, and balance is to prepare the soul for its next journey—whether in the halls of Ma'at or the realms of light. Both ancient and modern accounts agree: the soul is not judged arbitrarily. It is given the opportunity to reflect, to learn, and to choose how it will evolve. Whether through the esoteric rite of the Egyptians or the spontaneous experiences of NDEs, the message remains clear:

The heart must be light—free from deceit, regret, hatred, and fear.

And that lightness is not weakness—but truth in its purest form.

𓂀 𓂀 𓂀

Final Reflection

Manly P. Hall was not just a scholar of ancient mysteries — he was a bridge between worlds. Through him, the voices of Pythagoras, Plato, the Hermetists, and Theosophists speak anew, reminding us that the soul is on a sacred journey, and that the path to truth winds through life, death, and rebirth.

For Hall, to reincarnate unconsciously is fate. To reincarnate consciously is power. But to rise above the cycle entirely — to achieve harmony with the cosmic order — is freedom.

𓂀 𓂀 𓂀

Mystery Thread Sidebar: The Initiate and the Seven Spheres

In Hall's cosmology, the soul ascends through seven planetary spheres after death, each representing a level of consciousness. These spheres are not literal planets, but spiritual thresholds.

Each Mystery School taught how to pass through these realms in life, through ritual, meditation, and purification. The Egyptian *Book of the Dead*, the Greek *Chaldean Oracles*, and the Hermetic ascent through the stars all echoed the same truth:

The soul is not climbing toward heaven — it is returning.

𓂀 𓂀 𓂀

Mystery Thread Sidebar: The Pillars of the Temple

Manly P. Hall taught that the twin pillars of initiation — Boaz and Jachin — symbolize the polarities within the self. Strength and wisdom. Earth and heaven. Body and soul.

To enter the temple of wisdom, one must walk between them in balance.

Each reincarnation is a pass through the pillars — a return to the temple. Until, at last, the soul becomes the temple itself.

Manly P. Hall: Biography & Key Accomplishments

Birth & Early Life

- Born: March 18, 1901, in Peterborough, Ontario, Canada

- Raised primarily in South Dakota by his grandmother

- Influenced by his mother's Rosicrucian background

- A self-taught prodigy of metaphysics, Hall began lecturing on esotericism by his early 20s

Major Accomplishments

1. The Secret Teachings of All Ages (1928)

- A 700-page encyclopedia of esoteric wisdom

- Funded by patrons and still considered one of the most important occult texts of the modern era

2. Philosophical Research Society (1934)

- Founded in Los Angeles as a center for the study of ancient and mystical wisdom

- Continues to this day

3. Freemasonry & Esoteric Symbolism

- A 33° Mason and master of Masonic symbolism

- Saw Freemasonry as a modern remnant of ancient Mystery Schools

4. Prolific Teacher and Lecturer

- Gave over 8,000 lectures on metaphysics, Hermeticism, and universal religion

- Inspired the New Age, esoteric Christianity, and comparative religion movements

5. Esoteric Christianity

- Saw Christ as an eternal archetype of inner light, not confined to any single religion

- Viewed Jesus as an initiate of the Mysteries, whose life reflected universal esoteric truths

Death

- Died on August 29, 1990, under mysterious circumstances.

- Some suspect foul play due to missing manuscripts and unusual details surrounding his death.

- His legacy remains through his books, audio lectures, and the Philosophical Research Society.

Chapter 15: Esoteric Voices – The Soul, the Ego, and the Journey of Return

Throughout the ages, mystics and esoteric teachers have spoken of the soul not as a mere byproduct of the body, but as the eternal traveler across lifetimes. In the teachings of A.P. Sinnett, Helena Blavatsky, Rudolf Steiner, and Manly P. Hall, the soul is central to a great cosmic drama, wherein karma, reincarnation, and the purification of the ego guide us back to divine origin. These four thinkers, drawing from Theosophy, Anthroposophy, and Mystery School wisdom, provide profound insight into what we truly are, why we return again and again to Earth, and how the ego can ultimately return to God. Their perspectives can be strikingly compared with the modern accounts of near-death experiences (NDEs), which offer glimpses of the soul's continuity and the spiritual realms beyond.

Helena Petrovna Blavatsky

The Soul

Blavatsky describes the soul as a Monad—a compound of *Atma, Buddhi, and Manas*. It descends through the planes of matter to learn, accumulate experience, and ascend again, spiritualized. Each soul is divine in origin, yet cloaked in layers of illusion, karmic baggage, and forgetfulness.

The Ego

She distinguishes between the Lower Ego (the emotional and mental personality) and the Higher Ego (the soul's spiritual individuality). Only the Higher Ego endures. The lower personality becomes a memory, unless it becomes spiritually refined enough to merge with the immortal.

Karma

Karma is described as cosmic equilibrium, the sacred law of compensation. Every act, thought, and intention ripples across the soul's future, ensuring balance and opportunity for growth.

Reincarnation

After death, the soul ascends to Devachan, where it lives out the ideal results of its higher aspirations. The return to Earth only comes after this reflection. Reincarnation is not immediate — it is rhythmic and governed by both inner need and cosmic cycles.

NDE Comparison

Her teachings echo the experiences of those NDErs who warn of astral illusions — beings or realms that seem divine but are constructs of thought. Her emphasis on discernment aligns with NDE accounts where discerning the true Light is vital. The journey inward, the memory of the divine source, and the weight of moral life all resonate deeply.

The Ego's Return to God

The Monad must peel away the illusions of Maya, awaken fully within the Higher Ego, and ascend back to the divine origin. Blavatsky's path is one of occult discipline, clarity of mind, and inner vision.

Rudolf Steiner

The Soul

Steiner articulates three stages of soul development: Sentient Soul (emotional life), Intellectual Soul (thinking and judgment), and Consciousness Soul (spiritual will). Over many lifetimes, these aspects are refined to prepare for reunion with the Spiritual Triad: *Spirit-Self (Manas), Life-Spirit (Buddhi), and Spirit-Man (Atma).*

The Ego

Steiner's Ego is the divine "I" — the individualized flame of God within. It incarnates to develop consciousness and ethical insight, eventually becoming a vessel of higher spiritual perception and freedom.

Karma

Karma is pedagogical — it is a teacher, not a judge. Each life offers tailored experiences to develop virtues, confront shadows, and learn cosmic law.

Reincarnation

After death, the soul undergoes Kamaloka (a soul-purging reflection) and then Devachan (a celestial school of light). Steiner adds that the soul journeys through planetary spheres, absorbing spiritual influences before selecting a new life.

NDE Comparison

Steiner's vivid descriptions of panoramic life review, spiritual guides, and planetary ascent are echoed in advanced NDEs, where souls report cosmic journeys, reunions with divine intelligences, and experiences of overwhelming moral clarity.

The Ego's Return to God

The Ego, through conscious cultivation, transforms into a Christ-bearing being—a radiant soul who reflects divine love and wisdom. Steiner emphasizes that the true return to God is through the inner path, guided by Christ as the archetype of the fully awakened soul.

Manly P. Hall

The Soul

Hall portrays the soul as a traveler in subtle garments—clothed in astral, mental, and causal bodies. The soul exists between spirit and matter and seeks harmony through initiation, knowledge, and virtue. Its mission is illumination—the inner light awakened.

The Ego

The Lower Ego is the personality—bound to illusion. The Higher Ego is the divine presence within, capable of profound transformation. For Hall, the ego must become transparent to the Spirit.

Karma

Karma is a cosmic mirror, reflecting the inner state of the soul. Hall teaches that karma refines rather than punishes. It offers opportunities for inner alchemy — transforming suffering into wisdom.

Reincarnation

Hall holds that reincarnation is an initiatory process. The soul is drawn back to the earth by its unfulfilled lessons. But once it masters the lower vehicles, it transcends the cycle and lives consciously across dimensions.

NDE Comparison

Hall warned of false heavens and astral traps — echoed in NDE reports where beings of light test the soul. He stressed that true Light brings clarity, peace, and alignment with higher truth. His teachings resonate with those NDE accounts that describe crossing barriers or "tests" before reaching divine presence.

The Ego's Return to God

For Hall, illumination is the key. The initiate must pass through the fires of transformation, face the inner shadows, and rise — Phoenix-like — into union with the divine. The journey is not linear but spiral, returning upward toward the One Light.

Integration and The Path Home

Together, Sinnett, Blavatsky, Steiner, and Hall form a powerful esoteric tetrad—a chorus of initiates guiding humanity toward truth. Each one affirms the immortality of the soul, the veil of illusion, the justice of karma, and the necessity of reincarnation. Their voices resound across cultures and centuries, affirming the same hidden curriculum: *Know Thyself, Purify Thyself, and Return to the Light.*

Their teachings harmonize with modern near-death experiences—where souls speak of life reviews, astral illusions, guides of Light, and the ineffable reunion with a Love beyond comprehension.

To return to God, the ego must remember its source, shed its illusions, and become a vessel of Spirit. This is not blind salvation—it is the conscious Great Work of soul evolution, initiation, and sacred reunion.

Mystery Thread: The Hidden Curriculum

In the ancient Mystery Schools, initiates were taught that the soul is a divine exile, and the ego is its mask. Through rites of purification, symbolic death, and inner resurrection, the ego could be reborn in alignment with the divine will. This hidden thread runs through all four teachings—and through the deeper meaning of near-death experiences. Behind the veil, the soul remembers its true name.

Mystery Sidebar: Voices from the Threshold – NDE Quotes That Echo Esoteric Truths

"I left my body and felt an overwhelming sense of peace. But I saw another version of myself — calm, wise, observing. It wasn't my usual personality. It was like meeting the true me."

—NDE from *The Near-Death Experience Research Foundation (NDERF)*
(*Resonates with: Higher Ego / Reincarnating Self – Sinnett, Hall*)

"There was a life review. Not a judgment, just... complete understanding. I saw how every small act rippled out. It wasn't scary, but deeply moving."

—NDE account, documented by Dr. Raymond Moody
(*Resonates with: Karma as cosmic balance – Steiner, Blavatsky*)

"I went through a tunnel, but there were distractions — beings trying to get my attention. I knew they weren't 'bad,' but they weren't the Light. I kept going until I reached something beyond form."

—NDE testimony, anonymous
(*Resonates with: False heavens, astral traps – Hall, Blavatsky*)

"It felt like I merged with something vast, pure. There was no fear, no identity, just unity. I didn't want to return, but I was told, 'You still have work to do.'"

—NDE interview, *Dr. Jeffrey Long*
(*Resonates with: Atma, Devachan, and reincarnation by purpose – Sinnett, Steiner*)

"I saw planets, lights, even temples... it was like a cosmic school. There were guides who showed me how everything is connected."

—NDE archive, *IANDS.org*
(Resonates with: Planetary spheres and spiritual hierarchies – Steiner, Hall)

Esoteric Reincarnation Cycle Timeline

(With Parallels to Near-Death Experiences)

This timeline reflects the core afterlife sequence as taught by Sinnett, Blavatsky, Steiner, and Hall—alongside common NDE elements that mirror these stages.

1. Physical Death

- The body ceases; the soul begins detaching from the physical vehicle.

- *NDE parallel:* Feeling of floating above body, watching from above.

2. Separation of Vehicles

- The etheric and astral bodies begin to disengage.

- Lower emotional energies begin to dissolve.

- *NDE parallel:* Tunnel, passage, or veil—crossing to another realm.

3. Kamaloka (Astral Realm / Purgatory)

- The soul confronts unresolved desires and attachments.

- *NDE parallel:* The life review, emotional processing, or being held in a realm of reflection.

4. Devachan (Heavenly Bliss-State)

- The soul experiences a dreamlike heaven based on its highest aspirations.

- Assimilation of spiritual lessons occurs here.

- *NDE parallel:* Realms of light, presence of loving beings, feelings of home or wholeness.

5. Planetary Spheres / Spiritual Preparation

- Soul may travel through planetary influences (Steiner, Hall).

- Guided by spiritual hierarchies toward next birth.

- *NDE parallel:* Cosmic voyage, meeting soul guides, receiving a life mission.

6. Return to Incarnation

- The Higher Ego selects conditions for reincarnation based on karma.

- A new personality is formed for the next earthly experience.

- *NDE parallel:* Some NDErs report being "sent back," often after hearing, "It is not your time."

Repeat Until Liberation

- This cycle continues until the soul achieves liberation — mastery over the ego, integration of lessons, and conscious return to divine source.

𓂀 𓂀 𓂀

Chapter 16: The Planes of Consciousness – Descent into Matter, Ascent into Spirit

The concept of planes of consciousness is central to many esoteric, Theosophical, and mystical traditions. These planes represent different levels of reality, consciousness, and vibration. To incarnate as a human being, the soul must descend through these planes — gradually taking on denser forms and more limited states of awareness. Each descent marks a stage of increasing material entanglement, where the clarity of higher wisdom is veiled by the senses and ego. After death or through spiritual awakening, the soul must ascend back through them, shedding the veils of illusion and returning to its source. This ascent is not merely a reversal, but a conscious re-integration, where insight gained through earthly experience becomes fuel for higher realization.

Here's a breakdown of the main planes of consciousness, the process of descent, and the path of ascent:

The Seven Traditional Planes of Consciousness

Divine Plane (Adi Plane)

- Pure, formless unity. Source of all existence.

- No duality, only Oneness — Ptah in Egyptian terms, the Brahman in Vedanta.

- This is the original state of the soul before any differentiation.

Monadic Plane

- The plane of divine individuality.

- The "spark of God" begins to differentiate into individual monads—each carrying its unique destiny.

- Still pure, but with the potential for expression.

Spiritual Plane (Atmic Plane)

- Plane of the Higher Self, or true spiritual will.

- The realm of the Over-soul and divine purpose.

- Where the soul knows its mission and alignment with cosmic law.

Intuitional or Buddhic Plane

- Plane of direct knowing, spiritual love, and compassion.

- Where unity is felt and not just known—beyond thought, yet conscious.

- Mystics, saints, and enlightened beings begin to access this in flashes.

Mental Plane

- Divided into:

- Higher Mental (Causal Body) – the realm of archetypes, ideas, and soul memory.

- Lower Mental – rational thought, logic, ego structures.

- This is where karma begins to take shape as the soul's choices become crystallized.

Astral Plane (Emotional Plane)

- The realm of feelings, desires, passions.

- After death, many souls linger here in Kamaloka (desire realm).

- It is here that false heavens and astral traps often manifest.

Physical Plane

- The densest, material world.

- Includes the physical and etheric bodies.

- The realm of time, space, and physical incarnation.

Descent Through the Planes (Involution)

The soul descends from the Divine Plane, gradually putting on layers—from pure spiritual being down to mind, emotion, and physical form.

- This is often called involution, or the "fall into matter."

- It's not a fall in the negative sense, but a sacrificial journey of the soul to gain experience, individuation, and self-consciousness.

- Each plane adds a new limitation, but also a new tool for experience.

Ascent Through the Planes (Evolution)

After incarnating, the soul must ascend back through these planes, but now with the added gift of experience, wisdom, and awakened will.

- The path of return is the journey of spiritual awakening.

- Through purification, initiation, and gnosis, the soul releases itself from the chains of lower desires and false identities.

- Ascension involves:

- Transcending the physical through right living and service.

- Purifying the astral through emotional balance and compassion.

- Refining the mind through meditation and self-knowledge.

- Entering the Buddhic and Atmic planes through inner union, love, and divine will.

Initiation and the Mystery Schools

- The ancient Mysteries taught how to ascend through these planes while still in the body.

- Each degree of initiation symbolized mastery over one of these planes.

- The initiate was taught to die before death, freeing the soul from the prison of illusion.

Parallels in Near-Death Experiences

- Many NDEs describe ascending through layers or realms — often moving from darkness to light, from emotion to thought, from individuality to unity.

- Often, they are stopped before reaching the higher spiritual planes, being told it is not yet time.

𓂀 𓂀 𓂀

Mystery Thread Sidebar: The Temple Within

The ancient Egyptians taught that the body was a temple built in the image of the universe. Within it, the soul descended — first as divine breath, then as thought, then as feeling, and finally as flesh. The process of ascending was a sacred reversal — a climb through the inner temple, unlocking the seven seals or gates that bound the soul to earth.

In the Mystery Schools of Egypt and Greece, initiates symbolically descended into the underworld before rising again, reborn into higher consciousness. Each chamber of the temple mirrored one of the seven planes, and mastery of each level was required before stepping into the light of the inner sanctum — the place of union with the divine spark. This path still lives within every soul. The planes are not distant realms, but states of being waiting to be remembered.

𓂀 𓂀 𓂀

Chapter 17: Harriet T. Bartlett

Harriet T. Bartlett was a 20th-century esoteric author best known for her book *An Esoteric Reading of Biblical Symbolism*. She approached the Bible not as a literal historical record but as a spiritual and symbolic text, written to convey hidden truths about the soul, human evolution, and divine law. Her book entitled, "An Esoteric Reading of Biblical Symbolism" was published in 1916 by PHILOPOLIS PRESS in San Francisco, California. (COPYRIGHT 1916 BY HARRIET T. BARTLETT).

Introduction – A Voice of Visionary Symbolism

Harriet T. Bartlett was not merely an interpreter of scripture; she was a spiritual visionary whose inner insights brought forth a symbolic understanding of biblical figures that resonates deeply with the soul's esoteric journey. Her book 'An Esoteric Reading of Biblical Symbolism" is a guide to unlocking the metaphysical currents hidden within well-known passages. Rather than approach scripture as history or dogma, Bartlett explored it as an internal map of soul transformation, drawing on intuitive wisdom aligned with the Mystery Schools.

A very large problem has developed since especially in the 1300s. Translators began applying a literal modality to the ancient, esoteric teachings of what are known as the Biblical Texts. Understand also that what was written as to the ritual of The Mysteries are only such things as were given out to the public, not the true Mysteries. The true Mysteries were never written down, but are matters of expanded consciousness of each individual. Expanded consciousness eventually comes to us. We can choose to actively pursue this, or simply let the course of time fill that goal.

When the Mystery Teachings were lost to a "religion" because of a lack of qualified pupils, then the grosser extension of Mankind's consciousness ensued. Thus, the esoteric meanings were continually being swept away. This degradation continues up to the present day. How many times have you heard being preached from the pulpit of churches that Noah went around and collected male and female of every creature? Or how about that Samson was a drunk and a womanizer, yet he is 'mightily pleasing to God' at the same time? These are but two examples of the deformities because Mankind has not the abilities of symbology or has much of a thread left connecting his mind to the esoteric understandings. Yes, today, people demonstrate that they are infant-souls handling Sacred Texts.

In esoteric tradition, symbolism is often used. A symbol is imagery designed to convey many meanings simultaneously. No words are needed because the symbol speaks for itself. Before letters and words were created, ancient Mankind spoke the words of Symbolism. Going further back, we used communication as described by near–death experiences, and that was telepathic communication, which, of course, needs no symbolism, no hieroglyphics, and no organs of speech and hearing.

The Biblical Texts: Exerts From Bartlett's Book

"In the first chapter, we find Elohim creating, and in the second chapter, it is the Lord Jehovah who is carrying on the work. However, the word "bara" (create) is used but three times in the first chapter of Genesis. Recall that Rudolf Steiner explained that the Elohim and Aeons are helper or subordinate co-creators.

"The Lord Jehovah's **first work was to give Man a body in which to manifest.** We find **the egos of humanity** lying upon the **Buddhic Plane.** They are already human, having reached that stage of evolution upon the Moon Chain. **The Lord Jehovah builds Man a body of dust (the Kabbalah says "of finer etheric matter"). He forms the body out of atomic matter of the Mental Plane,** but must call upon the second breath, or Spirit, or the Second Great Outpouring, before it can become a "Living Soul", not a physical body. When Bartlett says that they are already human, this is not human as we see around us each day. She means the primordial essence of human, of a more spiritual substance. The vehicle had yet to become manifested.

"The first breath was given when Elohim **breathed upon the face of the waters** and impregnated all matter with the Holy Spirit, and brought forth the atomic structure of all planes, but no forms can be brought forth without the attractive force of the Great Second Outpouring of Spirit. **The egos are now ready to function on the Mental Plane. They have causal and mental bodies".**

"Lord Jehovah then **places humanity in a garden of trees.** Trees are symbols of teachers of wisdom. This garden is in the East. East represents intellectualism. **Eden means the Wisdom Plane (Chokmah). Four rivers flow through Eden.** This represents that the **four rivers are rivers of** wisdom that water the four planes for mental development in humanity. There are two Edens; a lower and an upper. "Pishon means sinking into a cleft, and is the one that waters the plane next to the one on which Eden is situated. Inferior Eden is on the Mental Plane, so Pishon must water the Astral Plane. Gihon, the rushing, roaring river waters the Physical Plane, or the land of Cush, the black land. Hiddikel, we are told by the Bible Dictionary, is a river in paradise, and so it is, for it waters the Mental Plane or the land of Assyria (Asshur son of Shem, Shem the Christ of the 4th Root Race). Euphrates, the great and abounding river, waters the Buddhic Plane or the Universal Love Plane, the Plane of Unity. Here is the Promised Land of the Race. The conquest of these four Planes is to be its destiny, and this is the Promised Land always referred to in Scripture".

"In the **rib story,** we find **Lord Jehovah providing an Astral Body for humanity,** and again He calls upon the Second Great Outpouring before the body can be made. This time, the symbolism is somewhat different. The **letter "Yod"** is the symbol for the first person of the Trinity, also the Monad. The shape of the letter Yod is something like **a rib with a vertebra** attached. The symbol is this: Adam was one Yod, and the Lord Jehovah took another **Yod** or a Second Outpouring of the Infinite at the side of Adam, and he closed up the rent thereof. That is Yod joined to Yod, making "H". **H is pronounced Hevah, which is translated as Eve".** The Lord Jehovah called this **production woman (Is-shah)** *"whom God lends,"* or as one translator puts it, *"the completion of man."* **In other words, a body for man (humanity) to function in."**

"He shall leave his father and mother" (the creative forces that brought him here), and cleave to his Eve, his vehicles that he has entered, until he gets control of them. But he and his body were naked (of experience)".

The Kabbalah states that inferior man (that which has descended from above, from cosmic man, which is Adam Kadmon) has two sides. The Right Side is the Holy Intelligences. The Left Side is the animal soul. (This is the animal–man that must be sacrificed. It does not mean to literally kill and sacrifice animals or anything else on an altar). Burning/sacrificing an animal is not to be taken literally. It is a metaphor for a purification by which the lower nature is burnt via the *purification* of 'fire'. This also relates to alchemy.

"So when Adam said to the Lord Jehovah, **'The woman Thou gavest me, she did it'**, he simply meant this new body that You gave me, she did it and passed the experience on to me her higher self."

"By breaking the law, humanity finds themselves so **naked of experiences** that they know not what to do next, so they hide from Lord Jehovah in fear. Breaking the law has also blinded their clear sight upon the higher planes. When the Lord Jehovah comes, they can see Him faintly, and it seems as though the dusk of evening had settled down upon them, as indeed it had, because by breaking the law they had densified matter and soon their sight of **those higher planes will be cut entirely off.**"

"In the **curse of the serpent,** we see the distinct cleavage of the **Mental Plane.** There will ever be a lower and higher Mental Plane, although in a sense they are really one. The serpent, or the teacher, or the Wisdom is represented as creeping when manifesting on the lower Mental Plane. Of dust shall ye eat, or of the Mental Plane, and Humanity will now gain wisdom only as he stumbles over the serpent hidden places and feels the pain of the experience."

"Unto woman, or the desire body (remember woman is the manifestation of the Second Person of the Trinity upon any plane) **"Thy desire shall be to thine husband", or thy higher self** (Thy maker is thine husband) and he shall rule over thee".

"This does not mean literally that a husband is to rule over and control a wife. Reread the above for clarity if needed. These esoteric explanations are not in the Physical Plane but are describing events during creation in the higher planes or the spiritual realms. As is the case most of the time, from the Conquistadors as just one example, down to men who seek to rule over their wives, they take the unlearned approach of literalism. Let us move onward."

"Humanity by gratifying desire, has sunken into animal bodies or, perhaps I should say, into physical bodies. These bodies have been evolving up from the animal kingdom, so Lord Jehovah does not make any new ones now; He wraps about them the skins of animals, their own skins, or circumscribes their development".

"And humanity knew Eve (became accustomed to his new vehicles), and they conceived and bare Cain Abel, the dual–nature first really physical Race".

"When **Eve (Heva)** the vehicle of humanity, brought forth the child (in Root Race 3, the Lemurian Race. This author's insertion for clarity), she said, 'I have gotten a man with IHVH', that is I have gotten a man with the Spirit of God within."

If one looks at the images of Isis holding baby Horus or Mary (Meriam) holding baby Jesus, one can't help but think of an image of Eve (Heva) holding the baby.

"**Abel means Spirit, and Cain means Possessor.** It is the dual–nature humanity. The first human Race is born. Abel, the first spiritual nature of man, naturally becomes a keeper of sheep or a teacher of the more evolved, and would gladly put his animal nature upon the altar in service to God, but Cain the strongly physical Cain, will offer up the first fruits of the Earth or anything else, but his animal nature never. When the Spirit remonstrates, he kills his Abel (Spirit) and buries it beneath the earth, or his dense physical. His animal propensities are in the ascendant".

This demonstrates our dual nature within. We have a war going on inside. The physical is trying to get the upper hand over the spiritual within us. **The Spirit is warring with the physical and materialistic desires and earthly trappings.** Near-Death Experiencers come back changed, where they no longer desire such earthly possessions. Their spiritual nature is in the ascendant. Let us continue.

213

"The curse is, because he has done this thing the natural law of cause and effect will force him to wander in the land; that is, he will have to reincarnate many times in the physical body, and wander upon the Physical Plane until he learns the lesson that his animal nature is his reasonable offering to God. It will take him ages to learn this lesson, **hence the necessity of reincarnation"**.

"He dwelt in the **land of Nod (wandering) on the east of Eden**, on the intellectual side of understanding".

"And Cain knew his wife (became used to his new bodies), and brought forth a new sub-race called Enoch, and the race Cain built a city and called it Enoch after the new sub-race".

So does this not explain as to why so many people ask this question: **"If Cain, Adam, and Eve were the only three occupants on Earth, who did Cain meet to begin a family?"** Do you see the confusions and misunderstandings that literal belief has caused on such an ancient and sacred text? It is not that the text is "screwy". It is the unlearned types out there that continue to rehash the same old arguments. So round and round they go, never once breaking out from the walls that enslave them.

Chapter VI entitled, Noah And The Flood.

"Intuition is one of the greatest of God's gifts to man, and it is one of the last faculties to develop, coming to its full growth only just before he finishes his compulsory earthly pilgrimages. These allegories are written in symbols to cultivate this wondrous gift and lead us to complete at-one-ment with the Father. Consequently, it is not surprising that at our stage of development, we are only just beginning to sense the great riches lying just beyond our reach. At best, at present, we are but catching glimpses of the sparkling treasure."

"Occultists tell us of the great Manu, the Noah of our Bible, also the Moses in one carnation, began to select the most evolved of the great fourth root race, to start the new fifth root race during the fifth sub-root race of the old race. In the Bible, we find him also incarnated as Enoch (Initiator), begetting sons and daughters (spiritual sons and daughters in this reading), three hundred and sixty-five, note the number, the number of days in a year, indicating that he worked to the full end of that race. The character of the Great One is indicated by the words, "And Enoch walked with God, and he was not, for God took him.". He was perfected in his Godhood, evidently a manifestation of a great perfected Soul. None of our own humanity had at that time attained that exalted position".

"At the beginning of the sixth sub-race he appears as Noah, "And Noah walked with God." He was a righteous man and perfect in his generations, not generation, but generations; that is perfect through many, many lives."

"He begets, or gathers about him, three distinct classes of peoples symbolized by Shem (the name), those of a spiritual nature, Japheth (the more evolved of the race upon the Physical Plane), and Ham (the remnant of the other races who are just sufficiently interested, probably for personal gain to follow the others)". Skipping forward now.

"The Bible says, **'there were giants in those days, which were mighty men of old"**, and the occultists tell us **the Lemurians were as tall as twenty-seven feet, and that the Atlanteans were also very large.** The Lemurians were dark colored, but the Atlanteans were white."

"**The fifth sub-race** from which Noah selected his people was the one spoken of as Semitic, from the name Shem, to whom the Jews always pointed as their ancestor, and so he was, but no less was he the ancestor of us all. Shem had the double significance of referring to both a man and to his followers, and without doubt meant the Christ of the race, from the significance of the name. 'The name' could refer to no one else. Noah, the great Manu, or lawgiver, and Shem, the Christ, together are shown leading the race to higher ideals. Shem is pictured as the son of Manu, as he always follows Manu. The Manu gives the race the law and teaches them to be moral, then Christ's influence begins to slowly awaken in them higher ideals."

"**Noah preached the way of righteousness, we are told, for five hundred years during the fifth sub-race as Enoch,** but the people would not listen; then he takes his followers and leads them to the Ark".

"All tribes upon the face of the globe have a tradition of the flood – a fine thing for an allegory, a historical fact that all understood and could be read literally, conveying a good

216

moral lesson, but was suitable to convey hidden spiritual meaning of greater significance, etc."

"Noah means rest, peace, harmony, harmony with God, a state of consciousness, as well as the name of an individual, even as Christ is a state of consciousness as well as the name of our Great Brother. **Theosophy says that Noah was the Seed Manu, or seed fifth root race Manu. He was Vaivasvata Manu, etc. "**

"In one sense, Noah, the Great Heirophant, **preached Righteousness to the people of Atlantis,** and those who believed in him segregated in the course of the ages in the north country, under the Pole Star, the Imperishable Land, it is called in Theosophical literature. This took place, we are told, about one million years ago. The Occultists agree with science in the tremendous length of time covered by the terse account given in Biblical records. Not that they agree exactly as to the number of years…"

"About eight hundred and fifty thousand years ago, Noah led them southward to Aryaavarta, from whence they scattered in the course of ages. Science finds them in this neighborhood; that is, finds ancient remains that indicate the fact that they were there."

" 'Ark' seems to have many meanings. The womb is sometimes called an ark, in the sense of containing and protecting the life germ. Baby Moses is represented as being placed in an ark of bulrushes. The Ark of the Covenant was a box containing the law of God, and in this allegory, a great ship is pictured. It would seem that the general meaning of

217

a place for safekeeping of valuables might cover the ground perhaps better than any other."

"Let us look at this symbol for a moment, and **see if it is really a ship that is meant.** May it not refer to the Imperishable North Land? First, the account says that the land was filled with violence; the Hindu accounts says that strife between the black art and the Great White Lodge grew very fierce, and that the White Brothers and their followers were driven to the North Land while the Black Brotherhood completely took possession of the southern portion of the country."

"Noah is told to build the ark of gopher wood. The Smith and Peloubet "Bible Dictionary" says that gopher wood in the Bible means 'any trees of the resinous kind', so let us say it meant to find a safe place among the pines and fir trees of the north, a high-lying land. **The ark was to have three rooms on each floor, even as man has three manifestations of God upon each plane, and it was to have three stories, even as man has three levels of consciousness. It shall be three hundred cubits in length, or three sub-races shall be the length of their stay, during the sixth and seventh sub-race of the fourth root race, and during one sub-race of the great fifth root race that is being born. In breadth, it shall be fifty cubits, symbolic of the cultivation of the fifth race type. So the dimensions indicate the length of their stay, the characteristics they are to develop, and the three planes of the consciousness of the race. A 'light' shall thou make; the margin says a 'roof'.** Strange that these two meanings should have been deemed a window. No other windows are mentioned.

Would it not seem more probable that the 'light' that could be read 'roof' may mean establish a vibration by which the light of God may pour, sheltering the people from harm? A light and a shelter. A door there was; that is, there was communication between the two forces for a while, but the day came when the Lord Jehovah sealed them up, and pitched the door; that is, put a stop to all communication between the two peoples. Those in the care of Noah were informed that there was danger for them in the low-lying lands, and they kept inside their ark, or their place of refuge, their highland home."

"If we read the account literally, we must take it that Noah, Shem, Ham, and Japheth and their wives cruelly left their children to drown, but if it means that Noah was to take the three classes of people that had listened to him and their schools of wisdom, or religious work to another land, then the difficulty clears up."

For clarification, the Great White Lodge and White Brothers are not referring to race as in ethnicity. For example, there is Black Magic and there is White Magic. This, too, has nothing to do with race as modern Mankind has come to use black and white. What Bartlett, Blavatsky, and others are meaning in occult language and explanations is that "Race" or "Races" are terms used in explaining the great shifts in humanity through the Seed Manus. Manus is the progenitor or archetype. Now let's move on to page 111 in Chapter XI of Harriet T. Bartlett's book entitled An Esoteric Reading Of Biblical Symbolism.

"The reader will remember that we discovered that the sun is used to symbolize the one occupying the position that our Christ occupies today, but at that time, Malchizadek held that chair, although the succession was understood by Initiates. Samson (little sun) – the name establishes the identity of the ego – is a son of a mother who is visited by an angel, and [she] is sufficiently evolved so that she can carry on a conversation with the supernatural visitor". At this point, I need to explain that the mother of the Buddha, John the Baptist's mother, and the mother of Jesus were all visited by an angel (messenger) announcing that they each would be giving birth. Let's continue on and look at Samson's mother. She is the wife of 'Manoah' whose name means peace, and she is told to purify herself, and touch no meator wine, or unclean thing, to go near no dead body, and to devote herself to the Lord, for she who has been barren is to bear a child, who is to be a Nazerite from his birth. Note the restrictions imposed upon her, for they also will be in full force upon the Nazerite from birth, and in addition to those named, he must be a celibate."

"Manoah belongs to the tribe of Dan, of whom Israel prophesied Dan shall be a serpent (wisdom) in the path (of the race), and the serpent shall bite the heels of the horses (the animal nature), so that the rider falleth backward. That is, Wisdom shall check the progress of the animal nature in its desires."

"Let us look for a moment at this beautiful little love story by which a child, man, might get, in the literal meaning, a sweet and pure idea of love and fidelity. Manoah, the peaceful man with his loving wife, who is so pure that the angels of heaven come to converse with her. When she gets the vision, she at once confides in her husband, and he accepts the story with unwavering trust, thinking only of the responsibility of the charge. Note how he at once begins to pray that the angel may come and tell them how to care for the little one who is of sufficient importance for such unusual steps to be taken to secure proper conditions. Again the angel comes in response to this request, and again it is to the wife that he appears, but in response to her request, and again it is to the wife that he appears; but in response to her request, he kindly stays while she goes to call her husband, and then, when the man would have offered hospitality in true Oriental fashion, showing that his mind dwelt on material things more than his wife's, the angel showed his nature by ascending in the flame, thus showing himself a Sun Spirit. The story is a beautiful one and reminds one of the birth of Jesus and of John the Baptist. The spiritual significance as well as the literal facts are very plain."

"Now let us note some of the points that give us the key to the inner meaning of the allegories connected with the mysterious character that we call Samson, that the orthodox will tell you drank, and associated with bad women, but that account tells us 'pleased God mightily'. Surely there is a misunderstanding somewhere. We note that the home of Manoah, the home of peace, was between 'Zorah', the place of hornets, or the hornet's nest. (Materialists are good home-makers but their tongues sometimes have a sting-----HTB), and Eshtaol, which means petition, prayers; so his home of peace lies between intense physical activity and prayer. Here it was that 'the Lord began to move the child."

"Before going farther, let us stop and consider what it meant to be a Nazerite by birth. From the earliest records preserved to the race from any source, we infer that the Nazerite was an old and established custom of recognition of the power and the sanctity of certain individuals, who incarnated from time to time, who took the vow of the Naserite, in order to be released form the ordinary routine of physical existence, to attend entirely to the affairs of God. The word is derived from Nazar, or serpent, a name given to the ancient wise men."

There were two kinds of Nazerites. The kind of birth which Samson was. The other kind became a Nazerite by living good, ethical, and righteous ways within the community. The Nazerites by birth never cut their hair. Their hair was long. The other type of Nazerite kept their hair shaved. They dressed a certain way and were also vowed to celibacy. He must bathe daily and touch no wine, eat no flesh, and never touch a dead body or carcass. Keep these in mind as we continue.

In Judges xiv, 2, 7, we find him asking his parents to find a wife for him from the daughters of Timnath, who were of the Philistines. Keep in mind that his parents know his vow to celibacy, but they did not object to the issue of having a wife. Their dismay was that Samson did not want a wife from his own people. A bit odd, is it not? It is not a question of physical women but a question concerning schools of Mystery. Not only did his parents not set Samson straight regarding his vows, but the Lord also showed His approval. Would the Lord lead Samson to break the sacred vows?

He insists that they go down to Timnath for him; that is, take steps to get the school for him, and he goes to the vineyard, or to spiritual exercises, to prepare himself for the new duty. Today, this would be the equivalent of psyching one's self up to prepare for what's coming. Remember, he is to touch no grapes, and the vineyard symbolizes the cultivation of spirituality.

Bartlett continues here. "Here he meets a young lion roaring against him (his own animal nature), and he slays it with no weapon. Then he, the Nazerite, is pictured as taking honey out of the carcass of that dead lion and eating it, absolutely an impossibility for a Nazerite if taken literally, yet we are assured that the Lord was 'with him mightily'. Can the reader not perceive the symbol? From the slain animal nature, the sweet fruits of the spirit are taken, so that he not only enjoys himself, but he gives to his parents, and they too enjoy the spiritual food. From the dead animal nature is the spirit fed."

'In the Leontiea or Lion grade of Mithriaea there was a honey rite,' Mysteries of Mithra, by G.R.S. Mead, page 60."

Samson has had a great spiritual awakening, and his soul overflows. He had a strong desire to give this great overflowing to others, so he went to the school to test their knowledge in symbols and the Mystery works. Samson began to test them. Bartlett continues. "They cannot tell what he means by 'out of the eater came forth meat, out of the strong came forth sweet'. They attempt to take advantage of him in unfair ways rather than own they do not comprehend, and when he perceives their spirit of being loath to acknowledge that anyone knows more than themselves, he turns the tables on them and tells them such truths that he slays (conquers) thirty of them, and takes their garments, or their arguments, and sends them back at the others, to satisfy them; but this spirit of unteachable hostility tries him and he leaves them, and the wife instead of going to the home of her husband as she would have done had it been a physical marriage stays with her father and is given to his friend."

"His wife beseeching him seven days to reveal his secret, and at last succeeded only to betray him, shows he had some kind of method of Mystery work that he tried upon them, but found then untrustworthy. After a time, he goes back with a kid, symbolic of a sin offering, but he is not allowed to enter the Mystery work, so he then thinks up another plan of reaching the people." [A kid is a young goat.]

"Now comes the fox story that has so puzzled the people of the ages since the Mysteries have been lost to Christianity. Let us stop a moment and consider what use a fox would naturally play in an allegory. A fox is considered the most cunning of animals; it quietly slips around the most hidden places and secures its prey with as little danger to itself as possible. Taking the position that Samson, little sun, is a great teacher who has shown that 'he pleased the Lord mightily', as we are continually assured that he did, then what more probable than that he had many students studying under him whom he could sen out two by two as he did two thousand years ago, bearing the torch of truth between them, and setting the grain and olive yards (or the followers of materialists and the inner schools), setting them on fire of the spirit, slipping about in their quiet unassuming way, One is reminded of the charge He gave two thousand years ago when He sent the disciples out, 'strive with no man'.

"So with these messengers, wise as serpents and harmless as doves, slip about among the people of the materialistic school, and with their torches of truth set on fire the error of the old doctrine, and it was utterly consumed; then in the enthusiasm of their conversation, the Materialists themselves took the new inspiration to the school that had rejected Samson, and burned the school and its promoter with the fire of spirituality, the sacred flame of truth."

Now let us jump forward a bit to page 117, still in Harriet T. Bartlett's, An Esoteric Reading Of Biblical Symbolism. Here we will cover the famous Samson and Delilah allegory. This paragraph begins with Samson finding a school in Sorek.

"After studying the different philosophies, he finds a school in Sorek. Now, Sorek means choice wine, as wine is a symbol of spirituality, we may infer that this school has some method of training the spiritual faculties, the only thing that would have tempted Samson, and from what follows, it may be inferred that they taught the negative methods of trance work. In Judges xvi beginning with the fourth verse, we read, 'And it came to pass afterward that he loved a woman in the valley, or by the brook of Sorek. Woman means symbolically Mystery work, brook symbolizes wisdom; so he is interested in the school of wisdom called Delilah."

"The meaning of the word Delilah is lost in antiquity, the only meanings given in the dictionaries being those derived from the literal reading of the allegory. It is possible that the Greek word Delphi may have come from the same ancient root primarily. At any rate, that word conveyed to the mind of the ancient of Ezra the idea of the oracle at Delphi, who gave her prophecies in a trance condition. This is a guess, of course, but it looks as though there was some connection between the words, as we note that Samson goes to sleep on Delilah's knees. It seems probable that the school taught negative methods of development."

"This method, while it opened up the Astral Plane to the student, has the danger attendant upon it that the students may be deceived by the illusion of the plane, and may become obsessed. One may infer from the previous experiences of Samson that he was able to function consciously upon the higher planes, and that he pretended to become unconscious while making his investigations in the Delilah school, but at each attempt to entrap him, he showed plainly that it was a ruse. Being able to function consciously there was no need for trance work, and when he allowed himself to be overcome by arguments of the school and really went into a trance condition, he, by that act, proved false to his Nazerite vow, and put his eyes upon the higher planes; that is he made himself the victim of hypnosis, which interfered with his doing the work of in the old positive fashion. But after finding that, this method causes him to be a prisoner of the Philistines, or the

226

progressive materialists, he regains his strength by the growth of his hair, or by renewal of his Nazerite vows, regains his own pure spiritual insight again and easily discriminates between the true and the false."

The symbolism of Samson's hair being cut means that he ignored the true source of his inner strength. His long hair is connected to his Nazerite training. He could consciously function on the different planes. He tested this in the Delilah Mystery School, which actually was not teaching righteous works. He discovered that such works closed his eyes to the truth in the higher planes. This 'put out his eyes'. Once he reestablishes his higher vibrations, does he have the strength to reassert himself? Once this is accomplished, he breaks the two pillars that gave the false teachings their foundation. The negative methods of the Delilah mystery works were using negative nature desires instead of the proper methods."

"Samson said, **'Let my Soul die with the Philistines'**. He had killed his animal nature when he killed the lion; he has now conquered the Astral Plane, and in one great struggle, he says, let my Soul die; that is, he finishes the conquest of the Mental Plane. The soul is now the vehicle for the God that he is. He is Master of all planes of matter; he has attained the full right to go into retirement to serve humanity from the secret places as the Christs ever do."

Let's move on to one more section of Harriet T. Bartlett's book, An Esoteric Reading of Biblical Symbolism, shall we? We will begin in the middle of the paragraph on page 120 of

Chapter XI entitled, Are These Some Incarnations Of Our Blessed Christ?

"It is very significant to find that Yeshua (Jesus), Noahdiah (Noah the beloved of God), and Moses, Ezra IV,3, and Eleazar (Master Koot Hoomi), Ezra VII,33, were Ezra's helpers at this time. What more natural than that they should have rewritten in The Books of Law, as it is stated that they did? That the incidents recorded happened at some date before they were compiled is, of course, certain, but the exact date of any of them cannot be proven. That Ezra lived during a part of the life of the great Buddha is probable, according to history, and that the great religious enthusiasm of the period must have reached Babylon is equally sure. Ezra was an Initiate, as were many of his associates, Daniel among them. That his nation was freed from its bondage at this time was undoubtedly due to the great events that had revolutionized the thought of the day. What more natural than that they should have woven some of these events into their new Book of Law that was to furnish the Scripture if the new fifth root race, and give to the new people the true Mystery teaching, hidden in these stories, giving them a record that they would eventually find complete when they arrive at the point of evolution sufficient to comprehend the full meaning,"

"The King David stories seem to date from this period, but, says someone, you do not mean to say you are putting King David in the same age as Buddha, when David lived about 1000 years BC and the Buddha only between 562 and 482, approximately? I answer, an allegory illustrating a truth is a different thing from literal history, although

228

usually based upon historic occurrences, and may be transferred to any age. However, from the symbolic reading of these allegories, the teaching seems to be that this David really did live at the same time that Buddha did, and that he was the same entity that we now call the Christ."

Skipping two paragraphs, we have this. "Many traces of the Aryan" [a root race and not a skin color, nor Caucasian, not an ethnicity] "origin of these stories still cling to them in spite of the Hebrew coloring that has been given them, and if one gets the full magnitude of the scheme of man's evolution, it will make no difference whether the incidents recorded took place in India or in Palestine. The important thing is to get at the truths they teach, and get a clear understanding of the great good law, at once the most perfect, the most just, the most soul-satisfying that it is possible to conceive."

"Let us take a moment to consider the meaning of the symbols used to bring the David stories before us. Saul (symbol of the established religion of the day), tribe of Benjamin, 'the wolf that raveneth', the church that swallows everything that comes near it. You will see later on how it tries to swallow David by putting him in charge of the Mystery work; the wolf that raveneth is surely a fitting name. Saul is introduced to us as hunting his father's asses, or looking after the common people who have strayed from the church fold. 'He stands head and shoulders above his brethren', by far the most promising religious movement of the age; and Samuel the Great Initiator, thinks that by giving the old church a new spiritual impulse that it may do to start the new fifth root race upon its career. So Saulis

229

taken to the mount of spirituality when he is anxious over his father's lost asses (common people), etc."

Next paragraph. "How different is David. He is found caring for his father's sheep (the fifth race people) on the spiritual hillsides. He is fearless because of his perfect confidence in God, and because he has slain his lion (conquered his stars – in this incarnation, he was born under Leo), and killed his bear (his animal nature). He has no use for Saul's material armor, so he picks up a few stones from the brook of wisdom, and throws them in the simple direction of a teacher (the shepherd's sling), and the great giant falls face downward. Materialism is conquered by a pebble of God's truth, for it sinks into the forehead, or the comprehension, and then David takes Goliath's own sword, or his arguments, the truths he has himself perceived to complete victory."

Let's now jump forward a few pages and begin there on page 130 of An Esoteric Reading of Biblical Symbolism by Hariett T. Bartlett. "In 'Inner Life', Mr. Leadbeater tells us that 'When our planet reached the place where it should provide a Buddha from the fruits of its own humanity, no one was found competent to fill the place." "Two Great Ones stood together at the head of the race, at the level of Bodhisattva (Messiah) of the fourth root race, and Lord Maitreya, or the one whom we call Christ. Guatama, because of his great love for humanity, decided to take the tremendous tests necessary to qualify him for the position of Messiah to our Christ, whom he dearly loved. This happened in the incarnation in which we know him as Guatama."

In other words, the Great Masters / Teachers of humanity that have risen among the ranks by their own efforts and will, incarnate upon the Earth to steadily guide Mankind along in its journey. Many have forsaken their spiritual destinations by putting that on hold so as to 'stick around' to assist us. It is similar to this image as an example. Think about a movie you have seen, and in this movie, two people are running, trying to escape a danger or a bear. The bear is in hot pursuit, and then one falls. Instead of the other person continuing to run for their life, he or she stops and return to his or her friend who has fallen. Even though they could have kept running to save themselves, they turned back and assisted their fallen friend.

In Biblical Texts, and specifically in 2nd Samuel 6:14-22, it is written that David danced naked or out of his clothes/garments. Now, a garment usually means a covering in esoteric literature. This clothing/ garment/ covering is not a material covering like we put on a sweater or a jacket. Recall that Samson was very pleased that he killed his (old) soul. In other words, Samson shed his old soul like an old coat, and he was clothed in his new and improved soul. This is part of our ascension process. Another similar view is presented by Bartlett. She explains it in the following: "he dances naked, that is, naked of bodies, or naked of earthly possessions. **Certain Initiates were called the naked because they renounced all worldly possessions."**

Hariett T. Bartlett's book has esoteric definitions in it, and I have placed some of them below.

Aaron... Lofty teachers

Angel... Messenger, or the higher self-awareness

Cedars....................................... Great men

Drunken..................................... Spiritual ecstasy

Famine......................................Symbol of a lack of truth

Fruit..Result of actions

Goats... Perverse people

Gommarah................................. Submerged

Grass... Weak humanity

Heaven...................................... State of consciousness

Mansions...................................Resting places

Manu... Father of a Race (progenitor)

Milk.. Weak food; elementary truths

Nazareth................................... A seat of Mystery work

Oaks..Strong teacher

Over against.............................. East of

Pestilence .... Purification

Rachel....................................... God's productive pupil

Shepherds.................................Teachers

Sodom....................................... Burning

Teeth (grinding)............................ Cruelty and greed

Temple..................................... Man's heart

Virgin..Virgin matter; not
used, yet to be vivified by Holy Spirit

Wall... The extent of one's
consciousness

Water..................................... Wisdom

Well... Symbol of deep
wisdom

Wine..................................... Spirituality

Woman..................................... .Completion of Man

Wrath..................................... Accomplished Karma

Wrath of God...............................Divine Karma

Here's a general outline of Harriet T. Bartlett's esoteric
interpretations on the topics mentioned—Noah's Ark,
animal sacrifices, the Nazarene symbolism of Samson, and
the allegorical meaning behind the Samson and Delilah
story—as described in her seminal 1916 work, *An Esoteric
Reading of Biblical Symbolism*:

Noah's Ark: Symbolism of Initiation, Consciousness, and Purification

In Bartlett's esoteric interpretation, the story of Noah's
Ark is far more profound than a historical or literal
narrative. She saw it as a symbolic representation of

humanity's cyclical spiritual evolution and individual initiation.

The Floodwaters: Symbolically, the floodwaters represent powerful emotional turbulence, delusion, ignorance, and uncontrolled desires that often overwhelm humanity. Bartlett aligns these floodwaters with esoteric teachings on the astral plane — a chaotic realm of emotions, illusions, and attachments. For Bartlett, the flood symbolizes an initiatory crisis — a necessary spiritual cleansing and testing that the soul undergoes in the journey toward higher consciousness.

Noah: Noah symbolizes the awakened initiate — an individual who has become spiritually attuned and guided by higher wisdom. His obedience to divine instruction represents spiritual alignment, intuition, and inner wisdom, qualities necessary to navigate life's turbulent challenges.

The Ark: The Ark symbolizes the protected inner state of spiritual consciousness that shields one from life's emotional and material turmoil. Esoterically, it represents the discipline and teachings of the Mystery Schools, meditation, inner contemplation, and intuitive wisdom. It is the secure inner sanctuary created by spiritual discipline, allowing the soul to weather external chaos and confusion.

The Animals: Bartlett further emphasizes the symbolism of the animals being brought in pairs. The pairs represent duality — opposing forces, instincts, thoughts, and emotions within every individual. In this allegory, the initiate must bring these opposing energies into harmonious alignment, symbolizing spiritual integration and balance.

Mount Ararat: Finally, the Ark resting atop Mount Ararat symbolizes spiritual realization—the elevation and stabilization of consciousness after surviving initiatory trials. Bartlett interprets this event as the soul's attainment of a higher level of awareness, spiritual clarity, and harmony.

Animal Sacrifices: Transcending Lower Nature: Bartlett offered a profound symbolic explanation of Old Testament animal sacrifices, transcending literal interpretations and illuminating spiritual truths:

Animal Nature as Lower Instincts: In Bartlett's view, animals symbolize the lower instincts, desires, habits, passions, and attachments within human nature. These primal forces, while natural, must be recognized, controlled, and ultimately transmuted for spiritual evolution to occur.

Sacrifice as Inner Transformation: The ritual sacrifice symbolizes the soul's willingness and conscious effort to relinquish or transform these lower impulses. Rather than literal violence, sacrifice represents the initiatory process of spiritual transformation—a process echoed in Mystery School teachings, Hermeticism, and various occult traditions.

Fire as Divine Energy: The sacrificial fire symbolizes spiritual purification and transformation through divine energy and conscious effort. Bartlett aligns this imagery with the esoteric process known as "alchemy," the inner spiritual practice of refining base energies into spiritual wisdom and illumination.

Samson as Nazarene: Symbolism of Spiritual Commitment and Power

Bartlett placed great emphasis on Samson's Nazarene vow, pointing out its powerful esoteric symbolism:

Nazarene Vow: The Nazarenes were individuals set apart through strict spiritual discipline, purity, and dedication to divine truth. Their vows (no cutting of hair, abstinence from intoxicants, avoidance of the dead) symbolize spiritual purity, intuitive wisdom, disciplined living, and avoidance of spiritual contamination.

Long Hair Symbolism: In Bartlett's analysis, Samson's long hair symbolizes a direct spiritual connection to divine power and wisdom. Esoterically, hair represents subtle psychic channels and intuitive connections between humans and higher realms. Samson's strength, therefore, derives symbolically from his direct link to spiritual truth, purity, and higher guidance.

Parallels with Jesus the Nazarene: Bartlett notes strong symbolic parallels between Samson and Jesus — both Nazarenes dedicated to spiritual purity, both representatives of spiritual awakening and power. Their lives symbolize the struggles and trials faced by all souls striving for divine truth in a material world, particularly initiates within Mystery School traditions.

Samson and Delilah: Allegory of the Soul's Fall and Redemption

The story of Samson and Delilah carries particularly deep symbolism, illustrating the spiritual struggle between higher purpose and worldly temptation:

Samson as Higher Consciousness: Samson symbolizes the spiritually awakened individual, endowed with divine wisdom and strength, who is nevertheless vulnerable due to his humanity. His initial purity and extraordinary strength are direct results of maintaining a disciplined spiritual life.

Delilah as Material Seduction: Delilah symbolizes lower materialistic seduction—representing worldly allure, sensory pleasure, egotism, and illusion. According to Bartlett, Delilah personifies lower energies that tempt individuals away from their spiritual commitments, leading to spiritual loss and suffering.

Loss of Hair as Spiritual Disconnection: When Delilah cuts Samson's hair, it symbolizes losing spiritual connection, divine inspiration, and spiritual purity. The result is the symbolic blindness Samson experiences—representing spiritual ignorance, disconnection from higher truths, and imprisonment within material illusion and limitations.

Temple Destruction as Redemption: In his last act, Samson destroys the Philistine temple, symbolizing the initiate's final victory and redemption. Bartlett emphasizes this as the soul's ability to recognize its mistake, regain strength through spiritual repentance, and ultimately transcend past errors, breaking free from the bondage of material attachments and delusions.

The Master Builder and the Fashioning of Man Through the Planes

An Outline -

1. **Mental Plane (Divine Archetype):** The Master Builder begins with perfected thought-forms existing on the **Cosmic Mental Plane**. These are the original blueprints for all kingdoms of nature — including humanity. These archetypes are not material, but ideal forms held in the divine mind. Mr. Leadbeater is quoted as saying that the Logos has thought out the entire system — past, present, and future — on this high plane, and through His thought, creation begins.

2. **First Great Outpouring – Forming the Bodies:** The Lord Jehovah constructs humanity by forming bodies from **finer etheric matter** on the **Mental Plane**. However, these bodies are not yet complete. The mental matter is shaped from atomic substance, but to animate it, **a Second Outpouring** (often called the *Second Great Outpouring* or the *breath of life*) is required.

3. **Second Great Outpouring – Breathing in the Spirit:** This is symbolized in Genesis as God "breathing into man the breath of life." Bartlett associates this with **Elohim**

breathing upon the face of the waters. Here, the *Holy Spirit* impregnates all matter with divine energy, making it responsive to the inner life. The breath (Spirit) animates the atomic structure and turns the inert form into a **Living Soul**.

4. **Buddhic Plane (Ego of Humanity):** The egos of humanity exist first on the **Buddhic Plane**, lying dormant until the astral and mental vehicles are prepared. Once prepared, they are ready to **incarnate** and begin their earthly journey. The Lord Jehovah builds "man a body of the dust," but this dust is *mental and etheric*, not physical in the early stages.

5. **Astral Plane (Desire Body):** Man's descent continues as he receives a **desire body**, symbolized by Eve being formed from Adam's rib. This body — **Hevah** — represents the *Second Great Outpouring* and the emergence of **sensual desire** and **emotion**, which complicates man's relationship with spiritual law. The desire body is "craving for sensation" and must be tamed through obedience, otherwise it leads to spiritual blindness.

6. **Physical Plane (Dense Matter):** As man breaks spiritual law, his form becomes more solid. The result is **dense physical embodiment**. Harriet Bartlett explains that this densification blinds humanity to the higher planes. The "thickening of the outer layers of atoms" is what locks man into physical incarnation, where he must learn the law of cause and effect.

7. **Separation and the Fall:** The symbolic act of Adam and Eve eating the forbidden fruit represents the **fall into matter** — a necessary step in evolution, but also one that

veils the higher planes. The more man breaks divine law, the more his form crystallizes and the harder it becomes to perceive spiritual truth.

Summary Insight:

The **Master Builder** (Jehovah) fashions man through an unfolding descent across spiritual planes:

- **Mental Plane** – Forming the archetype or ideal body

- **Buddhic Plane** – Hosting the ego or higher self

- **Astral Plane** – Adding the desire body, the seat of craving and passion

- **Physical Plane** – Final dense form, enabling experience but veiling the soul

Each layer adds both functionality and limitations. Bartlett shows that man's journey is one of descent for the sake of experience and eventual **ascent back to spirit** through mastery of the vehicles given to him by the Builder.

Mystery Thread Sidebar

The Descent of Man Through the Planes – The Builder's Work

According to Harriet T. Bartlett, the creation of man is not a single act, but a sacred process carried out by the Great Master Builder — the Lord Jehovah — across several planes of existence. Each stage of descent weaves a new layer into the human constitution, preparing the soul for experience in matter:

1. The Mental Plane – The Divine Blueprint

Before any form appears, the Logos holds perfected archetypes on the Cosmic Mental Plane. These are not physical bodies, but thought-forms — divine patterns of what will later manifest in matter. Jehovah, acting as the Master Builder, draws these patterns into manifestation.

2. The First Great Outpouring – The Formation of Bodies

On the lower Mental Plane, man receives a body made from etheric substance. This form is shaped but not yet living. It is the framework, prepared to receive the spirit. The first breath has not yet been given.

3. The Second Great Outpouring – The Breath of Spirit

Elohim "breathes upon the waters," symbolizing the descent of divine spirit into matter. This breath animates the etheric form, making it a Living Soul. The Second Outpouring brings life and motion, activating the latent potential within man's mental and astral structure.

4. The Buddhic Plane – The Ego Awaiting Incarnation

The egos of humanity dwell on the Buddhic Plane, prepared to enter into incarnation once suitable forms exist. Bartlett says these egos were present from earlier rounds and chains — specifically, from the Moon Chain — but waited for proper vehicles.

5. The Astral Plane – The Desire Body Emerges

Eve, drawn from Adam's rib, represents the desire body
—*Hevah*—linked to sensation, craving, and temptation. This
layer draws man downward into personal experience.
Bartlett warns that disobedience to spiritual law densifies
the form and clouds the perception of the higher realms.

6. The Physical Plane – The Fall Into Matter

As man breaks divine law, he becomes more fully
incarnated. Dense physical matter forms the final vehicle,
closing the veil over the soul's memory. With each descent
into matter, the planes above become harder to perceive,
and man becomes a wanderer upon the Physical Plane.

7. Redemption Through Evolution

Though man falls, the path to return is woven into his
being. He must now master the vehicles of his incarnation—
mental, astral, and physical—through understanding,
sacrifice, and obedience to higher law. The curse becomes
the catalyst for transformation.

The Planes and Near-Death Experiences – A Hidden Map of the Soul's Journey

Near-Death Experiences often report vivid encounters
beyond the physical realm—descriptions of light, beings,
life reviews, and otherworldly landscapes. These
experiences align strikingly with the **esoteric model of the
planes** through which the soul descends (during
incarnation) and ascends (during death or NDE). Here's

how each plane corresponds to what NDE experiencers describe:

1. The Physical Plane – The Point of Departure

The NDE begins with the cessation of physical functions. Many experiencers describe **hovering above their body**, watching doctors or loved ones. This marks the **momentary detachment of the etheric and astral bodies** from the dense physical shell. Consciousness is no longer rooted in the body but remains fully aware.

2. The Etheric Plane – The Life Force Layer

Immediately after death or during a crisis, the soul passes through the **etheric plane** — the layer of **life energy**. Some NDErs describe **seeing cords of energy** (the "silver cord"), feeling **vibrations**, or experiencing a **transition tunnel** of light. This plane retains impressions of the physical form, and often this is where the **life review** occurs, as the etheric body holds a record of the lifetime just lived.

3. The Astral Plane – The Realm of Emotion and Imagery

This is perhaps the most reported domain in NDEs. The astral plane is the world of **emotion, imagination, and form shaped by thought and desire**. People often encounter:

- **Deceased loved ones**

- **Heavenly beings** or religious figures

- Gardens, temples, or cities of light

- A **being of light** that radiates unconditional love.

These are real to the experiencer but are shaped in part by their emotional and spiritual condition. In esoteric teaching, this realm is also where **Kamaloka** exists — a place of purification where one faces desires and attachments. Some NDEs include disturbing or confusing experiences, which reflect **unresolved emotional or karmic material** within this plane.

4. The Mental Plane – The Plane of Archetypes and Wisdom

Few NDEs go this far, but when they do, they describe **limitless knowledge**, being shown the **true nature of reality**, or experiencing the **Akashic Records**. This aligns with the higher **mental plane**, where thoughts become objective realities and higher learning occurs. Some report **receiving missions**, meeting **guides**, or being shown Earth from a cosmic vantage point. Here, the truth is experienced directly, not in symbolic form.

5. The Buddhic Plane – Unity and the Christ Light

Very rare but profound NDEs include experiences of **oneness, cosmic unity**, or complete **ego dissolution** in light and love. This corresponds to the **Buddhic Plane**, where individuality blends with divine consciousness. The soul remembers its purpose beyond time and form. This is often where the experiencer is told, **"It's not your time,"** and must return.

6. The Return – Re-Entering the Lower Planes

Upon being sent back, many NDErs describe **a sense of contraction** or **descending through layers**, often with grief or resistance. They re-enter the **astral and etheric** bodies before settling back into the physical form. Many report lasting changes: psychic sensitivity, fearlessness of death, spiritual awakening—all signs that **higher planes have touched the lower vessels**.

Summary Insight:

NDEs are not hallucinations—they are real-time journeys through the **planes of consciousness**. Just as the soul descends through these layers at birth, so too does it ascend temporarily during death or near-death. What Harriet Bartlett and occult science describe as the *construction of man* across the planes is mirrored by the *deconstruction and ascent of the soul* in NDEs.

Noah's Flood According to Harriet T. Bartlett

Noah's Ark and the Esoteric Flood: Initiation, Segregation, and Spiritual Evolution

In Harriet T. Bartlett's esoteric interpretation of the Noah narrative, the flood is not merely a historical event or mythic deluge—it is a profound allegory of spiritual evolution, the purification of consciousness, and the initiatory trials of humanity. Through the lens of Theosophy and symbolic analysis, Bartlett unveils an inner meaning that reveals deep truths about the destiny of the soul and the rise and fall of civilizations.

The Floodwaters as Emotional and Astral Turmoil

In esoteric symbolism, water often represents the emotional body, the astral plane, or the chaotic realm of uncontrolled desires. Bartlett interprets the floodwaters not as literal rain but as symbolic of an overwhelming crisis of delusion, illusion, and spiritual ignorance. These floodwaters reflect the tumultuous astral forces that humanity must transcend in order to enter a higher state of being. The flood thus becomes an initiatory crisis — a necessary spiritual cleansing that forces humanity to evolve and shed its lower nature.

Noah as the Great Manu: Guide of the Root Race

"Noah is presented not merely as a man, but as a Great Initiate — specifically, the Seed Manu of the fifth root race. He is a manifestation of the divine archetype responsible for selecting and preserving the most evolved members of the previous fourth root race to begin the evolutionary cycle of the fifth. According to Bartlett, this transition occurred during the fifth sub-race of the old root race, marking the emergence of a new spiritual cycle."

"In one incarnation, Noah also appears as Enoch, who is said to have walked with God and was "not, for God took him." This phrase indicates a perfected soul, a being who had attained such spiritual development that he transcended the normal karmic cycles of reincarnation. Noah is thus both a person and a symbol — a hierophant, a Manu, and a perfected guide for the human race.".

Noah as Melchizedek: The Seed Manu and Eternal Priest of the Fifth Root Race

"In the esoteric tradition, Noah is not merely a historical patriarch or survivor of a literal flood. He is a cosmic figure — an aspect of the eternal Melchizedek, the high priest "without father or mother," whose appearance in the Book of Genesis is as enigmatic as it is significant. Harriet T. Bartlett's interpretation supports this deeper identity, connecting Noah with the Seed Manu of the Fifth Root Race, a divine archetype responsible for guiding humanity across great transitions.

Melchizedek, as described in both Genesis and Hebrews, is the timeless priest-king who blesses Abraham and is later declared by Paul to be the spiritual lineage from which Christ himself arises: **"Thou art a priest forever after the order of Melchizedek" (Hebrews 5:6).** This signifies that Jesus, as the **Christ, does not belong to a temporal priesthood, but to the same eternal priesthood of divine initiates** — a line of spiritual guardians and redeemers that includes Noah, Enoch, Manu, and Melchizedek as facets of a single divine function across epochs.

As Melchizedek, Noah embodies the archetypal priest of spiritual transition. His ark is not only a vessel for survival — it is a mobile temple of sacred knowledge. The segregation of animals symbolizes the gathering of soul types, and **the flood itself becomes a global baptism, washing away the karmic residue of the fourth root race (Atlantis) and preparing the emergence of the fifth.** In this way, Noah-Melchizedek becomes the High Priest of a New Humanity, carrying forward the flame of spiritual truth as the world undergoes purification.

This lineage is not one of blood but of consciousness. It is the lineage of those who serve humanity in its darkest hours, guiding souls toward the light not through conquest, but through wisdom, sacrifice, and initiation."

Shem, Ham, and Japheth: Spiritual Archetypes

Bartlett interprets the three sons of Noah as allegorical representations of spiritual types:

Shem represents the spiritually awakened, those aligned with divine law and higher ideals — the Christ principle in mankind.

Japheth symbolizes those on the path of evolution, beginning to awaken but still largely concerned with physical existence.

Ham reflects those primarily motivated by self-interest, who follow more evolved souls but are not themselves spiritually awakened.

These three archetypes are echoed throughout humanity and represent the soul's differing levels of readiness to respond to higher wisdom.

The Ark as Inner Spiritual Sanctuary

The ark itself is not merely a boat but a symbol of the protected inner state of consciousness. It is the place of refuge where spiritual discipline and Mystery School teachings shelter the soul during times of planetary or personal upheaval. It is built of "gopher wood" — symbolically, the trees of the high north, resinous and

248

protective—indicating a place among spiritual principles. The ark's three levels represent the threefold nature of man: physical, astral, and mental.

Bartlett also links the Ark to the Imperishable Sacred Land of the North—possibly referring to Hyperborea or Aryavarta—an esoteric center of wisdom where the faithful retreated during the fall of Atlantis. She explains that around 850,000 years ago, Noah (as the Manu) led this exodus northward to preserve spiritual teachings while the southern lands were overwhelmed by materialism and psychic decay.

Atlantis, Segregation, and the New Humanity

Atlantis, as Bartlett notes, was not only a lost continent but the symbolic seat of a great spiritual experiment that succumbed to corruption. The flood represents both a literal and symbolic event—the washing away of misused psychic power and the beginning of a new age.

Noah's mission was to segregate—not racially or geographically, but spiritually. He was to preserve the pure archetypes of spiritual humanity, together with the "animals" (symbolizing instincts, emotions, and karmic patterns) and transport them to a highland sanctuary. This place was under the Pole Star, the guiding light of the spiritual North, where the Ark symbolically came to rest upon Ararat—high ground or the "Holy Land."

The dove and the raven sent forth by Noah are also symbolic. The raven, a bird of ill omen, does not return—symbolizing the path of materialism and separation. The dove returns bearing an olive branch—a token of spiritual peace and the promise of a new covenant between man and the divine.

The Flood as Inner Transformation

Ultimately, Bartlett views the flood as a symbol of inner transformation—a karmic purge that gives birth to a new soul identity. The ark represents the inner chamber of truth, built by discipline and divine instruction. The journey through the waters is the soul's descent through chaos, and the landing on Ararat is its spiritual rebirth.

In this view, Noah is the archetype of the wise soul who prepares, purifies, and guides. His journey is ours. As the Atlantean world crumbles behind him, he preserves the spark of divine consciousness and becomes the father of a new humanity—not by blood, but by the lineage of the awakened heart.

From *An Esoteric Reading of Biblical Symbolism*. This page continues the rich esoteric thread, particularly regarding:

Egypt's role as a successor to Atlantean wisdom

- The **Mystery School lineage** through Abraham and Lot

- The division between **exoteric (outer)** and **esoteric (inner)** spiritual work

- The **barrenness** of Abram's wife symbolizing the inability to bring forth Initiates from those stuck in physical or literal interpretations

Page 50 from *An Esoteric Reading of Biblical Symbolism.*

- **Egypt's role as a successor to Atlantean wisdom**

- The **Mystery School lineage** through Abraham and Lot

- The division between **exoteric (outer)** and **esoteric (inner)** spiritual work

- The **barrenness** of Abram's wife symbolizes the inability to bring forth Initiates from those stuck in physical or literal interpretations

"In speaking of the descendants of Shem, it is only necessary to trace the lineage of Abraham.

The city of Ur, from which Abram (Abraham) and Lot started for Canaan, is in ancient Babylonia, and Ur of the Chaldees was a very ancient center of wisdom. According to occult sources, when the continent of Atlantis began to go down, colonies were started in many directions, one of which was Chaldea.

In those early days, Egypt and Chaldea were brother countries in the development of the remnants of the old civilization. Later on, the work was taken up in India. There is a connection between the Sphinx and the pyramid of Egypt, and the temples and towers of Chaldea.

The Sphinx represents man as he was at the close of the Fourth Root Race, the Atlantean, man with the strength of the bull and the lion, and the wings of the eagle (the symbol of the initiate), and the intelligence of man. These were the four faces of the Cherubim or the living creatures that Ezekiel saw in his vision.

The pyramid of Cheops is the most enduring and massive monument ever built, and it is built in the form of a triangle upon a square. It represents man as he will be at the close of the Fifth Root Race.

To quote Mr. Heindel, "The square is the symbol of the perfect man, and the triangle is the symbol of the higher self." These are the ideals toward which man is working.

The Sphinx and the Pyramid are companion pieces, one representing the highest attainment of the past, and the other the glorious goal that lies before the race."

Page 51 from *An Esoteric Reading of Biblical Symbolism*.

Significance of the Genealogy of Shem

This page deepens several symbolic teachings:

- **Abraham and Lot parting ways** as a metaphor for two spiritual streams:

- Abraham: ascending the current (toward spiritual return)

- Lot: descending the current (dealing with the fallen state of matter)

- **Lot's Wife** becomes a key esoteric symbol:

- She turns into a **pillar of salt** not because of a mere glance backward, but because she represents a **higher class of Initiates** who **fail to fully detach** from the degeneracy of the lower planes.

- *Salt* is explained as a **preservative** — a symbol of preserved wisdom and fixed spiritual principle that holds structure as the material world decays.

"As we follow the history of Abraham, we find him separating from Lot, and this is symbolic of the separation of the two classes of humanity. Abraham begins to climb the stream to make the journey back to his Father's house. Lot descends the stream to dwell in the vale of Sodom. That is to say, Abraham, the father of the sixth great root race, is led by the voice of God, by the spiritual impulses that come from above, while Lot, the representative of the last and most material sub-race of the Fifth Root Race chooses to dwell upon the material plane."

"The story of Lot's wife is one that is very beautiful when interpreted according to the esoteric key. She turned and looked back and became a pillar of salt. That is, she was an initiate of a very high class who had accomplished much in her efforts to live above the material plane. But she was not able to let go entirely. She was in danger of being drawn back again into the material plane. The chemical agent known as salt is a preservative, and her work had to do with the preservation of those qualities and substances of man's lower nature which are to be preserved for the coming race. So she became a pillar of salt, a permanent reminder that the lower nature of man must be purified before the higher faculties can be developed.

It is said that Lot's daughters made him drunk and lay with him and bore sons. This again is a very beautiful story if we but interpret it rightly. The expression "to lie with him" in Hebrew means to become united with him in spirit. The daughters of Lot were those Initiates who were able to become one with the wisdom of the great teacher. They were his children by the spiritual law. They became the mothers of Moab and Ammon."

Page 52 *An Esoteric Reading of Biblical Symbolism.*

This page offers a powerful **esoteric reinterpretation of Lot's descendants**, the **birth of Moab and Ammon**, and the **spiritual meaning of lineage and initiation**.

Key symbolic insights from this page:

- **"Lie with him"** is interpreted not sexually, but as **spiritual unity** with a great teacher — "to become one in wisdom."

- Moab and Ammon are described as **founders of initiatic lineages**, not sinful figures.

- Lot is seen as a **great Hierophant**, and his children represent **sons of wisdom** born from trials, guidance, and sacrifice.

- The chapter ends with a touching insight: even when humanity strays, **the loving elder brothers** (Initiates and Teachers) are never far away.

"These names have no significance to the ordinary reader, but to the student of the esoteric wisdom, they have a deep and beautiful meaning. Moab and Ammon were not degenerates. They were the founders of those Orders which were to carry on the work of the Initiates in later times. Lot was a great Hierophant. His daughters were those pupils who loved him with a devotion so pure that they were able to receive the highest instruction. They became the mothers of nations because the Initiate always works through the pupils whom he has trained."

"These stories, when rightly interpreted, show that although the race has gone far astray, although mankind as a whole has turned its back upon the inner life, there is always a band of loving elder brothers who watch over the race, and help those who seek the light to find it. These elder brothers do not leave the race without a witness. They see to it that the mysteries are preserved, and that at every great crisis there is a teacher, or a prophet, or a redeemer who is able to lead the people back to the path from which they have strayed.".

Moving forward to Chapter 7 are more examples of the esoteric interpretations.

Page 62, the beginning of **Chapter VII: The Significance of the Two Covenants of Abraham** from *An Esoteric Reading of Biblical Symbolism.*

"The meaning of the genealogies which appear at intervals in the Old Testament is very deep and beautiful when understood in the light of spiritual law. It is, of course, known to students of occultism that the Bible is the history of the fifth Root Race. We are told that Noah was the seed of Manu of the Fifth Race. Now the Manu is a great Initiate who is chosen to lead the people from one great cycle to another.

Noah was the Manu of the Fifth Root Race. Abraham was the Manu of the Sixth Root Race. But Abraham was not the Christ, the Initiator. He was only the chosen vessel, the one through whom the Christ was to work. The name Abraham in its Hebrew form is composed of the letters Aleph, Beth, Resh, He, and Mem, and these letters have a numerical value of 318. Jesus is said to have had 318 servants. These represent his qualities — manliness, courage, youth, and purity.

Abraham was told to leave Ur of the Chaldees and go to a land that would be shown to him. This meant that he must leave the place of the past and walk by faith into a future that was unknown. When Lot was taken by the kings of the valley, Abraham armed 318 of his trained servants and pursued them. The occult teaching is that Abraham left his body and traveled in the astral to plead with Lot. Lot is the representative of the astral body, and Sodom represents the Physical Plane.".

Key esoteric highlights from this page:

- **Noah** is identified as the **seed Manu of the Fifth Root Race**

256

- **Abraham** is viewed as the **coming Manu of the Sixth Root Race**, serving under a greater spiritual figure

- **318** is symbolically tied to **Jesus, purification**, and **the qualities of manliness, courage, and youth**

- **Abraham is said to send his astral body to plead with Lot—symbolizing higher spiritual forces reaching the physical world.**

Sodom is identified as representing the Physical Plane, linking the biblical narrative to occult cosmology.

Page 63: Melchizedek, Shem, and the **spiritual evolution of humanity through the root races.**

"Melchizedek was the Initiator. He was the Christ of the Fourth Race, or the Bodhisattva. He was either Shem reincarnated or some great Initiate of the Atlantean times who had continued to guide the people. Melchizedek was a Priest of the Most High God. He met Abraham and blessed him, and Abraham gave him tithes of all. The bread and the wine are symbols of spiritual nourishment.

The offerings of Abraham—turtle doves, pigeons, goats, and rams—are not literal offerings. They are symbols of the stages through which man must pass in order to purify his nature and become a vessel fit for the indwelling of the Christ. Every Initiate must pass through these four steps, which correspond to four planes of consciousness.

Abraham's seed was to be as the stars of the heaven and as the sand of the sea. This refers to the spiritual and physical descendants — the sons of the flesh and the sons of God. Isaac, Jacob, and Jesus are types of the same Great One — the three-fold expression of the Christ in the race.

It is necessary to understand that the true lineage is always spiritual and not physical. It is not blood descent but spiritual affinity that determines the chosen people. Many are called but few are chosen."

Here are some core esoteric takeaways from this page:

Melchizedek is said to be a **reincarnation of Shem**, or a being in service to the **Bodhisattva/Christ of the Fourth Root Race**

- He is called a **Priest of Righteousness**, tying him directly to ancient **solar and Christic lineages**

- Abraham's offerings to Melchizedek represent **transmutation of the lower nature**

- The **animal sacrifices** (goat, ram, turtle dove, pigeon) are not literal but symbolic of different aspects of **spiritual evolution**

- **Isaac, Jacob**, and **Jesus** are identified as **types or incarnations of Great Ones**, forming a spiritual **Trinity** guiding humanity toward the Sixth Root Race

Page 64 Abrahamic covenant in the context of Root Race evolution.

"When the covenant was made with Abraham, he was told that his seed should be a stranger in a land that was not theirs and should serve them and be afflicted four hundred years. This refers to the fact that the first four sub-races of the Fifth Root Race are to serve as the basis for the birth of the Sixth Root Race.

The land that is not theirs is the Fifth Root Race body in which the Sixth Root Race must be born. The bondage and the affliction refer to the limitation of the higher consciousness by the lower bodies which are not yet purified.

The boundaries of the land promised to Abraham are the boundaries of consciousness. The river of Egypt represents the wisdom of the Physical Plane. The river Euphrates represents the wisdom of the Buddhic Plane. All the other rivers mentioned represent the intermediate stages of consciousness. The land is the plane of life. To possess the land is to conquer the plane.

Abraham made two covenants — one with Hagar and one with Sarah. Hagar is the bondwoman, and Sarah is the free woman. Hagar represents the flesh, and Sarah the spirit. Ishmael is the child of bondage. Isaac is the child of the promise.

Here are the key teachings from this page.

Esoteric Highlights – Page 64

The covenant of Abraham marks a **transition between the Fifth and Sixth Root Races.**

- The **"four hundred years"** mentioned in Scripture is reinterpreted as **four sub-races** of the Fifth Root Race through which the Sixth Root Race will incarnate and evolve.

- The phrase *"a land that is not theirs"* refers to the **Sixth Root Race souls incarnating within Fifth Root Race bodies**—spiritually foreign to their environment.

- The **river of Egypt** is symbolic of **wisdom on the Physical Plane,** while the **Euphrates** symbolizes **Buddhic wisdom**—the higher spiritual faculties.

- The ultimate goal is to **conquer all the planes of consciousness,** completing the work of the Fifth Root Race (developing the mental faculties) and moving into the Sixth (developing the **higher mental and Buddhic bodies**).

- Sarai (Sarah) and Hagar are symbolic of the **bondage of the flesh** and the **evolutionary process** that leads to the purification of the soul's vehicles.

Here are the major symbolic teachings from this page:

Esoteric Highlights – Page 65

When Abraham was ninety-nine years old the Lord appeared to him and said, "I am El Shaddai; walk before me and be thou perfect." The number 99 is 3 times 3 times 11. It is the number of the perfected triune man — body, soul and spirit. El Shaddai is the Almighty God of the higher planes. The name El Shaddai means the nourisher, the giver of milk.

At this time Abraham received his second initiation. His name was changed from Abram to Abraham and Sarai's name was changed to Sarah. Name changes always follow initiations. The new name indicates a new stage of consciousness.

The land of Canaan represents the four planes of consciousness — the Physical, Astral, Mental, and Buddhic. The possession of the land means that man has conquered these plains. Circumcision is a symbol of purification. It has nothing to do with the physical body. It is a sign of the covenant between God and man.

The three visitors who came to Abraham are the three persons of the Trinity — Father, Son, and Holy Spirit. They came to announce the birth of Isaac. Isaac is Jesus. Jacob is Christ. Abraham is the Father. Together, they represent the three-fold expression of God in man.

Abraham's age (ninety-nine) symbolizes a **completed triune nature** — three threes or the perfection of body, soul, and spirit.

He meets **El Shaddai**, the **Almighty God of the higher planes**, and receives his **second initiation** — symbolizing spiritual maturity and purification.

Name changes are initiatory:

- *Abram* → *Abraham*: now father of a multitude

- *Sarai* → *Sarah*: no longer just a princess, but a spiritual mother of nations

- **Canaan**, the land promised to Abraham, represents **the four planes of consciousness** (Physical, Astral, Mental, Buddhic).

- **Circumcision** is symbolic of **purification and covenant**, not a physical rite.

- **Isaac** is identified with Jesus, and **Jacob with Christ** — forming a **Trinity of spiritual progression**:

- **Abraham** = the **Manu** (divine architect)

- **Isaac** = the **Son** (Jesus)

- **Jacob** = the **Christ** (perfected soul)

- The **letters IH, VH, IHVH** represent **departments of creative force**, corresponding to **Father (I), Son (H), and Spirit/Wisdom (VH)** — the esoteric **Trinity of Manifestation.**

Abraham Sacrifices Isaac page 66

When Abraham was told to offer Isaac as a sacrifice, it was not a test of obedience but a symbol of Initiation. Isaac was not to be slain but was to pass through the fire of

262

transformation. He carried the wood of Initiation and was laid upon the altar. But the lamb was substituted.

The lamb represents the Christ—the IHVH—who was slain from the foundation of the world. The sacrifice of Christ is the eternal offering of the Logos in man. Isaac is Jesus, and he must live to fulfill the promise. He is the child of joy and laughter, the symbol of the resurrected life.

The prophecy of Isaiah refers not to a man but to the divine principle in man—the Christ. "He was despised and rejected of men; a man of sorrows and acquainted with grief." This means that the Christ within is not recognized. "He hath borne our griefs and carried our sorrows." The Christ takes upon Himself the burden of the world.

The IHVH life is the life of God in man. It is the inner Christ who must be awakened. The whole story of Abraham is the story of the soul's journey from the physical to the spiritual plane. The covenant is the promise that man shall become divine.

Esoteric Highlights –

- **Abraham's willingness to offer Isaac** is not a tale of sacrifice, but of **spiritual consecration**. Isaac carries the "wood of Initiation," symbolizing that **he must pass through the fires of transformation himself**.

- The substitution of the lamb points to **the eternal sacrifice** of the *IHVH*—the Logos or Christic force —slain "from the beginning of the world," but present in each initiation stage.

263

- **Isaac is seen as Jesus,** not destined to die then, but to **live and teach the race** how to purify its vehicles in preparation for the Christ within.

- Isaiah's prophecy (quoted at length) is interpreted **esoterically,** referring not to vicarious suffering, but to **the path of divine service,** where the Master "bears the iniquities" through wisdom, love, and sacrifice.

- The **IHVH life** within man is the ultimate goal — to awaken the inner Christ. The whole sequence is about **awakening, not appeasement.**

The Covenants of Abraham – Guiding the Soul Through Root Races

In the esoteric view presented by Harriet T. Bartlett, the story of Abraham is far more than a tribal covenant — it is a divine blueprint for **soul evolution through the Root Races** and the **planes of consciousness.**

1. Abraham as the Manu of the Sixth Root Race

Just as Noah was the Seed Manu of the Fifth Root Race, Abraham is identified as the **coming Manu of the Sixth.** His life represents the preparation of humanity to ascend from mental development (the mission of the Fifth Race) to **higher mental and Buddhic faculties** — the mission of the Sixth.

2. The Covenant is Spiritual, Not Physical

The promises made to Abraham—lands, descendants, and signs—are **symbols of expanded consciousness**. The "land" refers to the **four planes of consciousness**: physical, astral, mental, and Buddhic. Circumcision is reinterpreted as **initiation and purification**, not a literal ritual.

3. Melchizedek and the Trinity of Masters

Melchizedek is described as a **Bodhisattva or Christ of the Fourth Root Race**, and Abraham's offering to him is a moment of **spiritual transfer and blessing**. This triad of Abraham, Isaac, and Jacob is seen as a **Trinity of Initiates**:

- **Abraham**: the Manu and Father

- **Isaac**: the joyful child, representing Jesus

- **Jacob**: the matured Christ, bearer of the spiritual mission

4. The Astral Journey of the Manu

Abraham sending his **astral body to Lot** is symbolic of higher spiritual beings reaching into the lower planes to awaken the sleeping masses. Lot dwells in **Sodom—representing the Physical Plane**—and must be rescued from material entrapment.

5. The Offering of Isaac – Fire of Initiation

Abraham placing Isaac upon the altar is not a test of obedience, but a symbol of **initiation by fire**. The wood Isaac carries represents his own lower nature, which must be purified. The lamb is symbolic of the **Christ force** that

265

must live within and guide humanity — not a one-time sacrifice, but a perpetual, inner transformation.

6. Destiny of the Races

According to Bartlett, the **Fifth Root Race** is destined to fully develop **mental faculties**, while the **Sixth** will begin developing **higher intuition and Buddhic perception**. Souls of the Sixth Root Race will pass through several sub-races of the Fifth before their full expression begins. Abraham's covenant spans these epochs.

Harriet Tuttle Bartlett – Biography and Accomplishments

Harriet Tuttle Bartlett (1870–1963) was an American esoteric writer, spiritual teacher, and visionary whose contributions to metaphysical Christianity and occult symbolism have only recently begun to receive the recognition they deserve. A deeply intuitive thinker, Bartlett authored *An Esoteric Reading of Biblical Symbolism*, a work that reinterprets the Bible as a spiritual allegory of the soul's journey, inner purification, and divine potential.

Her interpretations transformed figures such as Samson, Delilah, Noah, and David into representations of spiritual forces and psychological states. Samson represented the strength of the soul; Delilah, the false teachings that seduce it. Noah was a preserver of the purified astral body through cycles of destruction and rebirth, while David, dancing out of his soul, symbolized ecstatic liberation from the lower self. Bartlett viewed Christ not only as a historical savior but as an indwelling archetype of divine consciousness that must be awakened within.

Bartlett's work extended far beyond writing. She undertook spiritual outreach in India in the 1920s, where she studied sacred Hindu texts, learned from Indian mystics, and gave lectures to Theosophical and spiritual communities. She saw deep parallels between Christian mysticism and Vedic philosophy, emphasizing the shared inner light that unites all true religions. Her time in India further deepened her conviction that humanity was guided by a divine plan and that each culture carried unique keys to understanding the evolution of the soul.

267

Bartlett's quiet but profound influence is evident in her emphasis on sacred feminine wisdom, archetypal storytelling, and the idea that scripture must be read through the awakened heart rather than the literal mind. She represents the often-overlooked stream of feminine mysticism that helped keep the esoteric current alive in the modern age. Her legacy endures in seekers drawn to inner meaning behind religious texts and the soul's hidden history.

𓂀 𓂀 𓂀

Chapter 18: Zarathustra & The Egyptian Mysteries

The Spiritual Teachings of Zarathustra

Zarathustra, also known as Zoroaster, was an ancient Persian prophet whose teachings formed the foundation of Zoroastrianism, one of the world's oldest spiritual traditions. His vision introduced key esoteric concepts that later influenced Gnosticism, Theosophy, and Western mystical traditions. He is believed to have lived sometime between 1800 BCE and 600 BCE, though exact dates are debated. His teachings form the basis of Zoroastrianism, which became the dominant religion of the Persian Empire before the rise of Islam.

Ahura Mazda & The Cosmic Struggle – Zarathustra taught that the universe is governed by a battle between light and darkness, represented by the supreme deity Ahura Mazda (the Wise Lord) and the opposing force of Angra Mainyu (the Deceiver).

The Importance of Free Will – Humanity plays an active role in this cosmic struggle, with every thought, word, and action influencing the balance between good and evil.

Fire as a Symbol of Divine Knowledge – Fire was central to Zoroastrian worship, symbolizing spiritual illumination and the eternal presence of the divine.

The Saoshyant & Spiritual Evolution – Zarathustra prophesied the coming of a Saoshyant (Savior) who would lead souls toward final purification and unity with the divine source.

These teachings directly influenced later esoteric traditions, including Hermeticism, Manichaeism, and early Christian mysticism, all of which emphasize spiritual transformation and the struggle to overcome material illusion.

Key Aspects of Zarathustra's Teachings:

Ahura Mazda – The Supreme God

Zarathustra preached monotheism, teaching that **Ahura Mazda** is the one true God, the source of all good and wisdom.

Dualism – The Battle of Good and Evil

He introduced a moral dualism: **Spenta Mainyu** (the good spirit) and **Angra Mainyu** (the destructive spirit, later associated with Ahriman). This represents the cosmic struggle between truth (*Asha*) and falsehood (*Druj*).

Free Will and Moral Responsibility

Humans have free will to choose between good and evil. Ethical living, truthfulness, and good deeds bring one closer to Ahura Mazda.

Fire as a Symbol of Divine Light

Fire is central in Zoroastrian rituals, representing purity, truth, and the presence of Ahura Mazda.

The Coming of a Saoshyant (Savior)

Zarathustra foretold the coming of a **Saoshyant**, a messianic figure who would lead the final victory of good over evil.

Zarathustra's Influence:

- **Religious Impact**: His teachings influenced Judaism, Christianity, and Islam, particularly ideas about heaven, hell, angels, and the final judgment.

- **Philosophical Influence**: Nietzsche's *Thus Spoke Zarathustra* (1883) uses his name symbolically to challenge traditional morality.

- **Occult and Esoteric Thought**: Some occult traditions view Zarathustra as an initiate of ancient wisdom, linking him to the teachings of Hermes Trismegistus and other mystical traditions.

Zarathustra's Teachings and Their Connection to Esoteric Thought & Near-Death Experiences (NDEs)

Zarathustra's spiritual philosophy shares profound parallels with both occult traditions and NDE reports, particularly in the themes of cosmic dualism, divine judgment, and the afterlife journey.

1. The Battle Between Light and Darkness (Dualism in Esotericism & NDEs)

Zarathustra's concept of **Asha** (truth, cosmic order) vs. **Druj** (falsehood, chaos) mirrors the occult idea of spiritual ascension versus material entrapment.

- **Esoteric Parallel**: Occultists such as Blavatsky and Steiner speak of the soul's struggle to transcend lower astral realms (often associated with deception) and return to higher divine consciousness.

- **NDE Parallel**: Many experiencers describe encountering a realm of brilliant light **(Asha-like order)**, contrasted with darker voids or chaotic regions (Druj-like illusions), reinforcing Zarathustra's teachings on the soul's responsibility to *choose truth over deception.*

2. Ahura Mazda & The Light of the NDE

Zoroastrianism depicts **Ahura Mazda** as a being of pure light, guiding souls toward righteousness.

- **NDE Connection**: Numerous reports describe an overwhelmingly bright and loving Light, often perceived as God or a higher intelligence.

- **Occult Connection**: The Hermetic concept of the **Divine Pymander (the Mind of God as pure light)** aligns closely with Ahura Mazda's portrayal.

- **Zarathustra perceived a "Man" in the Sun which is named Ahura Mazda.**

3. Fire as a Symbol of Transformation and Judgment

Zarathustra emphasized **fire** as the purifier of the soul and a representation of divine truth.

- **Esoteric View**: Fire is central in alchemy as a transformative agent that purges impurity, just as the soul undergoes purification after death.

- **NDE Perspective**: Some experiencers describe passing through a barrier of fire or light, which feels like a purifying force preparing them for deeper wisdom.

4. The Chinvat Bridge and the Afterlife Journey

Zoroastrian belief holds that after death, souls cross the **Chinvat Bridge** — a mystical threshold where they are judged and directed toward either a blissful paradise or a shadowy realm.

- **Occult Parallel**: This aligns with Theosophical teachings on the **astral plane**, where souls encounter self-created realities based on past actions.

- **NDE Parallel**: Many who undergo near-death experiences report crossing a threshold, encountering past-life reviews, and facing the consequences of their choices.

5. The Saoshyant (Savior) and the Evolution of Souls

Zarathustra prophesied the coming of a **Saoshyant**, a messianic figure who would help souls achieve ultimate victory over darkness.

- **Esoteric Parallel**: In occult traditions, the Saoshyant aligns with the spiritual adept or Master of Wisdom who guides initiates through spiritual ascension.

- **NDE Connection**: Some experiencers report a presence or a guide who imparts knowledge, similar to the role of the Saoshyant in leading souls toward enlightenment.

Conclusion: Zarathustra's Relevance to NDEs & Esoteric Thought

Zarathustra's teachings resonate deeply with both occult initiatory wisdom and modern NDE narratives. His vision of a luminous, divine intelligence, the battle between illusion and truth, and the afterlife as a structured journey of purification all align with the broader esoteric tradition and near-death experience insights known.

The Egyptian Mysteries: Horus, Isis, and Osiris

The spiritual traditions of ancient Egypt preserved profound initiatory wisdom concerning the nature of the soul, the afterlife, and divine ascension. The sacred myth of Osiris, Isis, and Horus serves as both a cosmic drama and a guide for individual spiritual awakening.

Osiris: The Dying and Resurrected God – Osiris represents the soul's journey through death, transformation, and rebirth.

Isis: The Divine Mother & Keeper of Hidden Knowledge – Isis is both the protector of the soul and the revealer of mystical wisdom, guiding initiates toward enlightenment.

Horus: The Victorious Initiate – Horus, the son of Isis and Osiris, symbolizes spiritual mastery, having overcome darkness and reclaimed divine kingship.

The Initiation Process in the Egyptian Mystery Schools

Esoteric teachings reveal that Egyptian priests and initiates underwent a highly structured spiritual training, often symbolized by the death and resurrection of Osiris:

Symbolic Death & Rebirth – Initiates would experience simulated death rituals, designed to detach them from physical reality and awaken higher consciousness.

Navigating the Duat (the Egyptian Underworld) – The soul, after death, traveled through various spiritual planes, where it had to prove its purity and divine knowledge before reaching the afterlife.

The Weighing of the Heart – According to Egyptian belief, the soul was judged in the afterlife by Ma'at, where the heart was weighed against the feather of truth.

These teachings closely parallel later esoteric traditions, including the Gnostic concept of spiritual ascent, the Hermetic doctrine of inner transformation, and Free masonic rituals of death and rebirth.

This chapter reveals how Zarathustra's teachings and the Egyptian Mystery Schools provided profound wisdom on the nature of the soul, spiritual evolution, and the journey toward divine reunion. In the next chapter, we will explore the final return of the soul—its liberation from the cycle of reincarnation and union with the divine.

Chapter 19: Root Race 5

Ayre

The names **Ireland, Iran, and Syria** have deep linguistic and mythological connections that can be interpreted — especially in the esoteric traditions — as being linked to the Aryan (or Arian) Root Race, particularly as presented in Theosophical teachings by Helena Blavatsky and later expanded by Rudolf Steiner.

Here's a breakdown of each name and how they may relate to the **Aryan Root Race:**

Iran

Most direct connection: The name *Iran* comes from the word **Aryānām** (*Land of the Aryans*).

- In ancient times, the region was known as **Airyanem Vaejah,** which in the **Avesta (Zoroastrian scriptures)** is described as the original homeland of the Aryans.

- Esoteric significance: **Blavatsky, in** *The Secret Doctrine*, identifies ancient Persia (Iran) as a key stage in the evolution of the **Fifth Root Race (Aryan)**. Zoroastrianism, founded by Zarathustra (Zoroaster), is seen as a continuation of Atlantean spiritual wisdom, now refined through the Aryan mind.

- **Steiner** similarly emphasizes Zarathustra's role in spiritual evolution, indicating that the Persian epoch was essential in developing the etheric and life body as part of humanity's evolution.

Ireland (Ayre – Land / Eire - Land)

- Linguistic theory: The name *Ireland* is derived from *Éire,* which some researchers have linked to ancient **Indo-European** roots, possibly tying it to the same **Indo-Aryan** language family. While this is more speculative, there are intriguing mythological connections.

- Esoteric tradition: Some esotericists and fringe historians propose that **Ireland (and Celtic lands)** preserved Atlantean knowledge and that **the Tuatha Dé Danann (mythical beings in Irish lore) were survivors of Atlantis or a remnant of earlier Aryan or Atlantean migrations.**

- **Blavatsky** alludes to the **Celtic-Druidic traditions as having Aryan roots,** spiritually speaking, and believes that certain Druidic practices are Atlantean-Aryan in origin.

Syria

- Etymology: The name *Syria* is likely derived from the ancient name *Assyria,* which itself may be connected to *Surya* **(Sanskrit for "Sun").**

- Esoteric view: Blavatsky mentions that **ancient Syria, Chaldea, and Babylon** were critical transitional cultures through which Atlantean wisdom was handed down into Aryan civilization.

- Syria acted as a geographic and mystical bridge between the earlier Lemuro-Atlantean spiritual remnants and the emerging Aryan lineages — especially through Hermeticism, Gnosticism, and early solar cults.

The term "Aryan" has nothing at all to do with ethnicity, the color of one's skin tone, or geographical location. The unlearned perhaps may assume this, but it is a term used in defining Root Race 5, which came after Root Race 4, the Atlanteans.

Summary

In esoteric philosophy:

- **Iran** = *direct cradle of Aryan culture and root-race identity.*

- **Ireland** = *western outpost of Atlantean-Aryan wisdom, preserved in myth.*

- **Syria** = *mystical and geographic bridge between ancient root races and developing Aryan consciousness.*

In Blavatsky's framework, all three regions can be seen as carriers or remnants of Aryan-rooted spiritual knowledge, though they served different roles in the evolution of the Fifth Root Race. According to esoteric and Theosophical teachings, **Sumer** did indeed receive its development from the Atlantean Race, particularly as a **post-Atlantean civilization** that carried forward remnants of Atlantean spiritual science, technology, and priestly knowledge.

Here's how this is presented in the esoteric tradition:

Sumer as a Descendant of Atlantis

1. Helena Blavatsky (The Secret Doctrine)

- Blavatsky states that after the destruction of Atlantis, several colonies of the Atlantean Root Race migrated to new lands — some eastward into what would become Egypt, India, and Mesopotamia.

- Sumer, though not named specifically, is placed within this chain of development, seen as a civilization built on the remnants of Atlantean knowledge.

- The early Sumerians are thus descendants of the fourth Root Race (Atlanteans), but they also laid the groundwork for the emergence of the fifth Root Race (Aryans).

- The Sumerian gods and celestial lore — especially their focus on astronomy, astrology, and divine kingship — are reflections of Atlantean priest-kings and their advanced knowledge.

2. Rudolf Steiner (Cosmic Memory, Occult History)

- Steiner describes a migration of peoples from the submerged Atlantean continent into Eurasia, forming the foundation for later cultures like Sumer, Egypt, and Persia.

- He states that these cultures represent spiritual memory traces — preserved fragments of Atlantean clairvoyance and temple knowledge.

- In the Sumerians' ability to calculate celestial movements, track time, and create ziggurat temples aligned with the heavens, we see the Atlantean initiatory legacy transformed into material civilization.

Esoteric View of Sumerian Knowledge

- Ziggurats = Atlantean-style stepped pyramids, echoing the spiritual centers of Atlantis.

- Anunnaki / Divine Kingship = Descendants or memories of the Atlantean priest-kings, who ruled by divine right and cosmic knowledge.

- Cuneiform Texts = Early attempts to encode esoteric knowledge in written form, transitioning from telepathic and symbolic communication used in Atlantis to a more linear script suited for the Aryan mind.

- Planetary Religion = Echoes the Atlantean focus on cosmic forces and divine intelligences as guiding humanity's evolution.

In Summary

Sumer was a child of Atlantis in the esoteric timeline:

A post-cataclysmic civilization built by remnants of Atlantean migrants.

- Preserving fragments of higher knowledge through ritual, mathematics, astronomy, and temple science.

- Playing a key role in transmitting Atlantean wisdom into the Fifth Root Race, especially through Egypt, Chaldea, and eventually Greece.

Atlantean Echoes in Sumer – The Path Toward Zarathustra

Long before Zarathustra's divine revelation of **Ahura Mazda** and the Two Paths, the lands surrounding ancient Mesopotamia were already vibrating with the resonance of a forgotten age. Sumer, the cradle of civilization, did not arise in a vacuum—it carried within its sacred geometry, its priest-kings, and its star-watching temples, the fading pulse of Atlantis.

According to the esoteric teachings of **Blavatsky and Steiner, Sumer was a post-Atlantean civilization, seeded by survivors of the cataclysm that submerged the great western continent.** These early priest-scholars were not merely inventors—they were preservers. What they encoded into clay tablets and ziggurats was the outer shell of a once-living science—a cosmic spiritual system rooted in

Atlantis and now dimly reflected in the physical sciences of time, astronomy, and law.

This Atlantean inheritance flowed eastward through Chaldea and Babylon and laid the unseen groundwork for the emergence of Zarathustra, whose mission was to reawaken spiritual clarity within the Aryan Root Race. Where the Sumerians looked to the stars for order, Zarathustra would look beyond the stars to the **Spiritual Sun — Ahura Mazda,** bringing a purer, more conscious understanding of cosmic duality and moral evolution.

In this way, Sumer stands as a bridge — an intermediary step between the twilight of Atlantean clairvoyance and the dawn of Aryan awakening. What was once veiled in myth and rite would be spoken aloud through fire, word, and divine reason.

The Flame from the Sea: Sumer as an Atlantean Bridge

In the great migrations that followed the fall of Atlantis, remnants of its priestly castes and spiritual knowledge drifted eastward — eventually planting seeds in the land we now call Sumer. Far from being an isolated dawn of civilization, Sumer was a bridge between worlds: the spiritual science of Atlantis re-emerging in a new land, wearing the garments of kingship, astronomy, and temple ritual.

The towering ziggurats echoed the step-pyramids of the Atlantean era. The Sumerian priest-kings, guided by celestial cycles, mirrored the Atlantean initiates who once governed by divine alignment. Even their myths—of gods descending from the heavens, of tablets of destiny and the weighing of deeds—preserved distorted memories of the ancient Mystery traditions.

This Atlantean current did not end with Sumer. It passed through the sacred fire of Persia and found renewal in the mission of Zarathustra, who would offer not only moral clarity to the Aryan Root Race, but a purified vision of the spiritual world. Where Sumer preserved the flame, Zarathustra would breathe it back to life.

Thus, Sumer stands not as a beginning, but as a threshold—a sacred relay point in the great unfolding of the soul's journey through time.

This view is supported in Blavatsky, Steiner, and Edgar Cayce, who all speak of powerful remnants of Atlantean culture appearing in the Americas after the fall of their island-continent.

Here's how this connection unfolds:

Atlantean Migrations into the Americas (Esoteric View)

1. Central and South America – Carriers of Atlantean Wisdom

- **The Maya, Olmec, Toltec, and later the Aztec** are believed to preserve aspects of Atlantean astronomical knowledge, pyramid construction, and spiritual initiation rituals.

- **The Inca of Peru**, with their sun-worship and high-altitude temples, are often described as direct heirs of Atlantean priesthoods.

- The legends of **Viracocha (Inca) and Quetzalcoatl (Toltec/Maya)** speak of white-robed, bearded teachers who came from across the ocean, bringing knowledge of cosmic law, spiritual order, and agriculture — a recurring Atlantean archetype.

2. Edgar Cayce's Readings

- Cayce explicitly stated that Atlantean refugees settled in **Yucatán, Mexico, Peru, and even parts of the Mississippi Valley.**

- He described them as establishing colonies and temples, some of which preserved the initiatory schools and records of Atlantis.

- Some groups became corrupted and degenerated over time; others preserved a pure line of knowledge, hidden in underground chambers or passed through secret lineages.

3. Rudolf Steiner and the American Mystery Centers

- Steiner affirmed that America had spiritual centers connected to the past, though he warned that much of the Atlantean clairvoyance in these regions eventually fell into decline or was used in service of material power.

- Still, he believed a future awakening could re-ignite the ancient wisdom hidden beneath the American continent.

Mystery Thread Sidebar

The Western Flame – Atlantean Echoes in the Americas

As the final cataclysms shook Atlantis, not all of its priest-kings and initiates perished beneath the waves. Some sailed westward — guided by celestial knowledge and divine foresight — toward the rising lands of the future: the Americas. There, in the fertile valleys and high mountains of Mexico, Central America, and Peru, they planted the seeds of a second flame.

The great pyramids of Teotihuacan, the astronomical precision of the Maya, and the solar temples of the Inca all carry signatures of Atlantean architecture, cosmology, and ritual memory. In Toltec lore, the god Quetzalcoatl arrives from the sea, robed in white, bearing sacred knowledge. In the Andes, Viracocha emerges after a world flood to restore order and awaken mankind. These aren't isolated myths — they are veiled remembrances of Atlantean initiates bearing the light of the past into a new age.

Yet much was lost. As millennia passed, the wisdom of these ancient colonists was diluted, distorted, or buried — both literally and figuratively. What remains are symbols, stone alignments, and sacred legends that whisper of a forgotten greatness.

The soul of Atlantis did not vanish; it migrated, fragmented, and went underground — waiting for the moment when its light could rise again. The Americas, like Sumer and Egypt, are not beginnings, but echoes of a primordial fire still burning in the background of history.

Ancient Persia (especially Zoroastrianism):

1. Faravahar (Fravashi):

- Symbolism: This winged disc with a human figure is one of the most iconic Persian symbols. It represents the divine spark or guardian spirit (Fravashi) within each person, guiding them toward truth (asha).

- Meaning: Symbol of divine connection, moral righteousness, and the soul's evolution.

- Spiritual Parallel to the Ankh: Just as the ankh links to the eternal soul and divine breath, the Faravahar reflects the divine essence within and the journey toward higher consciousness.

2. Fire (Atar):

- Not a symbol in the geometric sense, but sacred fire was a living spiritual presence in Zoroastrian temples.

- Meaning: Fire symbolized purity, divine wisdom, and the ever-living energy of Ahura Mazda.

- Often enshrined in temples, fire is considered the visible sign of the divine.

Babylon (Mesopotamian Tradition):

1. Rod and Ring (Symbol of Divinity and Kingship):

- Seen in depictions of gods like Shamash, Ishtar, and Marduk. The god holds a ring and rod — interpreted as measuring tools, a looped rope and a rod, or symbols of law and divine authority.

- Meaning: Represented divine law, kingship, and cosmic order.

- Esoteric Reading: A precursor to symbols of spiritual governance — law not just as societal rule, but as alignment with cosmic principles (similar to Maat in Egypt).

2. Cuneiform Star (Dingir):

- A star-like symbol representing divinity or "god." Written in cuneiform as "Dingir" (Sumerian) or "Ilum" (Akkadian).

- Meaning: Used before the names of gods — essentially the spiritual signature of a deity.

- Mystical Function: Signified presence or invocation of a higher power — an abstract but powerful divine marker.

Summary Comparison:

Culture	Symbol	Meaning
Egypt	Ankh	Life, immortality, spiritual breath
Persia	Faravahar	Divine soul, moral purpose, spiritual ascent
Persia	Sacred Fire	Divine presence, purity, cosmic order
Babylon	Rod & Ring	Divine authority, law, measurement, order
Babylon	Star (Dingir)	Divinity, invocation of the gods, cosmic signature

𓂀 𓂀 𓂀

Chapter 20: Reincarnation & the Cycles of the Soul

The Eternal Return: The Soul's Journey Through Multiple Lives

The idea that life does not begin with birth, nor end with death, but is instead part of an eternal cycle, has been central to esoteric traditions, ancient philosophies, and spiritual teachings. Reincarnation is not merely a return to life but a process of refinement, growth, and self-mastery. **The soul, moving across lifetimes, carries the imprints of past experiences, karma, and the wisdom it accumulates.**

Sinnett's *The Mahatma Letters* and Theosophical Insights

A.P. Sinnett's *The Mahatma Letters* provides a unique insight into reincarnation, drawn from the wisdom of the Tibetan Mahatmas. According to these teachings:

1. After death, the soul transitions through **Kamaloka**, a realm where earthly desires dissolve.

2. From Kamaloka, the soul moves into **Devachan**, a blissful state where the higher aspects of the last incarnation are assimilated.

3. Once the lessons of the previous life are fully absorbed, the soul prepares for **rebirth**, guided by the karmic momentum of past actions.

These teachings align with many Eastern philosophies, particularly Hindu and Buddhist doctrines, which view reincarnation as a necessary stage in the soul's journey toward enlightenment.

The Role of Karma and the Higher Ego in Reincarnation

Reincarnation is governed by the law of **karma**, the principle that every action, thought, and intention leaves an imprint on the soul's future experiences. The **Higher Ego** — the eternal, spiritual aspect of the self — guides the process of selecting new incarnations based on what lessons remain unfinished.

- Karmic debts and rewards determine the circumstances of one's next life.

- The soul chooses experiences that will further its growth, sometimes reincarnating into challenging situations as a means of spiritual refinement.

- Esoteric traditions emphasize that conscious self-awareness and spiritual work can accelerate the process, allowing one to transcend cycles of karmic repetition.

Manly P. Hall and the Great Work: Self-Directed Evolution

Manly P. Hall taught that reincarnation is not merely a mechanical process but an opportunity for **conscious evolution**. Through the **Great Work**, an initiate can:

- Gain control over their cycles of reincarnation by choosing when and where they return.

- Break free from lower karmic cycles, accelerating spiritual progress.

- Achieve liberation, reaching a state beyond reincarnation where the soul attains mastery over the material world.

The Mystery Schools of ancient Egypt, Greece, and the East all emphasized that true initiates did not return blindly, but with knowledge of their past lives and a clear mission for their next incarnation.

The Purpose of Reincarnation: Growth, Liberation, and the Return to the Source

Reincarnation is not an endless loop but a structured journey that leads the soul back to its **divine origin**. The great esoteric traditions teach that:

1. The soul reincarnates until it has learned all necessary lessons.

2. Once mastery is achieved, the soul no longer needs to return and instead moves into higher spiritual realms.

3. Some enlightened beings choose to return as teachers and guides, aiding others in their journey.

4. Reincarnation is therefore not a punishment but a gift —an opportunity for the soul to perfect itself, awaken its divine nature, and eventually reunite with the Source.

"**Become actively involved in evolving your own soul**," taught Manly P. Hall.

Generally, there are two methods of one's soul evolving:

- **Exoteric evolution** – A life lived without conscious spiritual development. While the soul still evolves through experience, progress is slower. This is and has been the majority of people on Earth. They do not actively live a life from which they can grow or evolve their own soul. In my opinion, many of them desire to be good and live good lives, but they have not truly learned how to cultivate their own particular soul. The result of this is the slow "evolution" of their soul over long periods of time, and many reincarnations.

- **Esoteric evolution** – A life of active spiritual practice, aiming to reduce karmic burdens and hasten liberation.

Rudolf Steiner's Seven Virtues and Their Spiritual Significance

Each virtue aligns with a spiritual principle and a challenge that must be overcome for true evolution of consciousness. Manly Hall had also explained that we must overcome the impediments placed before us in our earthly life. Impediments/difficulties will find us, even the wealthy elite. It is how we react to those situations that is a measure of how our soul has evolved.

1. **Devotion (Reverence)** → *Strength of Character*

   - A deep reverence toward life, divinity, and higher truth.

   - Overcomes doubt and superficiality.

294

2. **Control of Thinking (Equanimity)** → *Clarity and Truthfulness*

- Focused, disciplined thought allows clear insight.

- Overcomes chaos and illusion.

3. **Control of Will (Steadfastness)** → *Inner Peace*

- Directs action with intention and patience.

- Overcomes inner conflict.

4. **Positivity (Tolerance)** → *Faith in the Spiritual World*

- Trust in cosmic order, even amid difficulty.

- Overcomes negativity and doubt.

5. **Openness (Unbiased Thinking)** → *Freedom of Thought*

- Embraces higher truth without dogma.

- Overcomes prejudice.

6. **Harmony (Balance)** → *Wisdom and Discernment*

- Balances all levels of being.

- Overcomes extremes and chaos.

7. **Love** → *Power to Heal*

- Selfless, transformative love.

- Overcomes separation and ego.

By cultivating these virtues:

- The **astral body** is purified.

- The **etheric body** is strengthened.

- The **Higher Self** gains mastery over the lower nature.

The Unfinished Incarnation: When a Fetus Dies in the Womb

From an esoteric and reincarnation perspective, the loss of a fetus is not a random event, but part of a larger **spiritual process**. *(The spiritual realm has dominion over the physical).*

1. Karmic Lessons and Soul Contracts

- A soul may need only a brief incarnation to resolve karma.
- Parents may experience loss as a catalyst for spiritual growth.

2. The Soul May Not Have Fully Entered the Body

- The soul links gradually to the fetus.

- It may withdraw if the conditions for birth are no longer ideal.

3. A Shift in Reincarnation Plans

- Reincarnation paths are not fixed.

- The soul can wait and choose another form or timeline if needed.

4. Influence of Astral and Spiritual Planes

- Astral interference or energetic misalignment may prevent full incarnation.

- Theosophical and Hermetic teachings suggest these disruptions reflect a greater cosmic realignment.

5. The Soul's Brief Return for a Specific Purpose

- A short incarnation may serve a focused karmic or spiritual mission.

- The soul may return later in another form or lifetime more aligned with its path.

Conclusion

No life is wasted. Even a brief incarnation has meaning in the grand cycle of evolution.

False Heavens and the Influence of Malevolent Energies

While the process of reincarnation is guided by higher spiritual laws and the wisdom of the Higher Ego, many esoteric traditions — including Theosophy, Hermeticism, and Gnosticism — warn that **not all realms encountered**

297

after death are benevolent. Just as the physical world contains both light and shadow, so too do the subtle planes.

Astral Traps and Illusory Afterlife Realms

Certain **near-death experiences**, particularly those recounted by spiritually discerning individuals, describe encounters with seemingly benevolent beings who encourage a premature return to Earth, or who project false imagery of "heavenly" realms. According to Blavatsky, Hall, and others:

- **The lower astral realm** is inhabited not only by kama-rupas (desire shells) but also by **disembodied energies**, including **thought-forms**, **wandering spirits**, and even **malevolent entities**.

- These entities may **impersonate light beings** or **pose as ascended masters**, especially to souls who have not trained their discernment.

- Some spiritualists and occultists have claimed that such entities feed on emotion, attachment, and belief — **perpetuating the cycle of illusion** to keep the soul bound to lower realms.

This echoes the **Gnostic idea of the Archons**, cosmic tricksters who construct false heavens to keep souls trapped in the wheel of reincarnation.

The Danger of Spiritual Passivity

Manly P. Hall and Rudolf Steiner both cautioned that without **spiritual training, ethical development, and inner**

298

clarity, souls are vulnerable to being misled in the postmortem state. Blind devotion or unexamined beliefs can create resonant frequencies that attract deceptive energies.

Thus, the key defense against such traps is **inner initiation** — the purification of the soul and the awakening of the Higher Ego, which naturally repels false light and recognizes the true spiritual current.

𓂀 𓂀 𓂀

Mystery Sidebar: Hidden Forces in the Astral Realm

"There are spiritual snares woven from illusion and desire. Some souls, enchanted by these false heavens, remain caught in realms where they are praised, adored, and deceived — never realizing they are not free." — Commentary on the Devachanic Illusion, inspired by The Mahatma Letters

In *The Mahatma Letters*, the Masters explain that most postmortem visions are **subjective projections** of the dying person's inner state. But there are also **astral parasites** that cling to souls, especially if those souls carry fear, confusion, or unresolved emotional patterns.

Esoteric Insight: Just as the body must pass through fire to be purified, the soul must pass through the astral to be tested. Only through **discernment, inner strength, and spiritual clarity** can the soul move safely from Kamaloka to Devachan, avoiding the magnetic pull of false afterlife realms.

Practical Wisdom: Training the mind, healing emotional wounds, and cultivating virtue during life builds **spiritual immunity** in death. These practices act as **keys of light** that unlock the gates of higher consciousness.

The Illusion of Light – Discerning False Heavens in the Afterlife

In the modern age, stories of Near-Death Experiences (NDEs) often describe encounters with light beings, idyllic landscapes, and overwhelming love. These accounts have helped shift public consciousness away from fear-based doctrines of eternal damnation, but they can also conceal deeper spiritual complexities.

As this book seeks to reveal, **not all luminous realms encountered during NDEs are necessarily divine**. Esoteric traditions — from Theosophy to Hermeticism to Gnostic Christianity — warn of **illusory astral realms** that mimic true spiritual states but are in fact subtle traps of the lower planes.

False Heavens and Astral Traps: In Theosophical and occult teachings, the lower astral realm is rich with imagery drawn from human belief systems. Souls conditioned by religious or emotional expectation may unconsciously project these realities after death or encounter beings who cater to them. While these realms can feel peaceful or blissful, they may be merely a **Devachanic echo** — a temporary dream — rather than the soul's true home.

Gnostic Warnings: The Gospel of Judas, an esoteric Gnostic text, speaks of false rulers (archons) who create imitation heavens to keep souls enslaved in cycles of rebirth. This aligns with the view that **some NDE realms, though filled with light, may be cleverly veiled prisons** designed to lull the soul into forgetting its divine mission.

The Role of Discernment: True spiritual evolution requires discernment. The soul must learn to distinguish between **genuine divine light** and its astral reflections. This book serves as a spiritual guide to help seekers **pierce the veil**, question what is presented, and seek the **higher light of truth** that transcends form, emotion, and illusion.

"There is a light that deceives, and there is a light that liberates. The initiate learns to tell the difference."
— *Inspired by Mystery School teachings*

Illusions of Light – The War in the Higher Realms

Many who undergo Near-Death Experiences report radiant realms, beings of light, and sensations of overwhelming peace. But the esoteric traditions — Gnostic, Theosophic, and Hermetic alike — warn that **not all that appears heavenly is divine**. The astral planes are vast and layered, and deception can wear the mask of beauty.

Helena Blavatsky wrote of **"false heavens"** — realms formed by the collective desires of humanity, maintained by astral intelligences who feed on illusion and spiritual stagnation. Rudolf Steiner similarly spoke of **"spiritual beings who oppose evolution"**, active in higher spheres and especially threatening to those awakening to their soul's mission. The Gospel of Judas even goes so far as to say the stars and aeons themselves can imprison the soul if it is deceived.

301

In this modern era, **there is a war in the higher realms** — a subtle conflict not waged with weapons, but with **illusions, false light**, and **spiritual misdirection**. Light-bearers — those awakening to their divine potential — are especially targeted. Deceptions are growing more sophisticated. **Dark forces may present themselves as angels of light**, offering comfort, false messages, or even reincarnation paths that detour the soul away from its true ascent.

"It is not the form of the vision that determines truth, but the vibration it carries." — Alisdaire Thorn

This book seeks to **educate readers about the esoteric landscape** that awaits beyond death. To help souls recognize the traps that look like paradise. The goal is not to induce fear, but to foster discernment.

Modern NDEers, though sincere and often transformed by their experiences, are rarely taught to question the **source** of the beings they encounter. They may return believing they've seen heaven, when in fact they may have touched only an astral mirror — a karmic echo rather than the true spiritual realms.

True spiritual light does not manipulate. It does not flatter. It awakens the soul and calls it toward selflessness, truth, and liberation.

The Deception of False Heavens and the War Against Light-Bearers

One of the primary reasons for writing this book is to **educate seekers that not all that appears heavenly is truly**

divine. In the modern era, as Near-Death Experiences (NDEs) become more widely reported, there is a growing danger in assuming that all experiences of "light" or "peace" are ultimately benevolent. This is not always the case.

The ancient Mystery Schools warned their initiates that many realms beyond death are **illusions or traps**, designed to **mimic the divine** but ultimately ensnare the soul. As more people undergo NDEs without spiritual training or proper discernment, they risk accepting as truth what may be astral deception.

These false heavens may offer comfort, light, and loving beings, but they are sometimes projections of the **kama-loka realm**, constructed from unfulfilled desires and illusions — residues of personality, not true spiritual realities. Even the presence of "beings of light" may not guarantee authenticity; **some entities assume forms that mimic goodness**, leading souls astray.

This is not fear-mongering. It is spiritual caution, echoed by mystics, Theosophists, and initiates of the ages. As the veil thins and spiritual perception increases on Earth, **the forces opposed to true liberation grow more subtle**, masquerading as saviors, guides, or even "higher selves."

There is, in a very real sense, a **spiritual war in the higher realms**, where the **dark side of the astral plane works to divert, deceive, and delay light-bearers** — souls with the potential to awaken others. These deceptions often come clothed in sweetness, but their end is stagnation.

The Role of Thoth and the Angel of Death: Guides to Truth

The ancient Egyptians understood that guidance was essential after death. **Thoth**, the ibis-headed deity, often called the "Lord of Divine Words," was not just a scribe—he was a **psychopomp**, a soul guide. In some Mystery traditions, **Thoth becomes the angel of death**, not as a punisher, but as one who ensures the soul is not waylaid by false lights.

Thoth measured truth. He weighed the heart against the feather of Ma'at. If the soul carried deception, fear, or illusion, it could not pass into the higher realms of truth. This weighing was not punitive—it was diagnostic. A soul unready for divine light would either be returned to the cycle of rebirth or diverted to realms suited to its inner vibration.

In the Hermetic tradition, Thoth (or Hermes Trismegistus) also guarded sacred wisdom. **Only the soul that had passed through initiation—through symbolic death, disillusionment, and spiritual purification—could safely navigate the upper worlds.**

Mystery Schools taught their initiates to **see through illusion**, to **distinguish true light from false luminescence**. They warned: **not all light is benevolent**, and not all beings claiming divinity are aligned with the Logos. Discernment was one of the final initiations.

Final Reflection

Today, as more people awaken to the reality of life after death, it is **imperative** that spiritual seekers **prepare themselves with knowledge and inner clarity**. Just as the body needs strength for physical journeys, the soul needs **wisdom, virtue, and discernment** to traverse the complex realms beyond this life.

Reincarnation is not merely a return — it is a test. And **those who awaken to the cycles must also awaken to the deceptions**. This book is a map, not only of the true path — but of the false trails, too.

𓂀 𓂀 𓂀

Mystery Thread: False Light and the Initiate's Warning

In the Mystery Schools of Egypt, Chaldea, and Greece, initiates were warned: **not all that glitters is gold, and not all light is of the Light**. The spiritual realms beyond death are not simple or uniformly benevolent — they are layered, filled with forces of varying intelligence and intent.

The untrained soul, still bound by desire or spiritual naiveté, is easily seduced by what ancient teachers called **"the false light"** — a radiant but deceptive force that mimics divine presence. In these realms, **astral entities may appear as angelic or familiar,** offering comfort and wisdom. Yet behind their form may dwell energies seeking to trap the soul in cycles of illusion, stagnation, or false enlightenment.

Only those trained in discernment — those who have faced their own darkness and passed through symbolic death — can see clearly. The initiate learns not to follow the first light, but to question, to test, and to wait. As the

Egyptian *Book of the Dead* states: *"Let the soul be weighed, let it be measured, and* **let it not mistake the door to Amenti.**"

The true light does not flatter, seduce, or promise ease. It challenges, strips away illusion, and burns with a fire that transforms.

In today's age of mass NDEs and astral awakenings, **the initiate's warning becomes urgent once more**:

"Do not follow every voice that calls you 'beloved.' Some lights shine only to bind."

𓂀 𓂀 𓂀

Mystery Thread: Anubis and Thoth – Guardians of the Soul's Passage

In the ancient Egyptian mysteries, **Anubis** and **Thoth** served as divine guides through the perilous realms of the afterlife. Together, they represented more than myth—they symbolized **inner discernment** and **divine order** in the soul's transition beyond the veil.

Anubis, the jackal-headed psychopomp, did not merely escort souls to judgment—he **guarded the threshold** against wandering spirits and illusionary forces. In the *Weighing of the Heart* ceremony, it was he who ensured the scales remained just, unmoved by fear, sentiment, or deceit. Anubis represents the **courage to face truth**—especially the truth of one's own soul.

Thoth, the ibis-headed god of wisdom and divine record, **witnessed and recorded** every deed of the soul. But

306

Thoth was more than a scribe — he was the **embodied Logos**, the inner voice of truth, and a master of the hidden realms. As some traditions hold, Thoth (or a being akin to the **Angel of Death**) helps **guide the soul where it is meant to go**, protecting it from false openings and deceptive lights.

Mystery School teachings preserved this core wisdom:

Not all light is benevolent, not all doorways lead home.
Only the soul guided by purity of heart and clarity of vision may pass through the true gate.

In our modern era of increasing NDE reports and astral experiences, the ancient warnings remain valid. **Anubis and Thoth live on** — not as distant deities, but as inner archetypes that awaken in those prepared to journey with discernment.

𓂀 𓂀 𓂀

Mystery Thread: Anubis and Thoth – Guardians of the Soul's Passage

In the ancient Egyptian mysteries, Anubis and Thoth served as divine guides through the perilous realms of the afterlife. Together, they represented more than myth — they symbolized inner discernment and divine order in the soul's transition beyond the veil.

Anubis, the jackal-headed psychopomp, did not merely escort souls to judgment — he guarded the threshold against wandering spirits and illusionary forces. In the *Weighing of the Heart* ceremony, it was he who ensured the scales remained just, unmoved by fear, sentiment, or deceit. Anubis represents the courage to face truth—especially the truth of one's own soul.

Thoth, the ibis-headed god of wisdom and divine record, witnessed and recorded every deed of the soul. But Thoth was more than a scribe—he was the embodied Logos, the inner voice of truth, and a master of the hidden realms. As some traditions hold, Thoth (or a being akin to the Angel of Death) helps guide the soul where it is meant to go, protecting it from false openings and deceptive lights.

Mystery School teachings preserved this core wisdom:

Not all light is benevolent, not all doorways lead home. Only the soul guided by purity of heart and clarity of vision may pass through the true gate.

In our modern era of increasing NDE reports and astral experiences, the ancient warnings remain valid. Anubis and Thoth live on—not as distant deities, but as inner archetypes that awaken in those prepared to journey with discernment.

𓂀 𓂀 𓂀

Chapter 21: The Gospel of Judas & the Hidden Teachings of Christ

Challenging Traditional Views of Judas and the Role of Christ

To begin, it must be understood that Christ and Jesus are not the same, nor is "Christ" the last name of Jesus. Jesus was a man, a physical being. Christ, however — as written in John 1:1-2 — is referred to as "the Word" (Logos), who *"was in the beginning with God."* The texts further clarify this in **John 8:58:** *"Truly, truly I say to you, before Abraham was, I AM."* And **Colossians 1:15-19** affirms: *"He is the image of the invisible God, the firstborn of all creation... For by Him all things were created, in heaven and on earth..."*

The Gospel of Judas, a Gnostic text discovered in the 20th century, presents a radically different perspective on Judas Iscariot's role in the story of Jesus. Unlike the canonical Gospels, which portray Judas as the ultimate betrayer, this text suggests that Judas was, in fact, an initiatory figure chosen by Christ to fulfill a higher divine purpose. This revelation challenges traditional Christian teachings, revealing hidden esoteric wisdom about the nature of salvation, spiritual ascension, and the illusory nature of material existence.

Judas as an Initiate: The Keeper of the Secret Knowledge

Because His apostles had been taught esoteric knowledge, they were not ordinary followers. (For the definitions of Initiate, Adept, and Master, please refer to the

Index of this book). The twelve were initiated into the Mysteries. As Jesus said in Matthew 13:11, *"Because it is given unto you to know the mysteries of the kingdom of heaven, but unto them it is not given."* Jesus spoke to the masses by using parables. The masses were unlearned regarding the Mysteries, so Jesus tried to explain as simply as He could by using parables.

So, what is a "Mystery" in this context? Esoterically:

• It is a sacred rite into which only initiates are admitted.

• It contains truths that are difficult or impossible to explain in ordinary terms.

• It refers to a divine revelation that surpasses ordinary human understanding.

When we speak of "Kingdoms," there are levels of being: Mineral Kingdom, Plant Kingdom, Animal Kingdom, the Kingdom of Man, and then — beyond all physical existence — the Heavenly Kingdoms. Humanity, as a hybrid being, exists on the threshold between the material and the divine.

Judas the Knower

In mainstream Christian theology, Judas is condemned for his betrayal. But in the Gospel of Judas, he is portrayed as the only disciple who truly understood Jesus' teachings. This aligns with Gnostic principles, which hold that salvation comes not through blind faith but through gnosis — direct inner knowing.

What the Bhagavad Gita Says About the Soul

The *Bhagavad Gita* echoes many of these ideas. The Atman (soul) is described as:

- Eternal: never born, never dies.

- Unchanging: even when the body perishes.

- Pure consciousness, undivided.

Key verses:

- 2:20 — *"For the soul, there is neither birth nor death at any time..."*

- 2:22 — *"As a person puts on new garments... the soul accepts new material bodies..."*

- 2:13 — *"Just as boyhood, youth, and old age come... so also does the soul take on another body."*

The soul is not limited to one incarnation but moves through many, shedding bodies like garments. This aligns directly with the Gnostic and Theosophical view of the eternal soul seeking liberation through knowledge and self-purification.

The Demiurge and False Afterlife Realms
According to Gnostic cosmology:

1. The Demiurge (a lower creator being) crafted the material world and the astral illusions surrounding it.

2. False heavens exist—created to deceive souls into returning to material life.

3. Jesus' mission was to reveal the true divine realms and liberate souls from these astral traps.

Though some Gnostic texts equate the Old Testament god with the Demiurge, this book does not fully agree with that interpretation. There are layers of symbolic truth in scripture, and discernment is key. Not all gods are the true God.

Barbelo and the Luminous Cloud: Barbelo, a prominent Gnostic figure, is sometimes described as the divine emanation of the true God—yet paradoxically, other texts imply Barbelo may also symbolize a false afterlife realm cloaked in radiant illusion. Again, discernment is key, and to assist us in this, we will dive into The Mysteries of Ancient Egypt in a later chapter of this book.

From the Gospel of Judas: • Judas recognizes that Jesus came from the Immortal Realm of Barbelo.

• He shares a vision where the other apostles are stoning him.

• Jesus replies: *"Lift up your eyes and look at the cloud and the light within it, and the stars surrounding it."*

So what is this cloud and the light within it, and the stars surrounding it? Ancient Egyptian and Mayan traditions point to Orion Nebula as the origin of souls. Within the Nebula lies the Trapezium Cluster: four bright stars arranged in a trapezoid, thus forming a triangle or pyramid. Pyramid is a Greek word and means "fire in the middle". So therefore, within the "pyramid" is a fire or a light. Note too that the All Seeing Eye symbol is an eye inside a pyramid. This "eye" represents the black hole in the center of the Orion Nebula.

Gnosis, Not Belief: Unlike traditional Christianity, which emphasizes obedience and faith, Gnosticism emphasizes gnosis — direct, inner knowing.

According to the Gospel of Judas:

• Jesus's death was not a sacrifice for sin but an act of liberation.

• Judas was not a traitor but a chosen one.

• The world is a trap, and truth lies beyond appearances.

This aligns with Hermeticism, Theosophy, and other esoteric schools, all of which agree that not all light is divine, and not all realms are heavens. This is one reason I chose to write this book and to share it. Hopefully, it will also be used for reference. Some experiences may be involved in deceptive trickery. Beware of "false light" and the big D-word – Deception. Lies are Deceptions and Deceptions are Lies.

Final Reflection: Stars, Candlesticks, and Kingdoms: Manly P. Hall spoke of "He who walks among the candlesticks" — a divine being moving among the stars. The "candlesticks" refer to the stars, and this brings us to NASA. NASA has concluded that the stars farther away from the black hole are older than the stars closer to the black hole (the swirling center). The Orion Nebula is a star nursery; stars are born or created there. NASA has also explained that not only do black holes, such as the one in the Orion Nebula, draw in materials, but material is also ejected out from it, into our dimension. It's like a 2-way street with materials being exchanged. Referring back to the claim of NASA about materials being ejected from the black hole, the matter that was ejected outwards at an older time, are more aged than matter being ejected outwards at a later time. Hence, the matter ejected outwards earlier are older and further away from the center of this black hole. NASA has described the Orion Nebula as a stellar nursery. It's a place where stars are born.

In the Pyramid Texts of Unis, discovered in Egypt, the King is said to become a star *in* the Kingdom of Osiris, located in the constellation of Orion. This again affirms the connection between soul origin, stellar realms, and divine return.

Now let's look at the exact communication taking place between Christ Jesus and Judas. (Jesus is speaking with Judas privately):

Judas said to Jesus, *"In a vision, I saw myself. The twelve disciples were stoning me and persecuting me severely. And I also came to the place where I followed after you. I saw a house, and my eyes could not comprehend its size. Many teachers were within it, and the structure*

had a roof of green plants, and in the middle of the house was a crowd."

Jesus answered and said, "Judas, your star has led you astray."

And he continued, "No person of mortal birth is worthy to enter the house you have seen. It is a place reserved for the holy."

And later Jesus said to him, "You will become the thirteenth, and you will be cursed by the other generations. But you will come to rule over them. In the last days, they will curse your ascent to the holy generation."

"You will not ascend with the others, but you will go your own way. For you will sacrifice the man who clothes me."

And Jesus said, "Look, Judas, lift your eyes and see the cloud and the light within it and the stars surrounding it. The star that leads the way is your star."

Esoteric Note: The Thirteenth and the Star of Judas
In esoteric numerology and ancient cosmology, the number twelve often represents completion within the material world — the twelve signs of the zodiac, twelve disciples, twelve tribes, and twelve houses. To become the thirteenth is to step outside the cycle, to break from the collective pattern and transcend the mundane order.

Thus, when Jesus tells Judas, "You will become the thirteenth," it signifies Judas's initiation into a higher mystery, one that separates him from the others and aligns him with a more hidden path of sacrifice and transformation. He is not simply excluded – he is elevated beyond the others, but at great cost.

The reference to "your star" leading the way draws from ancient astral symbolism. In both Gnostic and Hermetic traditions, the soul was believed to originate from a star, and its journey back to the divine realms was often guided by celestial forces. To say "the star that leads the way is your star" is to affirm that Judas's soul will ascend, guided by his own inner divine essence – despite the outer world cursing his name.

This language aligns with the teachings of Mystery Schools, where betrayal, sacrifice, and apparent failure were sometimes initiatory trials, preparing the soul for rebirth into higher understanding.

He saw the luminous cloud and knew Jesus came from beyond the veil. When he asked Jesus, "But what good is it to me?", Jesus answered that Judas would sacrifice "the man that clothes me" – indicating that Judas was helping to free the Christ from the shell of the Jesus-body. Judas's star – his consciousness – would eclipse all others.

This chapter reinterprets Judas not as a betrayer, but as an initiated liberator. Through this lens, the Gospel of Judas becomes a sacred key to understanding the deeper mission of Christ: to awaken divine knowledge in those ready to transcend illusion and return to the eternal light beyond the stars.

A few words about the veil or a veil. A veil is like a covering or as some put it, it is like a curtain. Us human beings in our current state of development, have the 5 senses. These 5 senses are physical senses and connected with physical organs. For example, sight. Sight is in relation to the physical eyes, and brain. Hearing is related to physical ears, and brain. These 5 senses and brain help us to navigate our physical realm or environment.

Now let us consider higher beings or angelic beings. They have no "eyes" or "ears", or brain for that matter, nor any of the other physical senses and organs. Near – death experiencers leave the physical body and its physical senses / organs, but still are conscious of their surroundings. Why? Well for one thing, they are using "super sensible organs" that function beyond our physical realm. This allows them to communicate with higher beings beyond the veil that divides the physical realm and the higher realms. (those with eyes to see and ears to hear does not refer to the physical eyes and ears, but the higher senses to perceive into the higher realms).

Although the Gospel of Judas is incomplete, it reveals three profound ideas:

1. Jesus entrusts Judas with sacred knowledge, revealing secrets about the false god of this world (the Demiurge).

2. Judas alone understands that Christ's mission is to liberate the divine spark within humanity. The divine spark is the Eternal Flame whose embers burn within our soul. The divine spark is similar to being in a cocoon entombed by the physical body. Ancient Egypt understood this very well. They explained that the body is a tomb.

317

3. The crucifixion, far from being a tragedy, becomes a necessary step to break free from material illusion.

This framework echoes the Gnostic teaching that the material world is a deception, created by a lesser being—the Demiurge—to trap souls in cycles of reincarnation. The soul must evolve, lifetime after lifetime, until it reunites with the Supreme Divine Consciousness.

Barbelo and the Luminous Cloud: Barbelo, a prominent Gnostic figure, is sometimes described as the divine emanation of the true God—yet paradoxically, other texts imply Barbelo may also symbolize a false afterlife realm cloaked in radiant illusion. Again, discernment is key, and to assist us in this, we will dive into The Mysteries of Ancient Egypt in a later chapter of this book.

From the Gospel of Judas:

• Judas recognizes Jesus came from the Immortal Realm of Barbelo.

• He shares a vision where the other apostles are stoning him.

• Jesus replies: "Lift up your eyes and look at the cloud and the light within it, and the stars surrounding it."

The soul takes flight to the world that's invisible, but there arriving, she is pure bliss. - Plato

How did the ancient Egyptians and Mayans know this when no telescopes existed in those times? The answer? The Mystery Schools. Mystery Schools held the truths of

Creation itself, and even beyond, into the Higher Realms. The fact that we can see the Orion Nebula with our earthly vision means that it is physicality. Mystery Schools passed down Wisdom and Knowledge dating back to Lemuria and Atlantis, and beyond.

If Barbelo is both the womb and trap of souls, then Jesus' mission was to help the awakened soul pass through Barbelo — not remain in it. The Egyptian "god" Anubis did likewise. He helped the soul of the deceased cross over to where the soul must go. Anubis was a Guide. In later centuries, the "Angel of Death" filled this role.

In the Pyramid Texts of Unis, the King is said to become a star in the Kingdom of Osiris, located in the constellation of Orion. This again affirms the connection between soul origin, stellar realms, and divine return.

He saw the luminous cloud and knew Jesus came from beyond the veil. When he asked Jesus, ***"But what good is it to me?"***, Jesus answered that Judas would sacrifice ***"the man that clothes me"*** — indicating that Judas was helping to free the Christ from the shell of the Jesus-body. Judas's star — his consciousness — would eclipse all others.

This chapter reinterprets Judas not as a betrayer, but as an initiated liberator. Through this lens, the Gospel of Judas becomes a sacred key to understanding the deeper mission of Christ: to awaken divine knowledge in those ready to transcend illusion and return to the eternal light beyond the stars.

The All-Seeing Eye and the Luminous Cloud

The symbol of the All-Seeing Eye, often misunderstood in modern times, holds deep esoteric meaning across cultures. One of the most striking artistic depictions is found at Karlskirche Cathedral in Vienna. High above the altar, the Eye of Providence radiates light from within a triangular frame, surrounded by angels and clouds. This eye gazes outward — not in judgment, but in illumination, watching over the soul's journey.

This symbol directly parallels the Free masonic All-Seeing Eye, the Mayan solar eye, and the Egyptian Eye of Horus. In all traditions, it represents divine omniscience, inner awakening, and spiritual discernment. It is the eye of God, but also the eye of the soul, turned inward and upward toward the divine.

When we speak of Barbelo — the luminous cloud from which Jesus descends in the Gospel of Judas — we are speaking of the same archetype. This is the radiant eye in the heavens, described across civilizations. The Egyptians portrayed this in their hieroglyphs, temple architecture, and cosmology. Barbelo is not just a Gnostic vision — it is the veiled light that the ancients tried to capture in stone, word, and symbol.

In Revelation, the phrase "He who walks among the candlesticks" refers to a divine being moving through the stars. In ancient Egyptian cosmology, this is none other than Osiris, the resurrected god-king whose soul resides in the constellation of Orion. The candlesticks are the stars, and the flame within them is the soul's eternal light. Thus, Osiris

walking among the candlesticks is the same as Christ
walking among the stars — a symbol of the guiding
consciousness that calls the soul home through the heavens.

The Black Hole and the Ancient Eye of Orion
One of the most astonishing discoveries of modern
astronomy is that a black hole exists at the center of the
Orion Nebula, specifically within the Trapezium Cluster — a
triangle-shaped stellar nursery that both draws in and ejects
matter in powerful flows of cosmic energy. This region is
visible to the naked eye and has long fascinated stargazers,
but only with advanced telescopes and space-based
observatories like Hubble and Chandra have scientists
confirmed the presence of a black hole at its core.

And yet — ancient civilizations already knew.

How did the Egyptians, Maya, and other ancient
cultures, with no telescopes or modern instruments, point
directly to this cosmic structure as the origin of souls and
the gateway to the divine realms? The answer lies in the
Mystery Schools, which preserved spiritual knowledge not
based on technology, but on direct perception —
clairvoyance, inner vision, and higher states of
consciousness.

The Egyptians referred to the Orion constellation as the
resting place of Osiris, the god of resurrection, judgment,
and return to the heavens. The Mayans associated the same
region of the sky with soul emergence and return. Both
traditions — separated by continents and centuries — revered
Orion's Eye as a celestial womb or portal of transformation.

This black hole at the heart of Orion is what many esoteric traditions have referred to symbolically as the All-Seeing Eye—the Eye of Providence, the Eye of Horus, the Watcher in the Sky. It is not merely symbolic. It is an actual astronomical structure, hidden in plain sight.

In this context, Barbelo—the luminous cloud seen by Judas and described by Jesus—is not a metaphor alone. It is the Orion Nebula, veiled in mystic light, a threshold between worlds. The light within the cloud and the stars surrounding it form the same triangular geometry depicted in the Trapezium Cluster—echoed in temples, pyramids, cathedrals, and symbols throughout the ancient world.

𓂀 𓂀 𓂀

Chapter 22: Ancient Egyptian Spiritualism – The Divine Science of the Neteru

The Hidden Science of the Soul in Ancient Egypt

When we think of ancient Egypt, we're often handed myths, funerary customs, and a pantheon of animal-headed gods from schoolbooks or documentaries. But behind the veil of imagery lies a far deeper science—an esoteric map of consciousness, encoded in symbols, temple rituals, and sacred texts. The ancient Egyptians did not worship gods in the Western sense. They revered Neteru—forces, principles, and aspects of divine mind manifesting as living energies.

These "gods" are not external beings but internal archetypes. Each Neter is a frequency, a mode of consciousness that shapes both the cosmos and the human soul. In this light, Egyptian spiritualism wasn't superstition—it was a sophisticated system of psychological and metaphysical mastery. The temples were not places of blind worship, but mystery schools where initiates studied the mechanics of the soul, the laws of cosmic order, and the journey after death.

One of the core esoteric truths echoed across Hermeticism, Theosophy, and the Kemetic teachings is this: Energy is Mind. The universe is not made of lifeless matter—it is a field of living thought. Everything that exists, from stars to souls, is a modulation of divine consciousness. The Egyptians knew this. Their gods were not idols of clay but blueprints of cosmic and personal transformation.

As we explore the Neteru, the Tree of Life, and the soul's journey through the Duat, we begin to understand that the spiritual path in ancient Egypt wasn't about obedience to the gods — it was about becoming them.

The Neteru – Divine Forces of Consciousness

In the Kemetic tradition, the term *Neter* (plural: *Neteru*) refers to divine principles that govern all aspects of reality. These are not gods in the way later cultures understood divinity; they are energetic intelligences — manifestations of cosmic law and spiritual function. Each Neter embodies a fundamental aspect of the divine mind. They exist within nature, the cosmos, and the human soul.

To know the Neteru is to know the structure of the self. These deities are mirrors of our spiritual anatomy — each one symbolizing a key psychological or cosmic principle. When invoked through ritual, meditation, or disciplined spiritual practice, they awaken dormant potentials within. Let's explore a few of the central Neteru and their esoteric significance:

- **Ausar (Osiris)** – Symbol of the eternal soul, Ausar represents divine will, resurrection, and the indestructible essence within. He is the blueprint of the perfected being, torn apart and reassembled, echoing the soul's fall into matter and its ultimate restoration.

- **Aset (Isis)** – Divine mother, sacred intuition, and the embodiment of hidden wisdom. Aset is the seat of inner knowing — the gnosis that leads to spiritual rebirth. She reassembles the soul from chaos, using the magic of love and inner power.

- **Heru (Horus)** – The Higher Self, born of spirit and intuition. Heru is the awakened soul, the spiritual warrior who overcomes the lower ego (Set). He represents vision, victory, and the reunification with divine purpose.

- **Set** – Far from being merely a villain, Set is the principle of chaos, ego, and necessary resistance. Set is what challenges the soul, sharpening its will and pushing it toward transformation. Without Set, there can be no Heru.

- **Tehuti (Thoth)** – The divine mind itself. Tehuti is the Neter of language, time, and the Akashic records. He governs sacred knowledge, esoteric sciences, and the laws of spiritual evolution. In many traditions, he is the messenger between realms.

- **Ma'at** – The foundation of the cosmos. Ma'at represents harmony, truth, justice, and universal balance. She is the feather against which the heart is weighed. Ma'at is both a cosmic law and an internal compass — guiding the soul to live in alignment with the divine order.

Each Neter is a door into the soul. They are not external rulers to be obeyed, but internal forces to be understood, balanced, and eventually integrated. In the Kemetic spiritual system, the path of the initiate is to awaken these energies within and ascend the ladder of consciousness back to the source — Ra, the One Light, the hidden source behind all manifestations.

The Tree of Life (Paut Neteru): The ancient Egyptian
Tree of Life, known as the *Paut Neteru*, is a spiritual map of
consciousness. Much like the Kabbalistic Tree or the Hindu
chakra system, it represents stages of development and
divine archetypes within the human being. In Muata
Ashby's work, this system contains 11 spheres, each one
associated with a specific Neter and a level of spiritual
awakening. Ascending this Tree means activating and
harmonizing these inner forces, gradually returning to the
Divine Source—Amen or Ra, the hidden Absolute.

An essential mystery embedded in this spiritual system
is the dynamic between Aset (Isis) and her twin sister
Nebet-Het (Nephthys). In the myths, Nephthys is mortal,
associated with the material world, while Isis is immortal,
representing divine wisdom. But the myth is not about two
separate women—it is a metaphor of the soul's dual nature:
the spiritual (immortal) and the material (mortal). Isis helps
Nephthys become immortal, just as the awakened soul
raises the lower self into union with the divine.

This duality and integration are perfectly symbolized in
the Caduceus—the twin serpents winding up the central
staff, often misattributed only to Greek mythology. In truth,
its roots stretch back to Egypt and beyond. The serpents
represent Ida and Pingala—the left and right energy
currents in yogic and Kemetic systems—while the central
staff is the Sushumna, the path of spiritual awakening. Isis
and Nephthys spiral around the soul's central axis,
activating each level of the Tree of Life until the crown (Ra
consciousness) is awakened.

326

In this light, the Tree of Life is not only a map—it is the soul's sacred anatomy. It shows the descent into form and the path of return. The temples of ancient Egypt were designed as literal blueprints of this inner tree, with each hall, pillar, and rite reflecting a stage on the initiate's journey.

The Book of the Dead and the Journey After Death: What we call *The Egyptian Book of the Dead* was known to the ancients as the *Pert Em Heru*—"The Book of Coming Forth by Day." Far from a grim account of death, it was a guidebook for the soul's liberation. It instructed the initiate, both in life and in the afterlife, on how to navigate the inner planes of existence—what the Egyptians called the *Duat*—the unseen realm of spirit.

At the heart of this journey lies one of the most profound esoteric teachings of ancient Egypt: the Weighing of the Heart. In this scene, the deceased stands before the goddess Ma'at, who represents universal truth and balance. The heart—considered the seat of consciousness—is weighed against her feather. If the heart is light, the soul moves forward. If it is heavy with ego, deceit, or imbalance, it is devoured by the fearsome Ammit, the devourer of the unjustified soul.

But this judgment is not about divine punishment—it is about vibrational alignment. The soul must match the frequency of divine order to ascend. Ma'at is not just a goddess; she is the law of spiritual gravity. The soul cannot fake virtue or bypass truth—the weight of the heart is determined by one's inner harmony.

Anpu (Anubis) plays the role of the psychopomp, the guide between worlds. With the head of a jackal — symbol of the desert and the unknown — he leads the soul through its transformation. He oversees the weighing, preserving both justice and mercy.

Near-death experiences echo these themes: the sensation of passing through tunnels of light, encountering luminous beings, facing one's life in review, and the overwhelming sense of judgment not from without, but from within. The ancient Egyptians knew this path intimately. They mapped it. And they left us their sacred keys.

Initiation and the Mystery Temples: The great temples of ancient Egypt were sacred theaters of transformation, mystery schools where initiates underwent rigorous training to awaken the higher faculties of the soul. Every statue, corridor, and hieroglyph was part of a multi-dimensional blueprint, designed to elevate consciousness and return the aspirant to their divine nature.

To enter the mysteries was to walk the path of the gods — not in blind reverence, but in living realization. The priests and priestesses who passed through the temple halls were initiates of cosmic science. Their work was not separate from the afterlife teachings — it was a conscious rehearsal of death, rebirth, and immortality.

Each temple mirrored the soul's journey through the Duat. The initiate would symbolically die, pass through trials of darkness and illusion, and then rise again as a new being — a Heru, victorious over the lower self. The story of Ausar being torn apart by Set and reassembled by Aset and

Nephthys is not just myth—it is the soul's own dismemberment and reintegration through inner alchemy.

The symbols found in Near-Death Experiences—tunnels, thresholds, radiant beings, judgment, and return—are all present in the Egyptian initiatory framework. The initiate, like the NDE experiencer, is given a glimpse beyond the veil. But unlike a passive vision, initiation is earned through discipline, purification, and alignment with cosmic truth.

The Eternal Return to the Divine: At the heart of ancient Egyptian spiritualism lies a single, luminous truth: the soul is divine, and it must return to its source.

The Egyptian term **Nehast**—often translated as **"spiritual enlightenment" or "awakening"**—describes this return. Enlightenment was not promised after death; it was cultivated in life. To live in harmony with the Neteru, to align one's will with Ma'at, and to awaken the higher faculties through initiation was to begin the return while still in the body.

The culmination of this sacred science is union with Ra, or Amen—not just the sun god, but the hidden, unmanifested source of all. In the deepest initiations, the initiate becomes Ra—the divine light that resurrects itself from darkness.

This process is mirrored in modern Near-Death Experiences:

- a passage through darkness or a tunnel (*the Duat*),

- luminous intelligences (*the Neteru*),

329

- judgment by one's own inner truth (*the Weighing of the Heart*),

- and the remembrance of spiritual identity.

Some experiencers describe being told they must return — not because they are unworthy, but because their soul's mission is unfinished. The Egyptian sages anticipated this — they knew death was never final, and that the soul's work continues until it becomes light itself. **The Emergence of Osiris, Isis, Nepthys, Set, and Horus – The Drama of the Soul**

As **Ra** enters the created worlds — moving forth from the divine stirring of **Ptah** and flowing through the cosmic principles of **Nut, Geb, Shu, and Tefnut** — he is not alone. With him come the five luminous archetypes who would become central to the Egyptian mysteries: **Osiris, Isis, Nephthys, Set, and Horus.**

Their appearance marks a turning point in the cosmological descent. Where Nut and Geb represent sky and earth in their *pre-physical forms*, and Shu and Tefnut the balance of breath and moisture, these five represent the beginning of polarity, conflict, death, rebirth, and ultimately, transformation. They are not abstract principles — they are the living drama of the soul made visible.

Nut, Geb, Shu, and Tefnut are the more Divine Principles that Ptah manifested. If you recall, Ptah was in the **Sea of Chaos** "lying on his back", which symbolizes stillness, no movement, so therefore no creation. This parallels the ancient Sanskrit term, Pralaya. When Ptah stirs, this signifies that creation begins. In Sanskrit, this is a Manvantara (Creative Forces). So from Ptah comes Ra, and accompanying Ra is Isis, Osiris, Set, Nepthys, and the principles of Horus. The four other than Horus are of a lower nature than Nut, Geb, Shu, and Tefnut, and they have a closer connection to physicality. To help illustrate this, let's take a simple example. Imagine Earth being a raindrop (moisture/water). Now, imagine Ra, Isis, Osiris, Nepthys, and Set being the cloud (cloud vapor). Now, you imagine what the elements derived from that manifested as the cloud vapor. The cloud vapor came to be from finer and more subtle elements that actually originate beyond our realm. This is the "realm" of Nut, Shu, Geb, and Tefnut. Notice that as you get further from our dense physicality, elements and energies become more subtle. Now, don't get the wrong impression that subtlety equates to weakness. Remember this. Physicality was manifested from Spirit, and these "Spiritual" laws supercede that which is below them in hierarchy. It is the same way that Earth is subordinate to the Sun. The Sun dictates all life on Earth. What is powering our local sun? That is referred to as the Sun behind the Sun or Black Hole Sun, but that subject will be explored in the next book. Let's return now to Ptah and His first manifestations.

Each plays a crucial role in the spiritual evolution of the individual:

- Osiris is the higher self, the noble soul that once ruled in truth but is dismembered — symbolizing how our divine nature is scattered and forgotten in the material world. Yet Osiris is also the *Resurrected One* — he who returns from the underworld with wisdom. He is the soul that remembers.

- Isis is the wisdom-bearing aspect of the soul, the divine feminine who uses her magical insight and sacred knowledge to restore what has been lost. She is the intuitive force that re-members — both literally (re-assembles Osiris) and spiritually (restores unity).

- Nepthys is Isis's sister and the mortal counterpart — symbolizing the earthly, veiled aspect of the soul. She represents the part of us bound to limitation, death, and forgetting — but with the potential to be raised into light through the aid of Isis. She is the twin flame of the soul, yet unawakened.

- Set is not simply evil. He is the chaotic force of ego, opposition, and trial — the one who dismembers Osiris, but also plays a role in the soul's eventual awakening. The set is the shadow. He is necessary for initiation. Without him, there is no test.

- Horus is the divine child, the product of resurrection and remembrance. He is the soul that integrates all polarities — divine and human, shadow and light — and rises in clarity. He is the inner Christ-force, the awakened initiate.

Together, these five deities form a sacred blueprint — not just of cosmic history, but of the individual human journey.

As Ra travels through the sky and underworld, these forces are at play in the soul's own cycle of forgetting, suffering, awakening, and return.

They are not only myths.

They are mirrors.

And they still live in us today.

𓂀 𓂀 𓂀

Mystery Thread Sidebar: Egypt as the Blueprint of Initiation
The Mystery Schools of Egypt formed the spiritual bedrock of Western esotericism. Initiates passed through symbolic death and rebirth, guided by principles embodied in the Neteru. These same principles are echoed in today's near-death experiences: the passage through darkness, encounters with radiant beings, the life review, the presence of a guide, the overwhelming experience of truth, and the call to return and transform.

Just as the initiate of old returned from the temple transformed, so too does the modern NDE experiencer return with new insight and purpose. The Mystery Thread reminds us that the path has always been known — engraved in stone, hidden in myth, and now reawakened in the hearts of those who cross the veil and return with light.

𓂀 𓂀 𓂀

Chapter 23: What Is Christ? – The Esoteric Path of the Inner Light

The Christ Mystery – Beyond Religion

To speak of Christ is to enter a realm far deeper than institutional religion has allowed. While Christianity has preserved powerful symbols, stories, and sacred echoes of the mystery, the true Christ—Kristos in the esoteric tradition—is not confined to any one doctrine, historical period, or religious label. Christ is not a man; Christ is a cosmic principle, a living current of divine light that enters into the soul to awaken it from the sleep of matter.

In the ancient world, this principle was known by many names. The Greeks called it the Logos—the divine Word or reason through which all things are made. In India, it appears as Krishna, the avatar of divine love and consciousness. In Egypt, it takes the form of Heru (Horus), the resurrected light emerging from the darkness of Set. In each case, we find a being—often solar in nature—who descends into the world, suffers, dies, and is reborn. This is not a coincidence; it is the symbolic language of initiation.

What we call "Christ" is not an external savior who demands worship—it is the seed of divine identity already within. Every soul carries within it the dormant flame of the Christos. The ancient Mysteries taught that we are not meant to merely believe in Christ, but to become Christ—to pass through the symbolic crucifixion of the ego, to awaken the divine spark, and to rise into spiritual mastery.

335

When Jesus of Nazareth walked the Earth, he embodied the Logos in flesh. He became the living vessel of the Christ principle. But the deeper mystery lies in what he demonstrated — that this divine force is not exclusive to him, but available to all who seek inner transformation. His message was not simply about moral obedience or sin avoidance — it was about initiation. "You shall do even greater things than I have done," he said. That was not a metaphor. It was an invitation.

To understand Christ from the esoteric perspective is to see the spiritual path as an alchemical journey of death and rebirth, of descending into the darkness of incarnation and rising again into divine remembrance. The Christ is not only above us — it is within us, waiting to be born.

The Descent of the Logos

In the esoteric traditions, Christ is understood as the Logos — the divine Word or cosmic intelligence through which creation takes form. This Logos is not limited to language — it is the structuring force behind all existence, the "pattern that connects" heaven and earth. It is the first emanation from the Source, the blueprint of divine order. To say "In the beginning was the Word" is to recognize that Christ is not the beginning of Christianity — it is the beginning of creation itself.

The descent of the Logos into matter is a sacred act of cosmic compassion. It is the light willingly entering into darkness so that even in the most veiled places of consciousness, the divine spark might be awakened. This descent does not only occur once in history — it happens every time a soul is born, and every time consciousness forgets its origin. But just as the Logos descends, so too must it rise.

According to Rudolf Steiner, the Christ Being is not merely one among many advanced souls—it is a singular solar entity, the central spiritual intelligence of our planetary evolution. Christ entered the Earth not just to transform human souls, but to infuse the very etheric body of the planet with a new spiritual substance. This is why Steiner called the Christ event the turning point of time.

But the Logos has appeared before. In ancient Egypt, it came as Heru (Horus)—the solar son who defeats Set and rises as king. In Persia, it appeared as Mithras, the light-bringer slayer of the bull. In India, as Krishna, the divine charioteer who reveals the eternal soul. These are not contradictory—they are rhythmic echoes of the same spiritual descent, playing out in different cultural keys. The Christ principle wears many names, but its essence is always the same: the divine descending into form to awaken itself in matter.

Each human being carries within them this divine seed —this spark of the Logos. It is not something earned, but something remembered. The goal of every soul is not merely to obey an outer deity, but to birth the inner Christ, to become consciously aligned with the higher order of truth, love, and light.

The Christ mystery, then, is not a doctrine—it is the journey of the soul becoming divine, and the divine willingly becoming human.

The Crucifixion and Resurrection – Inner Initiation

The story of the crucifixion and resurrection is perhaps the most well-known tale in the Christian tradition—but its esoteric meaning is often overlooked. Beneath the surface of the historical narrative lies a profound mystical teaching: the death of the lower self and the rebirth of the soul in divine awareness.

In ancient Mystery Schools, the crucifixion was not merely a historical event—it was a symbolic initiation rite. The initiate would undergo a series of trials representing death, purification, and rebirth. In this inner process, the "old self"—the ego-bound identity, clinging to illusion and separation—was symbolically put to death. Only by surrendering this self could the divine nature within be resurrected.

Golgotha, the place of the crucifixion, literally means "the place of the skull." This is no accident. In esoteric interpretation, the skull represents the seat of consciousness—the inner temple where transformation occurs. The cross, too, is a sacred symbol, representing the union of spirit (vertical axis) and matter (horizontal axis). To be crucified is to be stretched between heaven and earth—to hold both the pain of incarnation and the promise of transcendence.

The resurrection that follows is not simply a return from physical death—it is a spiritual awakening. It is the soul rising from the tomb of ignorance, reborn into the light of the divine self. In this light, the tomb becomes a womb—the place where true life begins.

The same process is echoed in Near-Death Experiences. Many experiencers describe a moment of surrender, a dissolving of the ego, followed by an overwhelming sense of rebirth and reunion with a source of light and love. They return changed—no longer afraid of death, no longer attached to the illusions of the world, but awakened to a higher truth.

This is the essence of the Christ Mystery. It is not about belief—it is about transformation. Every soul is called to carry their own cross, to die to the false self, and to rise as a vessel of light. This is not symbolic poetry—it is spiritual physics. The soul must pass through the fire of death to be reborn in truth.

Christ's path is not a historical event to be worshipped from afar—it is a living path to be walked within.

The Christ Within – The Higher Self Revealed

There is a line in the New Testament, often read but rarely understood in its full depth: "Christ in you, the hope of glory."

This was not a metaphor. It was the central teaching of the Mysteries—the inner Christ, the divine Self, dwelling in the heart of every human being.

The esoteric traditions teach that what we call "Christ" is not something separate or external. It is the Higher Self, the luminous presence at the core of our being. This indwelling presence is not bound by personality, culture, or belief. It is the eternal **"I AM"**—the pure spark of consciousness that existed before birth and continues beyond death. To awaken this presence is to remember what we truly are.

Rudolf Steiner spoke of the Christ Impulse as a cosmic force that entered into human evolution—not just as a historical event, but as a spiritual energy that continues to work within the etheric body of the Earth. According to Steiner, the Christ Being was unique among spiritual beings in that it took on not just a human form, but the task of transforming the very life-force matrix of the planet. Through this, every human being now carries within them the potential to realize the Christ within—to move from a consciousness of separation to a consciousness of unity.

The heart center, in both ancient and modern mystical systems, is the gateway to this awakening. It is the throne of the Higher Self, the place where divine will, compassion, and clarity converge. When the Christ within is awakened, the heart begins to radiate a light that is both deeply personal and universally transcendent. It is the light that NDE experiencers often describe as being more "real" than anything on Earth—a love so total, so knowing, that it dissolves all fear.

This is not emotionalism—it is soul recognition. When the inner Christ stirs, the soul remembers its origin. The false self begins to fade, and the individual becomes a vessel for divine will, creative power, and sacred love. This is not the end of the journey—it is the beginning of conscious co-creation.

To live with the Christ within is not to escape the world —it is to sanctify it. It is to carry that light into every thought, every action, every breath. And in doing so, we become what the ancient initiates knew was possible—not followers of Christ, but expressions of Christ in the world.

The Second Coming and the Age of Consciousness

Much has been said about the Second Coming of Christ —an event long anticipated by many, feared by some, and misunderstood by most. The esoteric tradition, however, reveals a radically different view: the Second Coming is not a future arrival from the clouds, but the rising of Christ consciousness within the human soul.

This awakening is already happening. It is subtle, gradual, and unfolding across humanity as more and more individuals begin to live not from the ego, but from the divine center within. The return of Christ is not a singular event, but a wave of inner realization sweeping through the collective spirit of the world. It is the birth of the New Humanity.

This inner resurrection was seen symbolically by John the Revelator, whose visions on the isle of Patmos form the cryptic final book of the Bible. Revelation is not a book of doom, but of initiation. The Seven Seals represent layers of spiritual ignorance being broken open, allowing light to pour into the soul. The Four Horsemen represent aspects of karmic cleansing and the purging of the ego's grip on the world. The New Jerusalem is not a city—it is the new consciousness, the golden light of the divine fully embodied on Earth.

John's vision of the glorified Christ—with eyes like flames, a sword of truth issuing from his mouth, and a voice
341

like rushing waters — is not the return of a man, but the revelation of the solar Logos within. He stands among seven golden lamp-stands — symbolizing the seven chakras, or inner churches, that must be illumined before the soul enters full union with the divine.

These inner teachings align powerfully with modern near-death experiences. Many who pass through the veil encounter a radiant being of light who knows them fully and loves them unconditionally. Often, they describe this as Christ, even when they come from non-Christian backgrounds. They speak of receiving divine knowledge, undergoing life reviews, and being told to return — to bring love and truth back into the world.

This is the Second Coming: each soul, awakening, one by one, until a critical mass tips the world into a higher octave of being.
We are not waiting for a figure to descend from the sky — we are the sky beginning to remember itself.

𓂀 𓂀 𓂀

Mystery Thread Sidebar: The Inner Sun and the Hidden Temple
The Mystery Schools of antiquity did not see the Christ as a distant deity to be worshipped, but as a solar archetype — the divine light within each soul, destined to rise. In the temples of Egypt, Greece, Persia, and even pre-Christian Palestine, initiates were taught that the true temple of God was not built of stone, but of consciousness.

To awaken the inner Christ was to open the "sealed scroll" of the self. Just as John of Revelation witnessed the Lamb opening the seven seals, the initiate was taught to open the seven centers of consciousness within—the chakras, churches, or temples of light—culminating in the full illumination of the divine spark.

This is why ancient temples were aligned with the sun, and why solar symbols were central to the rites of Mithras, Horus, Dionysus, and Krishna. These were not merely nature cults—they were reflections of an ancient truth: the sun in the sky is a mirror of the sun within. The outer rituals pointed to an inner awakening. The initiate was not called to worship the light—but to become it.

In this way, the Christ of the Mystery Schools is not confined to Jesus of Nazareth. He is the Solar Logos, the divine pattern that radiates through all traditions, appearing again and again to guide the soul from darkness to light. The cross, the tomb, the light-body resurrection—they are not exclusive events. They are universal experiences encoded in the path of the soul.

And now, as Near-Death Experiences continue to reveal glimpses beyond the veil, we are reminded: the ancient Mysteries have never died. They've simply gone inward, waiting to be remembered. The inner temple is awakening. The Christ is rising—from within us all.

☥ ☥ ☥

Chapter 24: The Holy Spirit, the Virgin, and the Womb of Matter in The Cosmos

In the esoteric tradition, the story of Christ's birth is not only historical — it is cosmic. Esoterically, it is not meant to be taken as a mechanical act. It is a sacred act, marriage - a union of spirit and matter, light and darkness, heaven and earth. This was encoded in myth, ritual, and symbolism across cultures. But at the heart of it all lies a single, luminous mystery: the soul's capacity to conceive the divine. It encodes the mystery of how spirit enters matter, how divine light takes on form, and how the Logos is continually born within the soul and the universe.

In the beginning, there is chaos — the sea of potential, the primordial waters known in Egyptian cosmology as Nun. This ocean is not evil or fallen; it is the unshaped body of the cosmos, awaiting the touch of divine order. Over this sea hovers the Holy Spirit — the breath, the light, the vibration that brings movement to stillness and life to inert matter. As written in Genesis, *"And the Spirit of God moved upon the face of the waters."* These "waters" are not the oceans in a geographic sense, but are the primordial substances of being. These waters were a chaotic sea of matter, but held the potential to become.

This Holy Spirit is the active intelligence - the vivifying principle — the flame that quickens matter, the spark that initiates creation. It is the active divine force that stirs the deep waters of chaos and makes them fertile.

But what receives this fire? What vessel holds the divine seed?

Here enters the Virgin—not as a woman bound by biological chastity, but as a symbol of pure, unformed matter, untouched by ego or corruption. The Virgin is matter before it is shaped by desire. In this sense, the Virgin is the receptive womb of the cosmos, the holy matrix awaiting divine conception. Virgin here does not imply chastity in the physical sense. Rather, the Virgin is elemental matter before it has been touched by ego, by corruption, or by distortion. It is pure potential – receptive, luminous, and ready to conceive divine light.

This cosmic virgin becomes Mary, who personifies the sacred womb in which the Logos is born. Mary is more than a mother—she is the symbol of spiritualized matter, divine receptivity, and the hidden temple where spirit takes form. She is also reflected in Isis, the Egyptian goddess who resurrects Osiris and gives birth to Horus, the solar child.

Thus, the Christ story reveals a universal trinity:

- The Sea of Chaos – the unformed substance of creation (Nun)

- The Holy Spirit – the fire/light that vivifies that substance

- The Virgin Womb – the cosmic matrix (Mary or Isis) that receives the seed of light

- The Christ – the Logos, born in matter, to awaken all souls to their divine origin

Mary is more than a historical figure – she is the personification of the sacred receptivity. As the angel says

346

in the Gospel of Luke, *"The Holy Spirit shall come upon you, and the power of the Most High shall overshadow you."* Mary becomes the temple, the ark, the hidden place where heaven and earth unite.

This mystery is not confined to Christianity. In ancient Egypt, Isis performed this sacred role. She gathers the scattered pieces of Osiris, reassembles them with love and power, and conceives Horus – the solar soul. Isis is the divine feminine at work within creation. She is the womb that births the light after darkness. Her sister, Nepthys, mortal and bound to form, represents the shadow of her lower self. The union of Isis and Nepthys – immortal and mortal, spiritual and material – is seen in the Caduceus, the twin serpents winding up the central staff, ascending toward enlightenment.

This symbolism framework reveals a universal structure:

- The Sea of Chaos – Primordial matter, formless and deepening

- The Holy Spirit – The fire/light that stirs creations

- The Virgin Womb – Matter awakened, purified, made holy

- Mary / Isis – The cosmic vessel, the bridge between spirit and form

- The Christ / Horus – Divine consciousness incarnated into matter

In esoteric terms, this process occurs within the soul. The Holy Spirit is the energy of awakening that moves through the depths of consciousness. The soul, purified and emptied of false self, becomes a Virgin once more – receptive to divine inspiration. And within the sacred interior temple, the Christ Light is born.

Thus, the Christ is not simply a figure from history. Christ is the pattern of the soul. Mary is not just a mother. She is the cosmic temple of inner realization. And the Holy Spirit is the breath that moves through the waters of being, calling Light upon the world. When He knocks, open that door.

This is the forgotten mystery of birth – the divine form within the finite, the Light born in the cave of the Heart.

This is not a doctrine — it is a spiritual science. It happens in the heavens, and it happens in us. When we surrender the false self and open the heart, the Holy Spirit moves upon our inner waters. The soul becomes a Virgin once more — pure, receptive, ready. And from this inner womb, the Christ is *born again*.

Chapter 25: The Universal Christ – Hidden Light Across the Ancient World

"The true Light, which enlightens every man, was coming into the world." (John 1:9-13)

The Light That Shines in All Nations: The Christ is more than a name, more than a man, and more than a religion. The Christ is a universal force, a Logos, a Light that has revealed itself to all peoples through symbols, archetypes, and divine patterns. From the **Tao of ancient China** to the Feathered **Serpent of Mesoamerica,** Christ's essence has been known under many names, yet always as the same sacred current: the guiding flame of spiritual rebirth. This chapter seeks to reveal how the Christ mystery lives across all ancient civilizations, showing that no one region, tradition, or theology holds exclusive parentage over this cosmic being.

Christ in Ancient China: The Tao and the Logos

Long before the birth of Jesus in Judea, Chinese sages spoke of a cosmic principle called **the Tao (道)** — **the Way.** **Laozi,** the ancient philosopher attributed with writing the **Tao Te Ching,** opened his teaching with a paradox: *"The Tao that can be spoken is not the eternal Tao."* Yet this Tao was described as eternal, the source of all being, ungraspable and unseen, yet manifest in the world. This aligns closely with the **Logos** described in the **Gospel of John: the Divine Word** through whom all things were made.

Jonathan Pageau, in his exploration of symbolic theology, draws the parallel between the Tao and the Logos: both are divine principles that enter into the material world to restore it, unify it, and elevate it. The Tao is not simply an idea but a living presence that sustains the cosmos. It is the rhythm of Heaven made manifest. The figure of the **Shengren (the sage)** within **Confucianism and Daoism** also reflects a **Christ-like role.** He is a righteous man, attuned to Heaven, who suffers for the sake of the people and becomes a bridge between the divine and the earthly. But even more striking are the ancient Chinese texts, which seem to prophesy the birth, life, and resurrection of a divine savior. As shown in the video you referenced, certain passages from classical Chinese literature echo messianic themes:

In the **Shu Jing (Book of History)**, it is written: *"The sky gave birth to the son of God who will save the world."*

In the writings attributed to **Confucius**, he speaks of the Shengren whose virtue will pierce Heaven and bring salvation. The **ancient Chinese character for righteousness (義)** is a combination of the symbols for 'sheep' over 'me,' visually representing atonement through a lamb — a clear symbolic echo of the Lamb of God** who takes away the sins of the world. The oracle bone scripts contain depictions that some Christian scholars have interpreted as prophetic symbols of crucifixion, resurrection, and divine mediation.

Most astonishing of all, at the moment of **Jesus's crucifixion**, Chinese imperial astrologers recorded an extraordinary celestial sign: a multi-colored halo, a rainbow-like corona, encircling the sun. This was interpreted by seers of the time as a sign of great spiritual significance. The

Chinese sages, well-versed in occult cosmology and spiritual observation, understood this event as the **death of the Son of Heaven.** These celestial records, combined with earlier prophetic texts, confirm that China held deep, esoteric knowledge of Christ's incarnation, death, and resurrection. These ideas suggest that the awareness of the Christ mystery was not absent in ancient China but encoded in their symbols, philosophies, celestial observations, and sacred characters. The Tao was already preparing people to recognize **the Light.**

Christ in Mesoamerica: The Feathered Serpent and the World Tree

Far across the oceans, in the temples of the Mayan and Aztec civilizations, another vision of the Christ emerged under the name **Kukulkan or Quetzalcoatl — the Feathered Serpent.** He was a god of wisdom, light, peace, and cosmic balance, who arrived mysteriously and promised to return. He rejected human sacrifice and taught moral law. In the esoteric tradition, he represents a solar Logos, a being who embodies both the serpent (wisdom, earth) and the bird (spirit, sky), uniting opposites in harmony.

The cross was also known to the Mayans. **The World Tree, or axis mundi,** was often depicted in the form of a cross, with its roots in the underworld, branches in the heavens, and the human soul ascending its center. This symbol deeply aligns with the crucifixion as a spiritual event: the bridging of all realms.

Some **Mayan** myths describe the descent of a god into the underworld, his suffering and death, and his return as a renewed force — another echo of the death and resurrection motif. The Long Count calendar, ending in 2012, was seen not as a doomsday prophecy, but a marker of spiritual renewal, the return of divine consciousness.

Of great symbolic importance to the Mayans was the Orion constellation, which they called the **"Fire in the Hearth."** Within the **Orion Nebula**, they saw the sacred fire that fuels creation—a divine hearth placed in the cosmic center. This spiritual fire was the origin point of the soul's journey. The connection between the Orion constellation and divine death-rebirth motifs is mirrored in ancient Egyptian beliefs, where Osiris is also symbolically identified with Orion. Both traditions pointed to the stars as gateways of higher knowledge and resurrection.

These cultures also held esoteric knowledge in their Mystery rites, reserved for the spiritual elite, where initiates passed through death-like trials and received visions of cosmic unity. The Christ mystery, in symbolic form, permeated these rites.

The Logos in Other Traditions: In India, **Krishna** is the divine speaker of the **Bhagavad Gita,** declaring: *"Whenever righteousness declines, I incarnate Myself for the protection of the good and the destruction of evil."* In **Persia, Mithras** slays the bull to bring forth new life — an initiatory sacrifice. In **Greece, Heraclitus** spoke of the **Logos** as the ordering principle of all things. In Egypt, Osiris dies and rises again, bringing judgment and renewal.

These are not copies of Christianity. Rather, they reflect the primordial wisdom that the Christ — the cosmic principle of redemption and unity — lives in all sacred traditions.

A Global Prophecyc - Christ Foretold Across the Ancient World: While Christianity holds the Incarnation of Jesus Christ as its central event, the presence of Christ—the Logos, the divine principle of Light, Wisdom, and Redemption—was perceived and prophesied in many cultures long before the birth of Jesus in Bethlehem. What is remarkable is that ancient Chinese sacred writings not only anticipated this reality but also described it with symbolic clarity that mirrors prophetic traditions across the globe.

China – The Ancient Vision of the Son of God: The Shu Jing (Book of History) speaks of a divine Son sent by Heaven: *"The sky gave birth to the Son of God who will save the world."* The oracle bone inscriptions contain symbolic prefigurations of a man crucified, mediating between Heaven and Earth. The Chinese character for righteousness (義) shows a lamb over the self, echoing the concept of atonement through the sacrificial Lamb, directly paralleling Christ as the Lamb of God. During the crucifixion in 33 AD, Chinese imperial court records describe a rainbow halo surrounding the sun, interpreted by royal astrologers as the death of the "Son of Heaven." These reveal not only a spiritual sensitivity to the Christ impulse, but an esoteric recognition of the actual events in Jesus's life —from birth to death and resurrection—recorded in a language of sacred symbols and celestial signs.

353

In the Bhagavad Gita, Krishna says: *"Whenever righteousness declines and unrighteousness increases, I incarnate Myself. For the protection of the good, for the destruction of evil, I appear from age to age."* This reflects the concept of the Christ as the divine incarnation of Logos, returning cyclically to realign the world to higher truth.

Greece – The Logos of Reason and Creation: Heraclitus described the Logos as the eternal ordering principle of the cosmos — unseen, yet present in all things. Later, Stoic philosophers viewed the Logos as the divine rationality guiding all creation.

These ideas were synthesized in John 1:1, where Jesus is declared the incarnate Logos, uniting the Hellenic and Hebrew traditions.

Egypt – Osiris and the Resurrection Mystery: The myth of Osiris contains death, dismemberment, and resurrection themes that align with the Christic pattern.

Osiris, identified with the Orion constellation, was believed to die and rise again to judge the dead and bring renewal — mirroring Christ's crucifixion, descent into the underworld, and resurrection. The "Fire in the Hearth" within the Orion Nebula, venerated by the Mayans and aligned with Egyptian star-lore, emphasizes a cosmic location for the soul's resurrection and Christ-like emergence.

Mesoamerica – The Feathered Serpent and the Returning God: Kukulkan/Quetzalcoatl was a bringer of light, law, and peace — who descended, disappeared, and promised to return. The World Tree, forming a cosmic cross, echoes the crucifixion. **Mayan records align the Orion constellation** with the soul's rebirth through the sacred hearth — a stellar Christ-center shared with Egyptian cosmology.

Conclusion – A Christ Known Before Bethlehem: These global traditions are not evidence of cultural borrowing, but signs of an ancient and universal Mystery — that Christ is the Logos written into the fabric of reality, recognized by sages, prophets, and mystics in every age. The ancient Chinese, with their celestial recordings, symbolic language, and prophecies, stand as powerful testimony to this hidden thread. No single tradition owns Christ. The Christ was — and is — the Light that lights every soul that enters this world. As Manly P. Hall once said, *"The Christ is not a man but the divine principle in every human heart."* Rudolf Steiner taught that Christ is the turning point of time, entering into the Earth not merely to redeem but to awaken a new capacity in the human soul: the ability to overcome death consciously. Helena Blavatsky saw the Christos as the higher self — the spiritual light latent in all. A.P. Sinnett taught that the perfected soul becomes one with the higher Ego, ascending to Devachan and beyond. Thus, Christ is not bound to history, but woven into the soul's eternal journey.

𓂀 𓂀 𓂀

Mystery Thread Sidebar: The Living Logos – How the Mystery Schools Prepared the Soul to Receive the Light. All Mystery Schools — whether Egyptian, Greek, Chinese, or Mayan — sought to initiate the soul into a vision of higher reality. Their rites symbolically mirrored death and resurrection, preparing the inner being to meet the eternal Light.

The Christ was known before the Incarnation, for He was the Light of the world from the beginning. And even now, He awakens in those who seek truth beyond dogma, beyond region, beyond form. He is the inner Sun rising in the heart of humanity.

𓂀 𓂀 𓂀

Chapter 26: Suppressed History and Forbidden Finds – The Vanishing Records of the Soul

We are not the first.

This modern world — with all its screens, satellites, and synthetic noise — rests on the ashes of a forgotten past. Beneath our feet are the bones of civilizations that rose and fell long before our textbooks began. But more than ruins were buried — an entire memory of the soul was scattered, hidden, or destroyed.

We live in an age of spiritual amnesia.

The idea that humanity is only a few thousand years old, evolving linearly from caves to smart cities, is a myth constructed by selective memory and institutional control. In truth, the further back we look — through myths, megaliths, and mysteries — the more we encounter a sophisticated, sacred science of the soul. One that modern history has conveniently dismissed, suppressed, or labeled as myth.

This isn't just about lost buildings or mis-dated bones. It's about a disrupted timeline of consciousness. A severing from our spiritual ancestry. When we forget where we came from, we forget who we are. And when we forget who we are, we become easy to control — spiritually, psychologically, and culturally. This amnesia is not accidental. The wisdom of the ancients — their star maps, initiation rites, teachings of the afterlife, and the soul's ascent — was deliberately silenced. Why? Because it pointed to something terrifying to the powers of this world: a human being who is divine, sovereign, and eternal.

In this chapter, we will explore the suppressed pieces of the human puzzle—archaeological anomalies, forbidden discoveries, and esoteric systems of knowledge that challenge everything we've been taught. These are not fringe fantasies—they are the whispers of a memory too powerful to stay buried.

It's time to remember what we were never meant to forget

1. The Timeline of Forbidden Finds

The official story of human history begins around 5,000 years ago—with Sumer, Egypt, and the first written records. But the evidence says otherwise. All around the world, anomalies exist—out-of-place artifacts, megalithic structures, and maps of ancient lands that defy the timelines taught in schools.

These are not isolated quirks—they are breadcrumbs from a forgotten golden age, pointing to a spiritual and technological sophistication that rivals, or even surpasses, our own.

Here are just a few of the revelations found on the Timeline of Forbidden Finds:

• **Göbekli Tepe (c. 9600 BCE, Turkey)**

This vast megalithic complex predates Stonehenge by 6,000 years. With astronomical alignments and intricate carvings, it reveals a level of planning and spiritual culture that shouldn't exist according to mainstream timelines.

• **Water Erosion on the Sphinx (proposed by Robert Schoch, c. 10,000 BCE)**

The weathering on the body of the Great Sphinx suggests it was carved in a time when Egypt was experiencing heavy rainfall—thousands of years earlier than the pyramids. If true, this places the Sphinx—and its builders—at the edge of the last Ice Age.

• **The Piri Reis Map (1513 CE, copied from older sources)**

This map shows the coastline of Antarctica without ice, something we only confirmed in the 20th century with satellite imaging. The original source of this data? Unknown —and officially impossible.

• **Vimanas and Ancient Tech (India)**

Descriptions from ancient Indian texts like the Mahabharata and Vaimanika Shastra tell of flying machines, propulsion systems, and even aerial battles. Myth? Or memory?

• **The Baghdad Battery**

Clay jars with copper cylinders and iron rods—potentially ancient galvanic cells. Their existence suggests electrical knowledge far older than we admit.

• **The Cradle of Humanity: Southern Africa**

Stone circles and advanced metallurgy in places like Adam's Calendar suggest a technologically advanced society dating back over 100,000 years—one tied to sound, resonance, and possibly consciousness manipulation.

Each of these finds on its own might be dismissed. But together, they tell a different story: that the rise of human civilization is not a straight line, but a cycle—of remembering and forgetting, of light and collapse. They speak of ages when spiritual knowledge, cosmic order, and the science of the soul were one. And they raise the question: what else has been hidden from us?

The War Against Ancient Knowledge

History is not written by the victors—it's edited by the survivors of power. The great knowledge of the ancients—their teachings of the soul, the afterlife, and cosmic law—was not merely forgotten. It was targeted. **The Library of Alexandria,** a center of global wisdom, held texts from **Egypt, India, Greece, Babylon,** and beyond. It was more than a library—it was the living record of a multidimensional civilization. It's burning was not just a tragedy—it was a ritual act of erasure. One flame to blind a thousand generations.

After Alexandria came centuries of conquest, crusades, and inquisitions. Temples were turned to rubble. Mystery Schools were driven underground. Sacred texts were banned or rewritten. The feminine principle, the divine soul, and the cycles of rebirth were demonized, fragmented, or buried beneath layers of dogma.

Why such aggression against wisdom? Because ancient knowledge pointed to a sovereign, eternal soul — a being whose authority did not come from kings, priests, or empires, but from within. A soul that could die and return, evolve across lifetimes, and ascend to divine awareness without the approval of institutions. This kind of soul cannot be taxed, threatened, or controlled.

And so the memory of who we are was attacked at the root. But it never fully vanished.

Near-death experiences are evidence of this suppressed knowledge returning.

Many who return from death describe realities that align with ancient teachings:

- The presence of light-beings (spiritual guides or Neteru)

- The weighing of the heart (life reviews)

- The multidimensional structure of the afterlife (planes of consciousness)

- The realization that we are eternal, not judged but known

These are not new discoveries — they are ancient truths reawakening. What the ancients taught in temples; people today are experiencing spontaneously through near-death. The veil that was torn down by fire and fear is now lifting again — through the soul itself. In a time of censorship and digital distraction, the most radical act is to remember

What Was Lost – The Soul's Original Science

Long before modern science dissected reality into atoms and algorithms, there was another kind of science — one that saw no division between matter and spirit, between the cosmos and the soul. It was the original science of consciousness, practiced in temples, preserved in symbols, and passed down through initiation. This sacred science wasn't theoretical — it was experiential. The ancients didn't guess about the afterlife; they prepared for it. They mapped the journey of the soul after death, understood the structure of the human energy body, and practiced techniques to master dreams, out-of-body experiences, and reincarnation. This wasn't mysticism in the modern sense — it was applied spiritual physics.

Consider the pyramids — not just in Egypt, but across the globe. These structures were not tombs. They were resonance chambers, precisely aligned with celestial bodies, designed for spiritual transformation. Initiates would enter them not to die, but to awaken — to leave the body, travel through the inner worlds, and return with higher awareness.

In India, yogis mastered the art of conscious death, leaving the body through the crown chakra, as described in

362

the Upanishads. In Mesoamerica, the shamans of Teotihuacan walked the Avenue of the Dead to rehearse their own rebirth. In Peru, Egypt, Tibet, and the Celtic Druidic traditions, the pattern repeats: initiation = death before death = illumination.

All of this was systematically erased, and replaced with fear-based doctrines — eternal damnation, blind obedience, salvation through external authority. But near-death experiences are now reactivating the ancient science. Those who return often describe a realm of knowing where everything is connected. They describe a blueprint-like world of light and energy, a place where thought creates reality, and where the soul sees its incarnations as part of a greater evolution. These insights echo the teachings of the ancient mystery schools almost exactly — yet the experiencers had never studied them.

What was lost is not lost forever. It lives in the soul. It resurfaces when the body dies. And now, in increasing numbers, people are remembering. The ancient science of the soul is rising from the ashes of false history — through us.

Why It Was Suppressed – The Power of the Soul

To understand why ancient knowledge was buried, burned, and rewritten, we must ask a simple question: What is the most dangerous truth in the world? It is not the existence of lost cities or forgotten civilizations. It is the truth that you are an eternal soul, sovereign, divine, and ungovernable.

The moment a human being realizes this — truly realizes it — the machinery of control begins to crack. No more fear of death. No more blind obedience to systems. No more worshiping outside what already lives within. A soul awakened cannot be manipulated, sold to, or ruled. And so, this truth had to be hidden.

Every empire — from ancient Rome to modern institutions — has known this. Control thrives in spiritual ignorance. When people are taught that they are fallen, broken, or born into sin, they become dependent. When the soul's power is externalized — placed in a distant heaven or a wrathful deity — it becomes easier to corral. And when the stories of the past are edited, the present becomes easier to shape. This is why the teachings of reincarnation were removed from the early Christian canon. Why the Gnostic gospels were buried in the desert. Why the initiatory knowledge of the Egyptians, the **Druids, the Vedic sages**, and the shamans was reduced to superstition or crushed by sword and fire.

But you cannot kill the soul, and you cannot erase the truth woven into its memory.

Near-death experiencers often return with a fierce clarity: they are not afraid anymore. They know they are souls. They know they chose to come here. They speak of love — not judgment — and of purpose — not punishment. They are no longer manipulable by the systems of fear that feed off forgetfulness.

This is the real reason ancient knowledge was suppressed:

Because it awakens the soul.

And a soul awakened… is free.

𓂀 𓂀 𓂀

Mystery Thread Sidebar: The Guardians of Lost Light

While empires rose and fell, and libraries turned to ash, the true knowledge was never entirely lost. It was guarded — not in vaults, but in lineages, symbols, and souls.

The Mystery Schools — those hidden sanctuaries of ancient wisdom — knew this day would come. They encoded truths into architecture, mythology, and sacred geometry. They whispered it across generations of initiates, preserving the light in the darkest times. Egypt, India, Tibet, Persia, the Celtic groves, the temples of Atlantis, and they understood that knowledge could be destroyed outwardly, but not inwardly. It could be burned from books, but not from being. The soul remembers. And now, that remembrance is accelerating.

Near-death experiences are not just anomalies — they are activations. The modern experiencer, like the ancient initiate, passes through the veil and returns with light. They echo the rites of the old schools, not knowing that they walk a path once carved in stars and stone.

In this way, the ancient knowledge lives on — not in museums, but in hearts.

You are not simply reading history.

You are part of it.

Lemuria — all carried fragments of the One Teaching. These schools were not simply keepers of ritual — they were **guardians of soul memory.**

Chapter 27: Barbelo and the Luminous Cloud – Escaping False Heavens

In 2006, the long-lost **Gospel of Judas** was revealed to the public—a Gnostic text buried for centuries and deliberately excluded from the Christian canon. In it, Judas is not the betrayer. He is the chosen one, the only disciple who understands the true mission of Christ. And it is Christ himself—Yeshua—who asks Judas to hand him over, so that the divine spark within may be released from the body.

This alone is enough to challenge centuries of theological doctrine. But the Gospel goes further. It reveals an entire cosmic architecture—one in which the so-called creator god is not the true source, but a lesser being, a **Demiurge,** who rules over the material and psychic planes. The real God— the Infinite, the One—is beyond comprehension, and only those with the gnosis (inner knowledge) can transcend the false heavens created by the **archons.**

At the heart of this system is a figure called **Barbelo**— described as a luminous, heavenly realm of light, the first emanation from the Source. But in the **Gospel of Judas**, Barbelo is not a place of final salvation. It is a realm of beauty, yes—but a deceptive one, where souls are trapped in cycles of illusion. A luminous cloud that seduces the soul into returning to a realm it believes is divine, when in truth it is still under the dominion of the archons.

In this telling, Judas becomes the true initiate—not because he betrays Christ, but because he understands the mystery. He alone perceives the trap of the material and astral worlds. He sees that salvation does not come through worship or blind belief, but through direct knowledge — gnosis — of the eternal Light beyond all forms.

The Gospel of Judas doesn't contradict Christ's message — it restores its initiatory depth. It pulls back the veil to show that the journey of the soul is not just about reaching the light — it is about discerning which light is real.

The Astral World – The Realm Between Realms

In the esoteric traditions — Theosophy, Anthroposophy, Hermeticism, and Gnosticism — the astral world is a transitional realm, a subtle plane that exists between the physical world and the higher spiritual dimensions. It is here, in this liminal space, that most souls first arrive after death.

The astral world is not heaven. It is a mirror-realm, formed from thought, desire, and archetypal memory. It contains both light and shadow — sublime beauty and terrifying illusion. It is the realm of dreams, visions, and mystic experience, but also of projection, seduction, and deception. In this world, what appears to be divine may only be a reflection of our own desires.

In Theosophy, the post-death experience begins in **Kamaloka** — the plane of desire — where the soul sheds its attachments to earthly cravings. From there, it may ascend to **Devachan,** a more blissful state where the soul processes its spiritual lessons before preparing for reincarnation. But both Kamaloka and Devachan are still within the astral veil

—they are not the final return to Source. They are intermediate realms, beautiful but impermanent.

This layered structure is echoed in the **Egyptian Duat, the Tibetan Bardo, and the Christian concept of purgatory**. It is even reflected in Near-Death Experiences, where many describe floating realms of light, radiant beings, and an overwhelming sense of love—but often with an invitation to return, as if the final journey is being withheld.

According to Gnostic thought, these realms are governed by the archons—beings who keep souls cycling through illusion and reincarnation, feeding on psychic energy and emotional residue. They are not demons in the Hollywood sense—they are cosmic bureaucrats, mindless enforcers of limitation, masking themselves as light.

And this is where Barbelo becomes a key figure. She is the luminous cloud, the false heaven that looks like salvation but binds the soul to repetition. It is not a punishment—it is a misrecognition. The soul sees light and assumes it has arrived. But the true journey has not yet begun.

Without initiation, the soul lacks the discernment to pass beyond the astral world. It confuses emotional bliss with spiritual truth. It accepts the beauty of the veil as the face of God. But those who awaken can see through it.

Barbelo – Womb of Return or Cage of Light?

Barbelo is one of the most mysterious figures in Gnostic cosmology—at once the first emanation of the True Source and the luminous cloud that veils it. In some Gnostic texts, she is described as a divine mother, the aeon of light that gives birth to all creation. But in the Gospel of Judas, her role is not entirely benevolent. She becomes the keeper of a beautiful illusion, a womb of return that leads not to liberation, but to reincarnation.

To the unawakened soul, Barbelo appears as paradise. Her domain glows with light, love, and familiarity. It radiates comfort—a cosmic sedative. But this light is not the formless radiance of the True Source. It is reflected light—astral light. The same "light" used in deceptive mysticism, false visions, and spiritualism disconnected from initiation.

She is a psychic seduction, a luminous net. Not evil—just binding. Like the sirens of myth who sang sailors to their doom, Barbelo draws souls back into the wheel of birth and death. Her realm is hypnotic, built of memory and longing. Souls arrive and believe they have reached their reward. They see beloved ancestors. They are praised. Some are even offered the choice to reincarnate "for the good of others." But this choice is already part of the trap—because the soul never truly left it.

In this sense, Barbelo is a threshold guardian. She guards the boundary between the astral heavens and the true spiritual realm beyond form. The danger is not in encountering her—it is in staying there. The initiate is meant to pass through—not to build temples in the cloud.

This insight is echoed in Near-Death Experiences. Many experiencers describe being told to return. But a rare few speak of going further—beyond the light, into a vastness

370

where there is no form, no being, only an infinite Presence. They say this is where the soul truly belongs.

The Gnostics warned that even light could be a trap, if it was not the right light.

And the mystery schools trained the soul to recognize the difference.

Near-Death Experiences and the Danger of the False Light

Near-Death Experiences (NDEs) have become a modern gateway into the mysteries once reserved for initiates. People from all walks of life — religious or not — report entering otherworldly realms, encountering beings of light, undergoing life reviews, and being offered a choice to return or remain. But among these radiant accounts lies a critical question, one the ancients asked with deep caution:

Is all light truly divine?

Many NDEs describe a blinding, loving light — an intelligence that knows the soul intimately. This light is often interpreted as God, Christ, or Source. And for many, it brings healing and transformation. But not all experiences end in clarity. Some report being drawn toward the light and feeling disoriented, confused, or even manipulated. Others describe a pressure to return, without a full understanding of why. Some speak of "contracts" they don't remember agreeing to, or missions imposed rather than chosen.

These testimonies echo the warnings of the Gnostics: that the soul must not mistake emotional bliss for spiritual truth. The astral realm, especially in its upper layers, can be radiant and convincing—a theater of mirrors shaped by belief, longing, and karma. The "beings of light" may not be deceivers in the traditional sense, but they are not always who they appear to be. In some cases, they may be constructs of the soul's own psyche, or entities bound to the astral hierarchy whose purpose is to maintain the cycle—not break it.

Barbelo, as described in the Gospel of Judas, represents this seductive realm of luminous containment. It feels like heaven, but it is still within the matrix. The initiate is not meant to rest there, but to see through it.

The esoteric teaching is not to reject all light—but to test it.

Ask:

- Does this light liberate, or bind?

- Does it expand my essence, or ask for surrender to something outside myself?

- Does it confirm what I want to hear—or call me to something deeper?

True light never imposes. It invites recognition. It does not command—it reminds. And it always points the soul back to itself, to the divine source that lives within.

In this way, the modern near-death experiences become a mirror of the ancient initiate—standing at the threshold, called to choose not just whether to return to the body, but which truth to return with.

Initiation as the Key to Discernment

The ancient world understood something that modern culture has largely forgotten: discernment is not natural—it is trained. The soul's ability to distinguish true light from false, liberation from illusion, is not granted by belief or intellect alone. It is cultivated through initiation—a sacred process of transformation that prepares the soul to see beyond the veil.

In the mystery schools of Egypt, Greece, Persia, and India, the initiate was led through symbolic death and rebirth. Not for spectacle, but to simulate the actual conditions the soul would face after physical death. Through fasting, darkness, dream-work, controlled out-of-body states, and the transmission of sacred symbols, the initiate developed the inner senses—spiritual faculties that allowed them to navigate the astral realms consciously. The key lesson? Not all that glitters is gold, and not all light leads home.

Initiation prepared the soul to recognize inner light—the Christ within, the divine seed that transcends the astral veil. This inner light is calm, steady, and rooted in gnosis, not emotion. It is often quiet compared to the dazzling seductions of the false heavens. But it is eternal. Once awakened, it becomes the compass that leads the soul beyond the cloud of Barbelo, beyond the temptations of form, and into the radiant unknown.

This is why the false light is so dangerous—it plays on the uninitiated soul's longing for love, belonging, and peace. It offers comfort in place of truth. Initiation does not eliminate these desires—it refines them. It transforms longing into vision, sentiment into clarity, and hope into knowing.

Near-death experiencers who return with deep transformation often describe this same shift. They no longer seek light—they carry it. They do not follow—they remember. And in that remembrance is the echo of every mystery school, every sacred teaching, every veil torn by a soul that chose to know rather than believe.

The soul is not meant to wander blindly through the afterlife.

It is meant to walk with eyes open, flame lit, and truth in hand.

That is what initiation was always for.

𓂀 𓂀 𓂀

Mystery Thread Sidebar: The Labyrinth of the Veil

Across every ancient Mystery School, from the sands of Egypt to the caves of Eleusis, there existed a central truth: not all veils conceal darkness—some conceal light. And not all light reveals the path—it can also blind.

The realm of Barbelo, the Luminous Cloud, is the astral labyrinth that surrounds this world like a shroud of divine mimicry. It is beautiful, yes—but it is binding. It offers peace, but not freedom. This realm, revered by the uninitiated, was seen by the Gnostics as a hallway of illusions, where even the sacred appears in costume.

Initiates were taught to pass through this veil, not to rest within it. The true temple lies beyond the veil of the veil — past the astral lights, past the archonic whispers, past the architecture of the mind. To reach it, the soul must awaken a light that does not flicker, a flame that does not burn — the Christ within.

In every Mystery School, this was the final trial.

The Labyrinth of the Veil.

To see through what appears true.

To walk past what appears beautiful.

To remember what appears forgotten.

In the end, it is not belief that opens the gate.

It is discernment born of direct knowing — gnosis.

This is the path of the initiate. This is the path of the soul.

And it is open once more.

The Cosmic Womb and the Virgin Veil

In Egyptian thought, Nut, the sky goddess, is often depicted arching over the Earth, enclosing the cosmos within her body. She births the sun every day and swallows it each night—a womb of stars, time, and rebirth.

- In Gnosticism, the Virgin is Barbelo—a divine mother and first emanation. While in some texts she is pure gnosis, in others (like the Gospel of Judas), she becomes a trap, a false womb that seduces the soul back into incarnation.

- In Kabbalah, the Shekhinah is the indwelling feminine presence of the divine—also considered a "virgin mother" of creation, often veiled.

- The Virgin Mary, esoterically understood, is not merely the mother of Jesus—she is the soul of the world, the container of the Logos. She is the sacred womb of manifestation. That's why the Christ is "born of a virgin"—because the spirit must emerge from pure potential, untouched by material corruption.

- In Hindu cosmology, the womb of the universe is called the Hiranyagarbha—the "golden egg," floating in primordial darkness. It is both the void and the matrix of creation.

The Esoteric Twist:

The **"cosmic womb"** is not always benevolent. In its highest form, it is the sacred matrix of divine potential. But when misunderstood, it becomes the illusory veil—a soft, luminous prison that binds consciousness to form.

This aligns perfectly with the Barbelo concept:

The soul mistakes the luminous cloud for the Source, and returns not to God, but to the womb of the world — again and again.

Initiation was the process of seeing through this veil. Not to escape the womb in fear — but to be born out of it, consciously.

𓂀 𓂀 𓂀

Chapter 28: Sleep and Death – The Soul's Nightly Journey Through the Veil

Every Night We Die

We tend to think of death as a singular, final event—a threshold we cross only once, and never return from. But the ancient initiates knew otherwise. They taught that death visits us nightly, not to end life, but to rehearse it. Every time we fall asleep, we step out of the body, cross the veil, and return—if only for a few hours—to the unseen world.

Sleep is not unconsciousness—it is a shift in consciousness. And in that shift, the soul detaches from its physical tether. In the stillness of deep sleep, our waking identity dissolves. Time disappears. The body lies inert, yet something within us continues to experience, observe, and receive.

This is not a poetic metaphor—it is a lived truth in many mystical systems. The Egyptians, Vedic sages, Tibetan Buddhists, and Christian mystics all described sleep as a minor death, and death as a greater sleep. In both, the soul exits the physical realm and enters another—the realm of spirit, symbol, and light.

We know this instinctively. Think of the language we use:

- "He passed peacefully in his sleep."

- "I was dead to the world."

- "She sleeps the eternal sleep."

We've always known that sleep carries us to the edge of something vast.

But what lies beyond that edge? Where does the soul go when it drifts into a dream? And what does this nightly journey reveal about the great crossing at life's end?

To answer this, we must turn to those who remembered what they saw — and to the wisdom of the Mystery Schools, which trained the soul to remain awake while the body slept.

Because death is not the end. It is what you do every night. And one day, you simply don't return.

Steiner's Teaching – Sleep as a Mirror of Death

Rudolf Steiner, the Austrian mystic and founder of Anthroposophy, gave profound insight into the hidden mechanics of sleep. For Steiner, sleep was not just a biological necessity — it was a spiritual operation, a rhythm woven into the soul's evolution. And it mirrored, with astonishing clarity, what happens in death.

According to Steiner, the human being is composed of four primary aspects:

1. The physical body

2. The etheric body (life force)

3. The astral body (soul)

4. The ego (the higher self or "I")

In waking life, all four are united. But when we fall asleep, a separation occurs. The physical and etheric bodies remain in the bed, while the astral body and ego lift out, returning to the spiritual world. This nightly departure is unconscious for most people—but it is real.

Just as in death, the soul leaves the form behind. But in sleep, the thread is not cut—it stretches like a silver cord between the realms. In this suspended state, the soul communes with higher beings, receives impressions from the spiritual world, and absorbs forces of renewal that the body alone cannot generate.

Steiner taught that spiritual development depends on becoming more conscious of this process. The initiate learns to observe the threshold—the moment between waking and sleep—and eventually to maintain awareness during sleep itself. This is not fantasy or dream control—it is the first stage of initiation, the reclaiming of what death will one day demand.

In this view, death is not a stranger. It is a sleep extended—a longer journey beyond the veil. And sleep is a daily invitation to prepare, to explore, and to remember. Those who learn to awaken within sleep are not surprised by death. They have walked its paths before.

The Womb of the Night – Sleep as Return to the Cosmic Virgin

Sleep is more than rest—it is return. Each night, when the soul slips from the body, it enters a realm that mystics and initiates have long described as a great, enveloping silence—a space beyond the senses, beyond thought, beyond time. It is into this space that the soul returns to be cradled, renewed, and reminded of what it truly is. This space has been symbolized in every ancient tradition as a womb.

In Egyptian cosmology, the goddess Nut arches over the Earth like the night sky—her body encloses the stars, and she swallows the sun each evening, only to give birth to it again at dawn. In this sacred gesture, she represents the cosmic virgin: the container of light, death, and rebirth.

In the Gnostic mysteries, Barbelo is that first emanation —the luminous veil, the vast cloud that envelops the soul. Though in some texts she becomes a seductress of return, at her core she is still the matrix of becoming—the womb that reflects the soul's longing for union.

In Kabbalah, the Shekhinah is the indwelling presence, the veiled feminine that carries the soul into the hidden chambers of God. She is also referred to as the **"Bride" or the "Holy Virgin"**—not in a bodily sense, but as the pure field from which form emerges.

And in Christian mysticism, the **Virgin Mary becomes the vessel of the Logos,** the untouched space from which divine truth is born into the world. All of these point to one universal idea. The soul sleeps in the arms of the Mother. To sleep is to return to the Cosmic Womb—not to dissolve, but to be held. In that space, the soul is not judged, commanded, or tested. It simply is. It rests in the primal sea of awareness—the same space it will one day return to at death. The same space from which it once emerged at birth. But the womb can also become a veil. The soul, seduced by comfort and light, may mistake the enclosure for the Source. That is why the mystery schools taught the initiate not just to return—but to awaken within the womb, to see through the veil, and to prepare for the day when sleep does not end in waking, but in liberation.

Dreams, Messages, and Astral Sight

If sleep is the doorway, then dreams are the messages slipped beneath it. They are not mere fragments of memory or imagination—they are echoes from the soul's journey into the hidden realms. In the Mystery Schools, dreams were not dismissed—they were studied, decoded, and revered. To dream was to receive a transmission from the deeper self.

In ancient Egypt, temples like those at **Abydos and Dendera were centers of dream incubation.** Initiates would sleep in sacred chambers, often after ritual fasting or purification, in hopes of receiving divine visions or instructions. These dreams were not random—they were structured experiences, intended to awaken insight. The gods spoke in symbols, and the soul responded in silence.

In Greece, the cult of **Asclepius** offered healing through dreams. In India, yogic and tantric texts speak of dream states as paths of initiation, leading to the awakening of astral sight—the ability to consciously perceive other realms. In Tibet, dream yoga is practiced to remain lucid during sleep and even in the after-death bardo.

These practices echo a truth confirmed by Near-Death Experiences: that the afterlife is structured like a dream. The world encountered beyond death is fluid, luminous, and shaped by thought and perception. NDE experiencers often report being in environments that respond to their feelings, moving through landscapes of the mind as if walking through imagination itself.

This is because both dream and death unfold in the astral realm — the realm of light-forms and archetypes. It is here that memory takes shape, where unfinished karma plays out, where the soul receives images meant to instruct, warn, or awaken. But not all dreams come from the soul. Some are born from the subconscious debris of the personality — fear, confusion, desire. And some are intrusions — psychic static or even misleading forms from lower astral layers. That is why ancient initiates were trained not just to dream, but to interpret. The dream was not the truth — it was the cipher.

True astral sight does not just see — it discerns. It recognizes what is symbolic, what is real, and what is projection. This same discernment becomes crucial at the moment of death. Because what the soul sees in dreams is a rehearsal for what it will encounter beyond the body. To dream is to listen. To interpret is to remember. To awaken is to walk with sight into the worlds beyond.

Near-Death and Near-Sleep – Echoes of the Threshold

There is a space — fleeting, silent, and deeply familiar — that exists between waking and sleep. A threshold where the body relaxes, the mind detaches, and the soul begins to drift. This space is often ignored, but it is one of the most potent spiritual doorways. The Mystery Schools called it the twilight of consciousness, the place between the worlds

Strangely, this same liminal state is described by those who have temporarily died. Near-Death Experiencers often speak of sensations eerily similar to what we feel just before sleep:

- A floating feeling

- A subtle detachment from the body

- The sound of rushing wind or vibration

- The pull toward light

- A sense of leaving, but not ending

These parallels are not coincidental — they are keys. They reveal that sleep and death are not separate realities, but different degrees of the same process. One temporary, one permanent. One is dimly remembered, the other life-altering.

Sleep paralysis is another window into this truth. Many who've experienced it describe being half-awake, unable to move, aware of their body yet completely conscious of another realm. Some feel watched. Others hear voices or see beings. While terrifying for some, initiates understood this moment as a gateway — the crossing point where the astral body is separating, and perception is in flux.

In this space, one can experience astral projection, lucid dreams, or even spontaneous encounters with spiritual guides. The soul is awake within the veil. It is at the same border NDEs describe — the moment before choice, the moment before return.

When you sleep, you rehearse your death. When you awaken inside your sleep, you rehearse your rebirth. Both death and sleep pull the soul into the same ocean. The question is: can you remember what you saw while submerged?

𓂀 𓂀 𓂀

Mystery Thread Sidebar: The Temple of Night

In the ancient world, night was not a void — it was a temple. The initiates knew that sleep was not idleness, but a sacred rite repeated nightly by every soul. To close the eyes was to step into the mystery — to walk the halls of the unseen world, where the gods whispered and the soul remembered. The temples of Egypt, the caves of Eleusis, the dream sanctuaries of India and Greece — all treated night as a portal, not a pause.

In these mystery schools, the goal was not simply to dream — but to awaken within the dream. To pass through the threshold of sleep and remain conscious. This practice trained the soul for its final departure: death. The more awake one could become in sleep, the more sovereign one would be in death. At the heart of this nocturnal temple lay a deeper truth: The universe is a womb, and night is the

386

return to its embrace. Each evening, the soul surrenders to the Cosmic Virgin — to Nut, to Barbelo, to the Shekhinah, to the veiled feminine that holds all things. But initiation teaches that this womb is not the end — it is the threshold of rebirth. The soul is not meant to dissolve into night, but to emerge from it illumined.

So the next time you sleep, remember:

You are walking a path carved by sages, guarded by stars, and lined with ancient echoes.

The Temple of Night awaits. Enter it consciously. And awaken in the place where sleep and eternity kiss.

Chapter 29: The Soul and the World to Come – A Vision of Spiritual Evolution

We Are the Ones Returning

There is a quiet revolution happening. It's not on the news. It doesn't carry banners or demand followers. But it is everywhere — beneath the surface of things. People are awakening. Not en masse, but soul by soul. They're remembering who they are. They're seeking, questioning, transforming. Many have never studied the ancient mysteries, and yet they dream as initiates, speak of past lives, and recount near-death journeys that echo the rites of long-lost temples.

This is not evolution in the Darwinian sense. It is spiritual emergence. According to many esoteric traditions, we are now moving through the final stages of a great cycle — a transition between the age of separation and the age of remembrance. The soul has wandered through matter, suffered amnesia, fought wars in the dark — but it was never lost. Only veiled.

Now, the veil is thinning. And what lies beyond it is us. We are the Atlanteans returning — this time with discernment. We are the initiates of Egypt, of Vedic India, of the Andes and the North — reincarnated to finish what we began. We are the ones who held the light in the dark — and now we hold it again.

This is the world to come — not a utopia imposed from without, but a sacred remembering rising from within.

Humanity at the Threshold – From Knowledge to Wisdom

We stand now at a great threshold—not just as individuals, but as a species. For centuries we have pursued knowledge: dissecting atoms, cataloging stars, wiring minds to machines. We have learned how to manipulate the outer world, but have forgotten the world within. The ancients would not have called this wisdom. Wisdom is not accumulation—it is alignment. It is not power over matter, but harmony with spirit. And it begins when the soul remembers itself.

This is why the sacred knowledge of the past is returning. Not as dogma, but as echo. The Mystery Schools, once hidden in mountains and temples, are now emerging in conversations, synchronicities, dreams, and near-death experiences. What once required lifetime initiations is now breaking through spontaneously in the hearts of everyday people.

This does not mean the world is becoming easier. In fact, initiation always intensifies before breakthrough. As humanity wakes up, so too does its shadow—the unhealed wounds, the astral illusions, the final tests of discernment. But this is not collapse—it is contraction before birth.

The soul of the world is laboring to bring forth something new.

- And here, the ancient teachings meet modern revelations:

- The soul is eternal.

- Life is a journey of becoming, not punishment.

- Death is a passage, not an end.

- The Light is not elsewhere — it is you, remembered.

To step into the world to come is to stop waiting for saviors and to begin embodying the divine Self. Not as fantasy. Not as rebellion. But as your birthright. And it begins not when you escape the world, but when you finally see it for what it is:

A sacred school, a mirror, a forge.

The fire is here not to destroy you,

but to reveal what cannot burn

The Soul's Future – Beyond Reincarnation, Beyond Form

Reincarnation is not endless. It is a means, not a destination. The soul does not return to Earth forever — it returns until it remembers, until it integrates the lessons of form and steps into the light of its own divine authorship.

In the esoteric traditions, the goal of life is not just moral improvement — it is spiritual sovereignty. The fully awakened soul is no longer bound to the cycles of birth and death. It becomes what the ancients called a liberated being, or in Theosophical terms, a Master — one who chooses incarnation not from compulsion, but from compassion.

As humanity moves into the age of consciousness, the veil over this knowledge is lifting. People are beginning to glimpse not only their past lives, but also the trajectory of their soul beyond Earth — into realms of light, purpose, and non-dual awareness.

Some near-death experiencers speak of this directly. After passing through the tunnel of light and the life review, they reach a realm beyond form — where there is no gender, no name, no body. Only being. Only love. Only the pure, vibrating recognition of truth. In that place, there is no "me" in the personal sense. There is only the awareness of the eternal Self — and the interconnectedness of all things.

This is where the soul is going.

Beyond Earth.

Beyond karma.

Beyond identity.

But this is not an escape. It is a return. The soul is not ascending to flee the world — it is ascending to remember that it created it. That it agreed to descend, to forget, to learn — and now, it returns with light.

The future is not linear. It is spiral. The more we awaken, the more ancient we become. And as the soul spirals upward, it takes with it the memory of Earth — not as a prison, but as a temple.

𓂀 𓂀 𓂀

Mystery Thread Sidebar: The Flame That Returns to the Flame

In every Mystery School, there was a sacred fire. It was not a symbol. It was not an object. It was the soul itself. The initiate learned not only to preserve this flame, but to recognize it as origin and destiny. It came from the One Light — the Source beyond gods and forms — and to the One Light it would one day return. But not as it was. It would return aware, conscious, radiant with the experience of the journey.

The Zoroastrians tended the holy flame.

The Egyptians carried it in the Ba and Ka.

The Vedic sages called it Atman, the divine spark.

The Gnostics called it the seed of the Pleroma.

The Christians called it the Christ within.

It was always the same flame.

And now, in our time, it flickers again in the hearts of those who remember — not through dogma, but through direct experience. Through Near-Death awakenings, dream visitations, spontaneous visions, synchronicities, and quiet moments of knowing. This flame cannot be inherited. It cannot be borrowed.

It must be tended, awakened, and chosen. And when it is, the soul becomes what the ancients always whispered it could be:

A bearer of light. A bridge between worlds. A living temple.

You are that flame.

And the path you walk, though long, leads home.

Not to a place.

But to the Source from which you came —

And which you have never truly left.

☥ ☥ ☥

Chapter 30: The Unified Truth – What the Soul Has Always Known

From the temples of ancient Egypt to the scrolls of the Gnostics, from the fire-lit sanctuaries of the Mystery Schools to the luminous testimonies of near-death experiencers — we have followed the soul as it has whispered its truth across ages, veils, and bodies. We have walked with those who remembered. We have sat with those who returned. And in doing so, we have begun to remember ourselves.

This book is not merely a map of death and rebirth. It is a mirror.

What it reflects is not something new, but something ancient and enduring:

The soul is eternal.

The soul is divine.

The soul has never been lost — only veiled.

We have seen how this truth was carved into stone, hidden in riddles, protected by initiates, and revived in visions. We have seen how empires tried to erase it — how ignorance disguised itself as religion, and illusion dressed itself as light. But despite all that was forgotten, something within the human being always remembered. Because the journey of the soul is not linear. It is spiral. It does not end at death. It does not begin at birth. It moves like breath — rising, falling, returning. We are not at the end of the road.

We are at a threshold — one walked by the ancients and now offered again. The soul stands ready.

Not to escape this world, but to transform within it. To carry the wisdom of countless lifetimes, and to plant it like flame in the soil of now.

Bridging the Ancient and the Modern

At first glance, the ancient world and the near-death experience might seem worlds apart. One cloaked in temples and ritual, the other in hospital rooms and heart monitors. But if you look closely — beyond symbols and time — you will see they are telling the same story.

Near-death experiences (NDEs) have become the modern mystery school. They offer spontaneous glimpses into the same truths initiates once spent lifetimes preparing to see.

- The tunnel of light? It's the soul's movement through the astral veil.

- The life reviews? The weighing of the heart, the soul's karmic reflection.

- Encounters with luminous beings? The Neteru, the devas, the spiritual guides of every tradition.

- The overwhelming presence of unconditional love? The Source — Ra, Atman, the Christ within.

Those who return from a near-death experience often speak with reverence, awe, and difficulty. Not because the experience was unclear — but because the language of Earth struggles to hold the light they saw. This same challenge faced the initiates of old. When the Eleusinian Mysteries ended, participants swore silence — not from secrecy, but from sacred inadequacy. Some truths cannot be spoken. Only remembered. And yet — those who've had NDEs and those who walked the ancient paths return with the same fire in their eyes. A knowing. A calmness in the face of death. A devotion to love, wisdom, and the invisible architecture of the soul. They may not use the same words, but they point to the same realm.

This is not coincidence.

It is convergence.

The near-death experience has become the doorway for many who never studied mysticism. It has reignited the very knowledge once passed in whispers behind temple walls. Now, the temple is your own life — and the initiation may come in a heartbeat, a moment of stillness, or a crossing you never expected. The ancients and the experiencers walk side by side.

And their message is this:

The soul is real.

Death is not the end.

You are far more than what you've been told.

The Real Purpose of Life and Death

Why are we here? It is the central question behind every religion, every mystery school, and every near-death experience. It echoes in the chambers of pyramids and in the hearts of those who've returned from the other side. And despite the diversity of traditions and testimonies, one truth emerges again and again:

Life is a school. And death is not the end — but a return, a review, and a renewal.

The purpose of life is not to accumulate wealth, achieve perfection, or please a deity — it is to grow the soul. To experience, to evolve, to remember. The soul enters form not to escape it, but to transform it. This Earth is not a punishment — it is an initiation ground. A temple of trials. A forge of consciousness.

Near-death experiences confirm this with stunning clarity. Many experiencers report being shown their life as a tapestry of choices — not judged by an external God, but by their own soul. They feel the joy or pain they gave others. They see where they forgot love, and where they became it. They understand, often for the first time, that the purpose of life is not perfection — but presence, courage, compassion, and awakening.

And death?

Death is the reset point. The return to the blueprint. The soul exits the body not to rest forever, but to reflect, integrate, and choose again. What religions once cast as heaven and hell are seen, in near-death accounts, as states of consciousness—not destinations imposed by judgment, but realities magnetized by vibration.

The ancient Mysteries taught this long ago. They saw death not as an enemy, but as a teacher. That is why initiates died before dying—so that when the real crossing came, they would know the path.

Now, those with near-death experiences are becoming modern initiates. They return transformed. Not simply to talk about death—but to live differently because of what they've seen. They know the soul's purpose is not to escape life—but to embody its truth within it. You don't have to nearly die to understand this. You are already on the path. Every moment of honesty, of love, of awareness—is initiation. And when the final crossing comes, you will not be afraid. Because you have walked this path before.

The Return of the Mysteries

There was a time when the Mysteries were hidden—veiled in symbols, guarded in stone, spoken only in sacred halls to those who had proven themselves ready. They were never secret to be exclusive, but sacred to be protected.

But now... something has changed.

The Mysteries are returning.

Not in their old forms—not in golden masks and priestly robes—but in the rising awareness of the soul itself. In the spreading stories of near-death experiences. In the quiet remembering that comes in meditation, in dreams, in synchronicities, in the space between breaths. They are returning through you.

You are the initiate now. You didn't need to be born into a temple — you are the temple. You didn't need a priest to guide you — your own soul is the guide. The rituals, the signs, the deaths and rebirths — they're no longer locked in myth. They're playing out in the theater of your life.

Near-death experiencers don't bring back new religions. They bring back the oldest truth: that life is sacred, death is not the end, and love is the law beneath all things. The very same truths the ancients preserved in stars, symbols, and sacred architecture.

What was once hidden is now revealed. What was once protected is now being passed freely — because the time has come. The veil has thinned. The torch is in your hand. This book has not been a guide. It has been a reflection — of what your soul already knows. The mysteries are not returning. They've been waiting. Waiting for you to remember.

𓂀 𓂀 𓂀

Mystery Thread Sidebar: The Book of the Soul

There is a book more ancient than any scripture. It is not bound in leather or ink. It is written in light, across lifetimes, carved into the very being of your spirit.

The Book of the Soul. The ancients called it the Akashic Record — the eternal memory field that holds every thought, every action, every moment of becoming. It is the real Book of Life. Not kept by angels in distant realms, but carried by you. Lived by you. You are both the author and the story.

The Mystery Schools taught initiates to read this inner book. To see not with eyes, but with insight. Near-death experiences often speak of it without knowing its name — describing life reviews where nothing is forgotten, and yet nothing is judged. Only understood.

This is the final thread of the Mysteries:

That the answers are not hidden.

They are within.

They have always been.

Every chapter of your life is sacred. Every page is part of the great scroll of the soul's unfolding. And this book you now hold is not separate from it. It is a mirror, a companion, a chapter in your larger story. So close it gently. But do not think for a moment the journey ends here. Because now — you begin to write the next page… with full awareness of who you truly are.

𓂀 𓂀 𓂀

Author's Reflection – A Note From the Edge of the Veil

If you've made it this far, then I already know something about you. You've remembered.

Not everything, not all at once – but enough. Enough to sense that this world is not all there is. Enough to know the voice inside you is older than your body. Enough to follow a thread woven through myths, symbols, and near-death experiences and realize: this thread is you.

This book was never meant to give you answers. It was meant to call something awake. To stir the waters of memory. To hold up a mirror to what your soul has always carried. Because this journey – the soul's journey – is not a fantasy. It is the deepest truth we have. I am not the teacher. You are not the student. We are fellow travelers, remembering together.

Everything you've read here – the gods, the veils, the initiations, the false heavens, the flame that cannot die – are real. Not because they are written in books, but because they are written in you. And if anything, here has stirred your heart, brought tears to your eyes, or silenced your mind into wonder, then you have already touched that inner truth.

And I thank you.

I thank you for walking with me through the temples of the soul. For looking beyond the veil. For letting this book be a companion as you spiral forward into your next becoming. The Mysteries are not behind us. They're ahead. They're within. And now...It's your turn to carry the light.

With wonder and remembrance,

– Alisdaire Thorn

Final Reflection

This book is a vessel of remembrance. It was written not simply to share knowledge, but to help awaken something ancient in the reader's soul. In these pages are fragments of truths lost and rediscovered, voices of forgotten teachers, and whispers from beyond the veil.

We are more than flesh and thought — we are eternal travelers, weaving through lifetimes toward a higher light. My hope is that this work becomes a lantern to those who sense that truth, and a map to those who have begun to remember.

— Alisdaire Thorn

406

Appendices

This section includes additional esoteric insights and summaries of key figures referenced throughout the book. These thinkers laid the foundation for modern spiritual science and helped shape the soul's map beyond death.

Appendix A

Glossary of Esoteric and Near-Death Terms

Akashic Records: A metaphysical compendium of all human events, thoughts, words, and deeds — past, present, and future — believed to be encoded in a non-physical plane of existence.

Angel of Death: An archetypal or spiritual being responsible for overseeing the soul's transition from physical life to the afterlife. Often portrayed as a psychopomp.

Astral Body: One of the subtle bodies of a human being, associated with emotions and desires. It operates on the astral plane and survives physical death for a time.

Astral Plane: A non-physical realm associated with thoughts, emotions, and desires. Often the first realm the soul encounters after death.

Barbelo: In Gnostic tradition, a divine emanation often symbolizing the spiritual womb or matrix. In some esoteric interpretations, it may represent a false afterlife realm or astral snare.

Christos (or Logos): The divine spark or spiritual principle within humanity. Often associated with the cosmic Christ or the spiritual light of truth that guides the soul.

Devachan: In Theosophical teachings, a blissful spiritual state following Kamaloka where the soul experiences a personal heaven before reincarnating.

Ego (Esoteric): Not the personality or prideful self, but the spiritual individuality or higher self that persists across lifetimes.

Etheric Body: A subtle energy field that interpenetrates and sustains the physical body. It dissolves shortly after physical death.

False Heavens: Illusory afterlife realms that appear as paradise but serve to trap the soul in cycles of desire, deception, or reincarnation.

Group Soul: The shared spiritual consciousness of beings at an earlier stage of evolution, before full individualization of the soul.

Guardian of the Threshold: A symbolic or spiritual being that tests the soul's readiness to pass beyond the veil into higher spiritual realms.

Initiation: A process of spiritual awakening and transformation taught in the Mystery Schools, often mirroring near-death or out-of-body experiences.

Kamaloka: A post-mortem state where the soul sheds earthly desires. Considered a purgatorial realm of emotional purification.

Logos: A Greek term meaning 'Word' or 'Reason,' used to describe the divine creative principle. In esoteric traditions, it is synonymous with Christos.

Manvantara: A cosmic cycle of manifestation. In Hindu and esoteric cosmology, it represents a period of activity between two periods of rest (Pralayas).

Mystery Schools: Ancient esoteric institutions that preserved sacred knowledge and initiated seekers into hidden truths about the soul and cosmos.

Near-Death Experience (NDE): A phenomenon in which a person comes close to death and experiences visions or journeys beyond the physical realm.

Pralaya: A cosmic rest period following a cycle of creation (Manvantara). A time when forms dissolve and spirit regathers.

Psychopomp: A spiritual guide who escorts souls from the physical realm to the afterlife. Figures like Anubis or the Angel of Death are examples.

Reincarnation: The belief that the soul returns to physical life in new bodies across many lifetimes for the purpose of growth and learning.

Root Races: In Theosophy, major stages of human spiritual evolution. Each Root Race represents a phase in humanity's physical and metaphysical development.

Seven Virtues (Steiner): A spiritual framework from Rudolf Steiner highlighting moral strengths such as patience, inner balance, and devotion that guide the soul's evolution.

Soul Memory: The enduring awareness within the soul that retains lessons, wisdom, and experiences across lifetimes.

Veil: A metaphor for the boundary between the physical and spiritual realms. Pierced in moments of initiation, death, or spiritual awakening.

Acknowledgments

To those whose voices have echoed across time, to the unseen teachers who guide in silence, and to the readers who walk this path beside me — thank you.

This work was not mine alone. It belongs to all who seek to remember the truth of who we are, and why we are here.

𓂀 𓂀 𓂀

To Those With Eyes to See

This work was not written for the world,
but for the remnant.

For those who remember who they are —
souls who carry a sacred fire within.
To you, I say: You are not alone.
The veils are thinning.
And soon, all things hidden shall be revealed.

𓂀 𓂀 𓂀

Further Reading

Recommended texts for deeper study:

- *The Secret Doctrine* by Helena P. Blavatsky

- *The Mahatma Letters to A.P. Sinnett*

- *Esoteric Christianity* by Annie Besant

- *Knowledge of the Higher Worlds* by Rudolf Steiner

- *An Esoteric Reading of Biblical Symbolism* by Harriet T. Bartlett

- *The Initiates of the Flame* by Manly P. Hall

www.ingramcontent.com/pod-product-compliance
Lightning Source LLC
Chambersburg PA
CBHW051411090426

42737CB00014B/2610